BARBECUED
HUSBANDS

BARBECUED HUSBANDS

and other stories from the Amazon

♦

Betty Mindlin
and indigenous storytellers

Translated by
Donald Slatoff

VERSO

London • New York

First published by Verso 2002
© Betty Mindlin and indigenous storytellers 2002
All rights reserved

1 3 5 7 9 10 8 6 4 2

Verso
UK: 6 Meard Street, London W1F 0EG
USA: 180 Varick Street, New York, NY 10014–4606
www.versobooks.com

Verso is the imprint of New Left Books

ISBN 1–85984–681–5

British Library Cataloguing in Publication Data
A catalogue record for this book is available from the British Library

Library of Congress Cataloging-in-Publication Data
A catalog record for this book is available from the Library of Congress

Typeset in Fournier by M Rules
Printed and bound in Great Britain by
Biddles Ltd, Guildford and King's Lynn
www.biddles.co.uk

Contents

Introduction

Barbecued Husbands is an anthology of indigenous myths about love. I recorded the myths in several indigenous languages and they appear here, in written form, for the first time. The stories are about love and hate, one of humanity's favorite themes. Work, food, love, the afterworld, and art are the fundamentals of life, and the myths collected here are united by the common thread of the experience of love.

Couples in love or in conflict may imagine their experience to be unique, they may think their happiness or sorrow derives from their personalities and personal histories, from what they share and how they differ.

Ancient myths (perhaps centuries old) such as these told by the Indians of Rondônia – handed down from generation to generation, recorded in the memories of those who tell them and of those who listen – suggest and reveal another perspective for inquiry into the meaning of love. They portray an eternal essence of love: a pattern of attraction and conflict between the sexes that is astonishingly similar across time, which bridges different societies, customs, life conditions, and languages.

Relations between the sexes form a fundamental aspect of our lives, and we like to think we are in control. We think that our own behavior, conduct, and destiny are responsible for everything that happens, but there is much that proves to spring, at least in part, from a common source. We live out our lives among given social conditions, but we unknowingly repeat what has already occurred in endless generations past: a lesson that can be comforting or devastating, depending on one's point of view.

The tiny villages in the Brazilian jungle present us with rich material to ponder over. The stories are surprising, contemporary, and, indeed, could provide new ground for modern novels. Some might also be selected as prime symbolic examples of the drama of love – old themes: seduction; mother–daughter relations; competition or cooperation; erotic solitude; greed; dreams of adventurous love, not to mention romantic love; magical men and women in the middle of the forest or underwater; incest and other illicit love; would-be lovers who reject and kill each other; widowhood and the image of death; violence, vengeance, and so on. Love is complicated in these stories, difficult to find and difficult to sustain. And yet, sometimes it appears as if a gift, seemingly out of nowhere.

The stories for this book kept growing in number as I collected them from many peoples over the years. I published two previous volumes of the mythology of the indigenous peoples of the same region: *Vozes da Origem* (published in English as *The Unwritten Stories of the Suruí*, University of Texas Press), and *Tuparis and Tarupás*. The present volume is part of a much larger collection of myths, recorded in various languages and translated into Portuguese, from 1993 on. As the size and scope of this research grows, it is inevitable that comparisons, explanations, commentary, and theory will present themselves. I think, however, that it is important not to spoil the pleasure, for the reader, of surprise and discovery. The myths must speak for themselves; our system of ideas need not be indispensable as an introduction. On the other hand, a bit of analysis might serve as a kind of Ariadne's thread, guiding us through the tangle of plots and demonstrating the contemporary nature of the imaginative contents of a society so different from our own. To help reconcile these two opposing impulses, I have included a short analytical discussion of the myths at the end of the book (pp. 253–80).

The stories I chose for *Barbecued Husbands*, always revolving around themes of love, are grouped by the peoples of the narrators: Macurap, Tupari, Ajuru, Jabuti, Arikapu, and Aruá (all of Rondônia). The six peoples speak different languages and have distinct cultures.

The Macurap, Tupari, and Ajuru speak a language from the Tupi trunk and the Tupari family; the Aruá language is from the Tupi-mondé family of the Tupi trunk; the Arikapu and Jabuti speak isolated languages. These six peoples live in two indigenous areas: the Rio Branco Indigenous Area and the Guaporé Indigenous Area (along Brazil's border with Bolivia), and have a total population of about 750 people. They have had contact with non-indigenous Brazilian society for about fifty years, they have experienced life as slaves on the rubber plantations, and they have seen the greater part of their population wiped out by epidemics of measles and other diseases. Today, with demarcated land and legal protection, free from invasion, their numbers are slowly beginning to grow. The majority speak Portuguese quite well, while the older people express themselves clearly only in their native tongues. It is these elders – many of them women – who told me these stories.

I was told these stories by thirty-two traditional narrators and translators, most of whom enjoy conversation in general and are endowed with expressive and creative gifts. (Later on they listened to the myths they had recorded.) Many of the narrators were born in the forest, before any kind of peaceful contact with non-Indians. The stories they tell come from an ancient era of life in small villages in the jungle, untouched by urban influences.

Most of the myths were narrated in the storytellers' native languages (although some of the narrators told their stories in Portuguese) and were almost always translated by younger people more fluent in Portuguese who are also wonderful storytellers. I took a certain degree of liberty when writing these stories (in a few cases almost recreating them), but I also attempted to retain the spirit with which the stories were originally told, as well as to preserve the style of the indigenous translators.

There was an urgency to record and understand these myths, to gather as many as possible and to listen to as many narrators as possible: to reach into the world of peoples who number only a few survivors, as is the case with the Ajuru, Aruá, and Arikapu. A more careful, faithful translation (such as I did with the Suruí myths in *The Unwritten Stories of the Suruí*, with transcriptions of each word of the native language) takes much longer, and is impossible in cases such as those of the Arikapu and Ajuru, among whom there is no one who speaks both their native language and Portuguese fluently. As *Barbecued Husbands* is made up of many myths, from many peoples who speak many languages, and is a work of wide scope, a greater degree of liberty in the translation is justified.

On the other hand, the material is presented in only one of several possible ways, and is not intended as a model; it would be desirable for other written forms to emerge later on. One of the aims of this, and of the other books of myths I have published, is to serve as reading material for an educational program for indigenous teachers promoted in Rondônia, since 1991, by IAMÁ, the Institute for Anthropology and the Environment, a non-profit, non-government affiliated-institution.

The indigenous readers compare literal transcriptions of the recorded myths with more elaborate renditions, listen to versions in the indigenous languages, experiment with writing narratives themselves, and do research among the elders. There is an ongoing project, still moving slowly, to write the myths in the various indigenous languages, Tupari in particular. One of the future goals is to produce bilingual editions.

One cannot overemphasize, in school and on other occasions, the importance of maintaining and stimulating the oral tradition: the transmission of knowledge through speech and memory instead of print. Writing changes ways of thinking, learning, knowing, and telling, but letters are part of today's world, which our society uses as an instrument of control. Most of the indigenous communities want to study in schools, but maybe writing and the oral tradition are not so incompatible as one imagines. The technological society is also oral, with radios, recorders, political debate, and videos, that can be used for the rebirth of cultural roots.

Remembering the myths is a path to cultural affirmation, to honoring the richness inherent in the diversity among societies and the right to preserve and maintain different traditions. Brazil counts more than two hundred little-known indigenous cultures and languages. The study of these myths broadens the field of imagination, the primal material from which works of fiction arise.

We only need to learn how to fish in the deep waters of Brazilian origins and not to push the myths aside as incomprehensible; for these stories are ancient, but they are also contemporary. The myths are always startling, but they cease to be frightening as they become more familiar.

The original title of this anthology in Portuguese was *A Guerra dos Pinguelos* (literally, 'The War of the Triggers' – but the Portuguese word, *pinguelo*, literally trigger, has several meanings), a perhaps elliptical way to evoke the liberty of the sexualized language of the narratives. In the regional oral Portuguese of many of the narrators, *pinguelo* means both penis and clitoris, as well as the trigger of a gun, and the feminine *pinguela*, which means a bridge made from a tree trunk; the multiple meanings are listed in Aurélio Buarque de Holanda Ferreira's *Novo dicionário da lingua portuguesa* (*New Dictionary of the Portuguese Language*), but not in the first editions of his *Pequeno dicionário da lingua portuguesa* (*Small Dictionary of the Portuguese Language*). Nothing could be more appropriate to symbolize the battle between the sexes. And it's important to preserve the richness of the narrators' uninhibited way of referring to sex and to the human body, although now, unfortunately, in Portuguese, the narrators have been influenced by our repressive concepts of shame and modesty and no longer express themselves so naturally). Finally, we think the title, *Moqueca de Maridos* (*Barbecued Husbands*), with its comic violence, best expresses the mystery of the battle of the sexes.

The final essay is intended to stimulate the reader's curiosity – already primed by a first reading – about the rich, dense universe of the myths, bringing what is strange and little known together with more familiar concepts. A profile of each narrator and his/her people is also presented at the end of the book.

MACURAP

Botxatoniã,
the Women of the Rainbow

Narrator: Iaxuí Miton Pedro Mutum Macurap
Translators: Niendeded João Macurap and Rosilda Aruá
Other Macurap narrators and translators into Portuguese: Buraini Andere
Macurap and Menkaiká Juraci Macurap

All the women fell in love with a being who lived deep under the water. His name was Amatxutxé and the women thought he was extremely handsome. They were so crazy about this man, or creature, that they scorned their husbands and didn't even take care of their children any more. All they could think about was their new love.

Now the husbands lived like single men, and the women who used to be their wives lived like single women. They didn't even look at their husbands any more. They didn't lie in their hammocks at night and they didn't make love to them. Poor abandoned warriors, all that remained for them was to hunt and to take care of the children. They hunted for days on end, trying to distract themselves from their pain, trying to forget the piercing thorns in their heads. Meanwhile, the small boys cooked the game for the men and wandered on their own about the forest. They went swimming whenever they wanted to.

One day, while shooting arrows on the bank of the river, they saw a baby alligator.

"Let's kill it!" they shouted happily, in chorus.

Their arrows were so small that the boys couldn't even get the little alligator's attention, much less kill him. He just lay right where he was and didn't move, so the boys decided to push him. They kept pushing until he fell into the water. Then the boys also fell down to the bottom of the river.

What a surprise awaited them under the water! There were people there, women who looked like their mothers, who were very affectionate and nice to the boys. They fed them *chicha*, a fermented drink, *tacacá*, a kind of stew, and fish. The boys believed they really were their mothers.

These women were Botxatoniã, the Rainbow People. They were enchanted women. When they had finished spoiling the boys, the women sent them home to their fathers, carrying clay pots overflowing with *chicha*.

"We want you to take our *chicha* to your fathers! Explain to them that this food is sent by real people. It's not from Txopokods, or ghosts, or creatures."

The boys took the path back to the game huts and soon ran into one of the hunters carrying a deer on his back. He asked if they were bringing home any *mandim* (a kind of Brazilian catfish), or other kinds of little fish. He was very happy when he saw the *chicha*.

When the boys arrived at the campground, they set the pots of *chicha* and the food on top of some tree stumps. There was plenty for everyone. They gave their fathers the Rainbow Women's message.

"Our mothers" (that's what the boys called the enchanted women) "asked us to tell you that this food is really very good. It's human food, it's not from Txopokods!"

The men ate until they could eat no more. They were happy and their bellies were full. Only one of the men was suspicious of the enchanted food. He only ate deer, mashed up with peanuts grown on their own plots. The others didn't even want to know where the delicacies had come from. They sent the boys back to the Women of the Water to ask for more.

The mothers – they weren't the boys' real mothers, they were Rainbow Women, Women of the River Bottom – sent more *chicha*, *tacacá*, and fish.

The men ate again. They ate and ate. They ate what the Rainbow Women had sent and they ate deer's head and peanuts.

That's how it was every day. The men couldn't wait to visit the Rainbow Women. The women said they were going to make lots of *chicha* and sent the boys to invite the men.

After a long time, the chief called the men together.

"Tomorrow is the last time we will go hunting – it's time to go to the village of the Rainbow Women. And while we are out on our last hunt, you boys will go tell the women that we are coming."

The hunters left their campground that same day, and the boys no longer put *chicha* on the tree trunks. The men bundled up their game with strips of *embira* fiber and, carrying heavy loads, they went on their way. They were not returning to their village – not to the village where they had lived with their wives, the mothers of their children, who didn't want to make love to them any more. They were going to the Women of the River, the Rainbow Women.

They were still far away when they heard the clamor of the *chicha* feast, from deep down under the water. They could hear the sound of the straw rustling under the dancers' feet. There, deep in the water, the Botxatoniã vomited up the *chicha* and the vomit made bubbles in the water. The women threw up and the water bubbled.

The hunters remained for many days under the water. They danced and drank and made love to the beautiful, enchanting women. When the *chicha* was all gone, the men decided to go hunting, to kill deer and gather *gongo* larvae from the *ouricuri* palm tree. The women promised to wait for them and said they would make more *chicha* and more food.

Even in the midst of all this happiness, the men were a little suspicious. The women made a lot of *chicha*, but they didn't drink any. The chief felt uneasy and sent Socó (the Heron) to look around and find out what was going on.

Meanwhile, the women who had been infatuated with the creature from the bottom of the river, the women who had scorned their husbands, had made necklaces and *chicha* for their lover, but it seems that Amatxutxé didn't really appreciate their food. They started to wonder about their husbands and their children, about what they might have been doing all this time.

The women walked and walked, and from far away they heard the party under the water. They saw the water bubble up from the vomiting down below.

They returned to their village and decided they should get rid of Amatxutxé.

"This man we fell in love with, this man we thought was so beautiful, is really an ugly, broken-down old creature! And he seemed so attractive! Better to kill this piece of garbage."

They freed themselves from their love.

The suspicious man, the one who didn't want to drink the Rainbow Women's *chicha*, had stayed alone in a hut while the others went down under the water to dance with the Botxatoniã.

The men were also thinking about returning to their village, but there was still plenty of the Rainbow Women's *chicha* was still left. Even so, the chief, who was suspicious, decided to send his son back to the village to explore a possible reconciliation between the men and their wives upon their return home. The men were already turning into Rainbow People, Botxatoniã. It was time to go home, or it would be too late.

Before the boy left, his father warned him not to touch any of the women at all, and told him to ask his mother to make *chicha* for when the men returned.

The boy went. His mother was overjoyed to see him again, but he made sure to keep his distance from her. He talked to her, but he wouldn't hug her. In spite of his being so reserved, he created quite a stir: he was handsome and strong, with a broad, muscular chest; his body was painted with genipap, and his large soft eyes gleamed; his long black hair was decorated with beautiful feathers. One of the girls of the village fell in love with him at first sight and couldn't stay away. She wasn't the only one – they were all crazy about him.

But he said, "Don't come near me! My father gave me a stern warning to keep away from women! And he told me to ask my mother to make *chicha* and have it ready for the men to drink when they come home."

But what woman could believe that such a handsome warrior would heed his father's warning when it came to making love? The girl wouldn't leave him alone, and when night fell, she slipped into his hammock. And it happened, the very thing he had said he would refuse.

The next day, downcast and ashamed, he went looking for his mother.

"Mother, I'm going away. My father asked you to prepare a lot of *chicha* for us, but I ruined everything. I made love. It was a transgression, *kawaimã*, a crime. I have to go."

He ran to his father and warned him that a girl would be following soon behind him. He told his father that he had broken the rule, that he had succumbed to the young woman. Before long she arrived – but she died from the contact with the Rainbow People. However, her spirit stayed there and lived with the boy.

Since that day, the men remained enchanted, living with the Botxatoniã women, the Women of the Rainbow, for ever. They still live deep down under the water, over there by the source of the Rio Branco. They forgot all about their wives from the village, the mothers of their children.

As for the women of the village, they went looking for husbands somewhere else.

The ghost lover and the girl with the giant clitoris

Narrator: Iaxuí Miton Pedro Mutum Macurap
Translator: Alcides Macurap
Other narrators in Portuguese: Buraini Andere Macurap and Menkaiká
Juraci Macurap

A married woman didn't like her husband at all. She hated sleeping with him and stayed as far away as she could. Her eyes were always on the other young men of the village. She was graceful, as light on her feet as a doe – it seemed as if she was always dancing! There was no shortage of admirers.

One day, while walking in the forest on her way to pick some fruit, she ran into one of the bravest warriors. The two of them didn't need to talk much before they were rolling on the ground, in the leaves, fondling each other, their young bodies on fire.

Now, at night, she burned with desire. She imagined herself in his arms, gently stroking his back, his chest and his legs, blending her skin with his, holding him tightly to her.

At sunset, when everyone was usually out gathering firewood or taking a bath, the two would try to meet somewhere nearby, in the thick of the jungle. But there was always someone on the lookout, especially the children, so she had to be careful not to come home with dirt or twigs stuck to her body. Her greatest desire was to receive her lover in her own hammock, quiet and relaxed, without being seen and without being bitten by ants or the other little creatures that are always crawling around on the ground.

The better to escape her husband's advances, the young woman hung her hammock in a corner of the hut, a little apart from the others, and slept with her back pressed against the straw wall.

One day, while drifting off to sleep, she felt someone's hands caressing and fondling her body. The hands started gently touching her face. The fingers tenderly traced the outlines of her eyes, her nose, her mouth, her cheeks and neck. They went slowly down her body; they lingered tenderly over her breasts and nipples. She remembered her lover's caresses on their rare getaways and she kept very still and quiet, scared to death that someone might interrupt. The experienced hands descended, leaving no spot untouched. They took their time, delighting in her pussy. The fingers of the mysterious hands groped and teased her clitoris. They entered boldly inside her as though they were not just fingers, but a man's eager cock. She trembled with desire. She tried to touch her lover's body, she wanted to repay his gift, his gift of night magic, but she found only the smoothness of his arms, sleek like the flesh of the *pariri* fruit. She wanted to dig through the barrier of the hut's wall to her lover on the other side, but she was afraid of making a noise by rustling the straw.

Every night she waited anxiously, and every night the arms came to play with her. Now she didn't even run to the forest to meet her lover, and during the day, he hardly spoke to her; it was as if they had nothing to do with each other. But, at night, how he used his hands! They were a nice substitute, in fact they felt even better than the usual parts of a man's body, of the man who was forbidden to approach her, separated by the straw! The able hands seemed to take special pleasure enchanting her clitoris, tugging and pulling it with caresses of fire.

Day by day, the girl noticed that her clitoris was growing. She felt alive with the warm glow of erotic satisfaction, but that tiny piece of flesh, so small, imperceptible to the others even in the nudity of the village, was starting to trouble her. A week passed, and it was the size of man's cock in the ecstasy of making love. Dying of shame, she hid herself from everyone. She never went anywhere any more.

"Why are you always hiding? Why don't you go with us to the fields any more, or even sit near us or your husband?" asked her mother, worried about her daughter.

She realized it was impossible to deceive anyone and confessed the truth to her mother. She even told her about her lover in the forest.

"How naïve you are, my young daughter! It's not a man, it is a Txopokod, a spirit, a phantom, who comes to make love to you through the straw! And you thought it was one of our warriors! If it was one of us, he'd invite you to hide with him and make love near the river, far away from the hut."

"He comes to me every night, Mother, like a person. He's such a good lover and he's so tender with me!"

The girl's clitoris had now grown so big that it dragged along the ground. She cried and cried and cried. Feeling sorry for her, her mother called together her relatives and they agreed to put an end to the Txopokod. The betrayed husband was the one who incited the others to take vengeance.

"Tonight we'll tear the arms off this foul beast!"

The men spent the day sharpening their bamboo arrows until they were as sharp as razors. Then they waited silently for night to fall, peeking at the embarrassed young woman as she lay in her hammock, with her heavy clitoris.

It was very late at night when the Txopokod cautiously called and whistled to the girl. He put an arm through the straw and soon reached her most sensitive spot, it was gigantic . . . and tchok! She grabbed the arm and screamed for the men to come. They lit a candle made of resin from the *jatobá* tree and ran to her side. Zapt! They cut off the arm.

There was a bloodcurdling howl and the Txopokod ran away to the jungle. Everyone in the village gathered around the strange arm. It was covered with decorations: bracelets made of coconuts from the *tucumã* palm, teeth, and feathers. When they had finished looking at it, they threw the arm-lover into a clay pot to cook.

They boiled the arm soup over a roaring fire, but nothing happened. The arm stayed exactly the same! It didn't even soften or grow tender. It was as if the Txopokôd didn't have any bones. The flesh wouldn't come loose.

Then something terrible happened. It was time for sunrise, but the dark night continued. There was no light at all. The morning had turned into night. The night had stretched out — just like the poor young woman's giant clitoris.

The villagers couldn't afford to let the fire go out. For it is in total darkness, when there is no light at all, that the Txopokods come to eat men's flesh. And there were many Txopokods! And they must have been beside themselves with anger, thirsting for vengeance. Everyone went running to gather firewood. Everyone searched for wood to burn.

Now all the firewood was gone, but the darkness remained. There was no sign of the sun. One night had already lasted three days.

The villagers had to start using corn and manioc meal for fuel. They trembled with fear of the Txopokods, of the deep shadows of the night. They kept cooking the arm over the fire so the Txopokod couldn't come and eat the whole village.

"Throw out that phantom's arm!" ordered the chief. "Why should we cook this strange beast? Our corn is running out! Now we have nothing left to burn!"

Kupipurô, the Rabbit, arrived. He sang beautifully, just as we did a little while ago. The people all asked him to come inside the hut and sing with them.

The villagers saw things moving in the darkness. The yard was full of Txopokods, encircling the people, preparing for a final banquet.

The Kupipurô rabbits decided to help the men. They got up and sang to distract the Txopokods.

"Throw the arm away, so the Txopokods won't eat us!"

The villagers gathered together to lift the pot and poured the contents into a stone mortar. They tried to beat the arm with the stone pestle, but it was just like a stubborn clam that doesn't want to open — it wouldn't disintegrate — it kept its shape. Even the Txopokod's bracelets wouldn't break.

Finally they gave up and threw the arm into the yard. The owner, the Txopokod lover, ran and stuck the arm back to his body again. His arm was burning up so he ran to the river bank as fast as he could and threw himself into the water. That part of the river is always warm and they say it's because the Txopokod with the burning arm dove in there.

The Txopokod went swimming in all the rivers and streams he could find, to help him cool down. Finally his arm stopped burning, near the Paulo Saldanha waterfall. That is why the water in that stream is always cold.

When his burning arm finally cooled down, the long night ended, dawn came, and once again there was peace in the village. Many lost days of light had slipped away and now it was almost nightfall again.

They cut off the young woman's clitoris and threw it in the middle of the river – it turned into an electric eel. The drinking gourd they used to carry the clitoris turned into a crab. The betrayed husband didn't want the girl any more. He was afraid. As for the lover, no one knows if he still wanted her – everything is secret. But the Txopokod never returned.

Akaké, a groom with three cocks

Narrator in Macurap: Iaxuí Miton Pedro Mutum Macurap
Other narrators in Portuguese: Aienuiká Rosalina Aruá
Translators: Graciliano Macurap and Alcides Macurap

Going to a party and looking for a husband

Two sisters and their niece were getting ready to go to a neighbor's party. The neighbor was the master of a large plot of corn and it was going to be a lavish party, with lots of animals (that in those days were also people) as guests. The girls didn't know the way, but their sister-in-law, the wife of one of their brothers, offered to show them.

The three young women went to gather tobacco leaves from their plot. They wanted to offer cigarettes to their host, who was generous and would give them lots of *chicha* and plenty of food to eat.

The sister-in-law was wicked and didn't like the girls. She went ahead, promising to put leaves alongside the path to mark the way. But she hated the girls so much that she carefully placed the leaves so they pointed the wrong way – to the path of the Txopokods, ghosts, evil spirits.

Feeling carefree and happy, the three adventurers went walking through the jungle, mistresses of their own time and destiny. Each of the young women thought about meeting a husband, maybe on the walk or maybe at the party – maybe even the same husband for all three of them. It was time for them to get married.

Time passed and, already quite tired, they caught sight of a small hut in the distance. Just then, very near them, an armadillo caught their attention. The niece beat the animal with a stick and killed it without the least difficulty. She cut up the armadillo and the three girls wrapped its meat in leaves, planning to give it to the host of the party, the master of the corn. They headed for the little hut.

An old woman was by the door of the house, tidying up the corncrib. Little did the three know that the armadillo was the old woman's son.

"Grandma, we're dying of hunger! Give us some ears of corn to eat with the armadillo we killed. Come eat with us!"

The old woman started to cry when she saw that her armadillo-son had been slaughtered like game. The three girls gave her bracelets, necklaces and tobacco to help make her feel better. But the two aunts sensed that something was not quite right and nudged the niece, who thought they meant her to offer the old woman some armadillo meat. So she did. The niece was much crazier than her aunts and was always doing things she shouldn't.

And how! The old woman cried even more when she caught the scent of her dead son. But suddenly she grew quiet; she was thinking how nice it would be to eat these three young women.

The aunts didn't notice, but the niece saw that the old woman brought the armadillo back to life and that the pieces of meat disappeared from their mouths and hands. She watched uneasily as the old woman climbed up to the loft where the ears of corn were stored. She kept rummaging around up there. Was she looking for a club to kill them with?

"Let's get out of here, Aunts! This old woman isn't a person! She must be the armadillo's mother! She brought him back to life! She's a Txopokod, a ghost!"

The road of no return

The aunts were enjoying the food and didn't want to leave. But the niece pointed to the door of the hut. It was closing! She pulled her aunts outside and the door slammed shut behind them – they had escaped just in time! The three girls went back to their path, but the trail they had arrived on was now covered with thick, impenetrable jungle. They were frightened. They knew they were lost and that something mysterious was making the forest cover the path they had just been walking on. There was no choice; they had to follow the path in front of them; they couldn't return home.

Farther along the road they met another being. He looked like a man but was really some kind of strange creature. He was high up in a grove of snake-wood trees, cutting down fruit.

"Ai, Grandpa, we're so hungry! Give us a little food! How about some of that fruit?"

They say he turned upside down and started to creep down the tree. He thought they looked good to eat too! The girls were terrified and ran away as fast as they could: people can't turn upside down in a tree! The path kept closing behind them and there was no way to go but forward. It was scary to see the jungle grow so quickly over where they had just passed. What had just been such a clear trail was now nothing but dense, impassable forest.

They kept walking – there was nothing else to do. Soon they saw another man-creature at the top of a tree, cutting down *ingá* fruit. They asked him the way and asked him for some fruit because their stomachs were rumbling. Who knows? He might make one of them a good husband. But they ran away more terrified than ever, when the man – or monster – also turned upside down and came slithering down the trunk, his nose and mouth dribbling saliva, his teeth bared, excited about the unexpected treat.

All they wanted to do was go back home, but the road behind them covered itself with trees and thorns, creepers and vines – from underneath you couldn't even see the sky. There was only one way they could go and that was in front of them, along the trail ahead through the forest.

A husband, master of the piss soup

The girls had no idea where they might be able to sleep and their legs were feeling weak by the time they arrived at Snake's house (Snake was also a man). The chief, Vine Snake, Txadpunpurim, was standing in the doorway. He invited the girls to come in and said they were welcome to sleep there.

They stayed – where else could they go? Vine Snake treated them well. He offered them *chicha* and gave them a place high up in the corn loft to sleep. It was a way to hide the girls from the other snakes (all the people who lived there were really snakes).

The snakes came home in the late afternoon and the crazy niece saw that they weren't people. She tried to tell her aunts but she forgot to lower her voice.

"Be quiet! It's because of you that we got into this mess in the first place! You killed the armadillo and gave it to the old lady!" whispered the aunts.

The girls sat and listened to the snakes' conversations. The other chief, Baratxüxá, the Rattlesnake, wanted to work on the corn loft. He wanted to fix it up and clean it so they would be able to store more corn. Vine Snake, Txadpunpurim, tried to discourage him so he wouldn't find the girls. He suggested a hunting party.

"Let's throw a party, with lots of meat!"

No one would ever miss a chance to go hunting. The snakes – everyone except Vine Snake – went out that night and planned to hunt for several days. But before he followed the others, Black Snake looked in the *chicha* pots and saw that they were all dry and empty. He pissed in the clay pots and filled them all to the brim. He didn't know about the niece who had been watching the whole time from her hiding place in the corn loft.

At sunrise Vine Snake called to the girls and told them to climb down and drink some *chicha*.

"I'm not drinking any of this *chicha*, Aunties, it's snake piss!"

Their protector insisted that they eat and drink. The aunts drank the *chicha* but the niece kept her mouth shut tightly.

"Go on, you can drink it. That's just how we like it. That's what our *chicha* is like," offered Vine Snake pleasantly.

But she really didn't want it. This Vine Snake would not do for a husband.

The three girls left before the other snakes returned from their hunt. The generous Vine Snake showed them the path to take — but of course there wasn't any other way: behind them was nothing but jungle. There was no way back.

Stealing the pestle and the sister of the winds

They walked and walked until they arrived at a house. The woman who lived in the house had a small pestle made of stone and even from far away they could hear her pounding corn, "tak, tak, tak . . ."

It was a beautiful pestle and the girls wished it belonged to them. The niece was crazy about it but the aunts warned her not to take it.

Piribubid, who owned the pestle, was the sister of the winds. she called to the winds, shouting,

"My brothers, come protect me! Three women are coming who want to steal our pestle!"

The aunts tried to stop her, but the moment Piribubid stopped shouting for her brothers and looked the other way, the niece ran up, grabbed the pestle, and put it in her *marico* (straw basket). The three young women ran away.

Just when they thought they had finally escaped, the girls heard a terrible storm approaching. They were frightened as a violent wind rushed towards them, blowing down even the biggest trees. The trees fell one on top of another with a deafening roar, just missing the three girls. They would have been crushed! The winds were chasing them.

"Throw away that cursed pestle, the winds are almost here!" the aunts begged.

The niece took the pestle out of the marico. She carried it a little way on her shoulder, and when she saw a pile of big rocks, she hurled the pestle against them as hard as she could. It shattered into pieces.

The winds came rushing through the air, while their sister, mistress of the pestle, ran along the ground. Suddenly they stopped. They felt heartsick at the sight of their beautiful pestle broken into shards, scattered among the rocks. But they glued all the pieces back together again and managed to restore the pestle. Then they turned around and took their pestle home with them.

The niece turns into bamboo

The young women felt very relieved to have escaped from the winds and went on their way. Soon they heard a knocking, "tok, tok, tok . . ." It was Woodpecker plucking *gongos* out from inside a tree. He too wanted to eat the girls and they ran away.

A little while later, the crazy niece pricked her foot on a bamboo thorn and after two days she turned into bamboo herself. The aunts were sad and didn't know what to do. They saw a man digging larvae out of an *ouricuri* palm.

"You've arrived?" he asked.

"We've arrived," said the sisters sadly, because their niece had turned into bamboo. "Our niece turned into bamboo!"

The man gave them some larvae from the *ouricuri* palm to eat. But all they could think about was how to save their niece and turn her back into a person again. They showed the man where their niece had been bewitched and turned into bamboo. He wanted to help.

"Look here. Close your eyes – I'm going to smoke. I'm going to try something."

The two sisters closed their eyes while he smoked and smoked. When they opened their eyes, their niece appeared! She had turned back into a person.

The husband with more than what's necessary

By now the three girls were exhausted and started to look for a place to spend the night. They saw an old man sitting and picking *gongos* out of an *ouricuri* palm. His name was Akaké.

"Grandpa, *Awatô*! We want to eat *gongo*!"

"Then come and eat, pretty ladies! There's corn and a bit of *gongo!* Go ahead and eat. Then I'll pick out some more!"

The hungry girls ate their fill. They liked having a man to feed them. Too bad he was so old.

Akaké sent the girls to the river bank to take a bath. He told them there were fruit rinds to wash their eyes with and leaves from the annatto tree for them to use as well.

On their way to the river they passed Akaké's mother, who was sweeping the yard.

"I'm so glad these young women escaped! Now I'll have someone to help sweep my son's yard." Soon she was calling the three young women her daughters-in-law.

Akaké's mother didn't look like a woman and the three girls didn't even notice her. She looked just like a clay pot. The girls sat down next to the pot and the crazy niece happened to scratch it with her fingernail. Blood came out. The pot screamed.

"Aunties, this pot has blood just like we do. It must be a person!"

The old man approached. He was already calling the three girls his wives, but the niece didn't call him husband. She didn't want to have anything to do with such an ugly old man.

However, Akaké's mother, the woman-pot, promised to give him a bath of ashes and hot water which would turn him into a handsome young man again.

After giving him the bath, the old woman warned, "He'll be here any minute – such a good-looking young man! But don't look at his body, only at his feet!"

The niece wondered why they weren't allowed to look at his body, if now he really was young again. She decided to look anyway.

The young women saw him arriving in the distance a little while later, playing a bamboo flute to announce his presence. The aunts kept their heads lowered and obediently looked only at his feet. The niece secretly raised her eyes. What a fright! Young he was, nothing like the ugly old man he had so recently been. But what a huge, unusual penis sheath she saw swinging between his legs, hiding his triple gift! No wonder they weren't supposed to look! She could see that instead of just one, he had three cocks! It was only then that she remembered that akaké means straw basket, or penis sheath.

Many hammocks of love

Night fell and Akaké called the young women to his enormous hammock – it had plenty of room for the four of them. The niece refused – how could she marry a monster like that? Just imagine what those three things would be like when they were hard and ready for making love! Just one would make her happy, but three was too much! While her aunts lay down and slept she went out looking for a different hammock to sleep in.

She found one nearby. It belonged to Tree Man, who was covered with twisting *sapopemba* roots. She stretched out to try and get some rest but the branches and twigs started to squeeze her. They almost strangled her. It was impossible to sleep.

"What kind of a man is this? I have to escape!"

"This is just how I am. I belong to Akaké's tribe."

The crazy niece jumped out of Tree Man's hammock and went to look for another one. She tried out many different hammocks, each one belonging to a different man. But none of them worked out. One of the men was nice and warm but he was a monkey and kept biting her. How could she sleep?

"I don't like men who bite!"

"But I'm from a monkey tribe. I'm not a man!"

Then Cold Man, Pitigboré, called her to his hammock. She breathed a sigh of relief and finally went to sleep. But she had barely had a chance to doze off when she woke up shivering with cold. She felt like ice.

"Now what kind of a man did I choose?"

"That's how I am. I am Frost."

Still shivering, she went back to Akaké's hammock.

"Aunts, I'm freezing cold!"

"Make a fire for her. Then the two of you lie down between her and me, so she won't be scared!" said Akaké happily.

But the niece was still scared.

"These men who work for Akaké and his mother aren't people. Each one is stranger than the other, Aunts, let's get out of here!" she begged.

The niece lay down in the hammock, but as far away from Akaké as she could. She was pretty sure he couldn't reach her, but just the idea of his triple threat made her very anxious.

Until then, Akaké hadn't even tried to make love to any of the young women. But now that he saw the three girls sleeping peacefully beside him in his hammock, he stripped off his akaké, his penis sheath, the straw protector that covered his triple treasure. He thrust himself into all three women at the same time – even the niece, who was the farthest away. How this is possible, how they had this four-way orgy, no one knows – his phalluses hung one right next to the other, more or less in the place where a single one belongs, on a normal man.

And so the three young women became his wives, all at the same time. Morning came, and the three girls, who had never had a man before, said to each other: "I'm menstruating!

"Me too!"

"Me too!"

The mother-in-law told the three new wives to make *chicha* and she made them work all day long without stopping. They pounded the corn with a pestle, then they stirred and watched over the great clay pots full of *chicha* as they cooked over the smoky fire. The mother-in-law kept watch to make sure the girls didn't stop working and she wouldn't let them relax for a single minute. She wanted the food to be really delicious.

The three young women became pregnant, all three of them walking around with big bellies at the same time. Even the crazy niece calmed down a little. At last the three girls had their babies.

The pet birds

When the three girls lived in their own village they had raised some pet birds. But when they started on their journey, they left them behind with their mothers. One day when they came back from Akaké's plot and were on their way to fetch water to make *chicha*, they saw some pretty birds that looked a lot like the ones they had left in their village. The birds were singing beautiful melodies.

"Could these be our birds, Aunties?" asked the crazy niece.

"No, they can't be. They must be from the jungle. Our home is too far away!"

But the birds flew fearlessly into their hands and let the young women put seeds right into their tiny beaks. They were indeed the girls' pet birds. The birds flew back to the mothers' village.

"Where are your owners?" asked the mothers.

Birds don't know how to speak; they only know how to fly. Three times the birds came to visit the girls and three times they returned to the mothers' village. The crazy niece made up her mind.

"I'm going home with our birds. I'm going away from here!"

The aunts didn't want to leave, but still, one day, the three girls all went home. The birds were their guides and showed them the way. The young women brought their children in their arms. They were very happy to see their mothers.

A young man from the village liked the niece and wanted to make love to her. He took a hot coal from the fire, fanned it with *taxi* leaves, and put it under her baby's hammock. The child sizzled and crackled until it died.

The *koman* song (the frog song), or the women who barbecued and devoured their husbands

Narrators: Überiká Sapé Macurap and Iaxuí Miton Pedro Mutum Macurap
Translators: Biweiniká Atiré Macurap and Alcides Macurap
Other translators in Portuguese and Macurap: Buraini Andere Macurap and Menkaiká Juraci Macurap

Katxuréu, the mistress of music, little frogs, and Genipap

The women sent their daughters to the lake to catch fish and small frogs for dinner. The girls obeyed happily, for the lake was full of fish and other little swimming creatures that would be fun and easy to catch.

The girls had already captured lots of tasty little tadpoles, when a hideous old woman appeared, floating in the middle of the lake. Her name was Katxuréu. She saw the girls catching the little fish.

"My little granddaughters, you're ruining our music and our genipap!"

"We're not ruining anything, Grandma! Our mothers sent us fishing so we'd have something good to eat for dinner!"

"You think you're catching fish and tadpoles, but it's really our music and our genipap dye that we use for body paint! I'm going to teach you to sing."

The old woman started to sing and her song was so beautiful that the girls could hardly breathe; they found themselves seduced by the beautiful music and tried to learn it.

"And now my little ones, go call your mothers and tell them to come learn my songs too. Tell them you were stealing our music and our body paint, not just little tadpoles!"

When the girls returned to the village their mothers complained that they hadn't brought back any fish or baby frogs.

"How could we have fished?" They explained, "There's an old lady named Katxuréu in the lake and she told us to fetch you so you can learn her beautiful songs. She said the little tadpoles are her music and her genipap and that we'd better not take any with us!"

The mothers were curious and went with the girls to visit the old woman Katxuréu.

"The girls spoke the truth, my daughters," confirmed the woman of the lake. "It is our music and our genipap that swim in these waters, not fish or frogs. Come, I'll teach you."

The women and their daughters formed a circle and danced and sang for hours on end. The music possessed them and they felt transported into a state of wonder and enchantment. They were so engrossed in the music that they weren't even aware of time passing – but they did start to get hungry.

Old Katxuréu floated in the water, almost her entire body visible, as she taught the songs in a strong, full voice. Her hair was jet black and so long that it reached all the way down to her feet. It was almost scary how thick and abundant her hair was – but it was very pretty. Katxuréu saw that the women were enjoying themselves and said:

"Tomorrow you must come again to sing the frog song with me. But before you come, you must kill one of your husbands – one each day – so we can eat them while we sing. Now that's real food, not our little fish and tadpoles."

At first the women were shocked, but they kept thinking about it and kept remembering the old woman's heavenly song. Before long they were all excited and ready to start killing the men.

"Who will be the first one to kill her husband? Who will kill her husband today?"

"I will! I will!" responded several voices at the same time. And they chose one from among them to be the first to murder her husband.

The roasted husbands

The woman killed her husband at dawn, while he was asleep. She put him in her *marico* and covered the top with straw. It was still early when she told everyone she was going to the field with the others. She brought the basket to the lake and they cooked the dead man in a clay pot. Old Katxuréu and the other women ate him all up.

And so it was, every night. Each night another man disappeared, and the women spent the day by the lake, singing with the old woman and eating their husbands' flesh.

The men didn't understand what was going on, why they were disappearing one by one. Their wives said they went to the field, but they were always so late coming home, and they seemed so strange when they returned, that the men started to think they might be lying.

The men decided that they must find out the truth. They couldn't just let so many men disappear without doing anything about it. Every time one of them went to gather straw to make a headdress for a *chicha* party, he ended up disappearing for ever. And while this was going on, as if nothing unusual was happening at all, the women went to make *chicha* and went to the field. Could it be true? Before long there wouldn't be a single man left, only women! Didn't they miss making love, lying down with those-with-whom-they-always-played? Had they found some new playmates?

It was decided that the men would all go hunting to put the women off their guard, but that one young man would stay in the village and try to discover their secret.

When all the men had gone off hunting, the boy pretended he had a fever and lay down, shivering, near the fire. The women took care of him. They felt sorry for him – even the women who had already killed their own husbands.

They gave him a pot of *chicha* and left him stretched out comfortably in his hammock. He appeared to fall asleep and the women left the hut.

The *danse macabre*

The women had killed one of their husbands the night before and had hidden the corpse by a sapopemba root near the village. Before going to sing with Katxuréu they ran to get the dead husband's body. They assumed they were safe from being seen by masculine eyes – the only man close by was the sick boy, who couldn't move.

Meanwhile, once the boy found himself alone, he climbed up into the corn loft and made a small hole in the straw of the ceiling, hoping that from there he would be able to see what the women were up to. He saw clearly as a woman pulled her dead husband out of the hiding place, threw him in her *marico* and lifted him onto her back.

The boy climbed down as fast as he could and ran to find the men in their campground in the jungle.

"It *is* the women who are killing us off! They're murdering us one by one!"

The men were taken by a terrible, inexpressible rage. They filled their quivers with arrows made of *mamuí* wood and went into the jungle after their wives. They wanted to track the women down and kill all of them.

"Let's kill these disgraceful women!"

The men followed the women's footprints and soon arrived at the lake. They moved in a deliberate, menacing silence.

Still hidden in the jungle, the men surrounded their wives. The women were dancing in a big circle, and eating the well-cooked flesh of one of the men they had killed. They sang to the accompaniment of the old woman playing her bamboo flute, gripped by a terrible, ferocious joy. Even in the midst of their hate and pain, the men could not help but be impressed by the force of the music, by the old woman's *koman* song. She danced too, blowing into her bamboo flute, her black hair flying around wildly, covering her withered breasts.

The dead men's bones were strung up all around and some decorated the old woman's and the dancers' legs. Even from where they stood in the jungle, the men could hear the rumble of the women's feet hitting the ground as they danced in their circle, ". . . pá, pá, pá . . ."

"Who will kill today? Who wants to give us a husband to eat?"

Vengeance

At that moment, in the middle of the dance, the cord the bones were hanging from broke. It was as if the women guessed they were surrounded, as if they had received a sudden warning. At just the same time the men shot their arrows at the women. They killed all the women and piled their bodies into a big heap. Then they called to Katxuréu, who had escaped into the water.

"Grandmother, come out of the water, come teach us how to sing! Your music is so beautiful!"

They called her and called her but the old woman had disappeared. She wasn't stupid. She dove down to where she lived, in the deepest part of the lake. But the men begged and pleaded so much that finally she floated to the surface carrying her beautiful bamboo flutes.

"Sing your beautiful song for us!"

The old woman sang the same song she had sung for the women and now it was the men's turn to be overcome by the divine music. They didn't want the exquisite music to stop, but they remembered what had happened.

"Your song is beautiful, Grandmother, but you killed many men, and we must take revenge!"

Katxuréu opened her mouth, bared her teeth, and boasted, "Yes, and it was with these sharp teeth that I ate you! I ate many men!"

Her brilliant white teeth glittered in the middle of the lake, and one of the men took careful aim and shot her in the mouth with an arrow, and shattered all her teeth. But even so, the old woman didn't die. She is still alive today.

Men without women

The men returned to the village but now they had no women to cook for them or to make love to.

Only two little girls survived the men's revenge. They had been hiding behind a tree trunk and the chief was the only one who saw them – they were his sisters. He saw them crying and they told him that their mother and their aunt had killed their brother and their uncle.

"Did you eat your uncle and your brother?"

"No, our mother didn't let us!"

The chief brought the two girls back to the village and hid them high up in a corn loft. They were the only ones to escape the men's revenge and no one knew about them. They grew up.

Now the men were the ones who made the *chicha*, who chewed the corn and yams and manioc to help it to ferment. It tasted terrible – it wasn't sweet at all. But without women, what else could they do? They complained and spat out their *chicha*, but there was nothing they could do about it.

They took turns. Every day one of the men stayed in the kitchen instead of doing men's chores, like hunting or working in the field. Finally, the chief offered to cook the *chicha* and the next day he sent everyone else out hunting.

Once everyone had gone to the jungle and he was alone in the hut, the chief let the two sisters come down from their hiding place. He wanted them to help him cook, to chew the corn kernels to sweeten the *chicha* – that's what the men didn't know how to do.

The two girls were happy to come down and help. They did their work and then they returned to their makeshift bedroom high up in the loft. The chief carefully swept up the cornhusks and scraps of chaff so there would be no trace of the girls' work.

Everyone loved the *chicha*.

"This is different! Now this is how *chicha* is supposed to taste! It's delicious! Our chief makes sweet, delicious *chicha* – while ours is no good at all."

"It's only because I know how to do it, my friends. I learned the trick," he said modestly.

The men didn't know the *chicha* they were drinking was made by real women.

The chief sent everyone out hunting every three or four days, whenever it was time to make *chicha*. The girls, who by now were full-grown women, would climb down and make the seasoning, chewing to sweeten the *chicha*. The others would drink it all up eagerly upon their return.

Finally the chief sent the men out hunting so often that they started to get suspicious.

"There must be a woman around here somewhere! The chief must be hiding her from us!"

The chief told them the truth.

"I didn't let you kill my little sisters. They didn't eat men's flesh!"

"It's really true that when men try to make *chicha* it just doesn't taste right!"

The world's new beginning and
the women's *Koman* song

The two girls came down from their hiding place. They were young women now. They got married and the population started to grow once more. Their brother, the chief, didn't start a family right away – only much later, when there were women who were not his sisters – when his nieces grew up.

If it wasn't for these two sisters, there wouldn't be any more Macurap in the world. The sisters didn't forget; they taught the *koman* song that they had learned from old Katxuréu to all the women. Until today we sing the *koman* song.

The women without men, the Amazons, the Kaledjaa-Ipeb, the black women

Narrators: Iaxuí Miton Pedro Mutum Macurap
Translators: Niendeded João Macurap and Rosilda Aruá

The huntress

It was the dry season. Today, we would say it was August – but in those times we didn't reckon in months: we only knew winter and summer.

One day a very handsome hunter went wandering in the forest searching for wild boar and curassows. As he approached a river bank he heard a rustling in the nearby leaves. Hoping to find some kind of game, the hunter drew closer in silence, but then he almost shouted out loud with admiration. For leaning over the water was an enchanting young woman. Her body was painted and around her neck were beautiful necklaces made of *tucumã* palm. She was stirring *timbó* (a woody vine that contains poison the Indians use to kill fish) into the darkening water and plucked out the fish as they died. The hunter gathered his courage and asked:

"Who are you? And why are you alone in the jungle? Don't you think it's dangerous to come here by yourself with so many animals around?"

"I came to fish with *timbó*. And you, who come wandering in our land, who might you be?"

"I went out hunting and have ended up far away from my village."

"Well, now you are going to stop hunting. I want you to help me gather up the fish as they get dizzy from the poison I put in the water!"

The hunter couldn't have dreamed of anything better than staying with this beautiful young woman, making a game of filling the palm leaves with fish – laughing, brushing against her as if by accident, his body gently touching hers.

That's how they spent the whole day, in the warmth of the sun, gathering all kinds of fish. They kindled a fire on the river bank and once in a while they stopped fishing and the young woman grilled some fish for them to eat. Finally, at the end of the afternoon, she insisted that the young man accompany her back to her village – and to the astonishment of the hunter, she was already proposing that he stay and live in her village.

When they arrived at the huts, the hunter saw that there were only women and girls. His new friend had told him she was single, but he didn't know she was a Kaledjaa-Ipeb: one of the black women who never have a man, who lived only with other women, doing all the chores of the field, as well as hunting, fishing, and building houses – as if they were strong, brave men. The only man of the village was the father of the young woman and her sisters, but he was away. He'd gone to find *taquara* (bamboo) to make arrows with.

The young women were sitting together on straw mats inside one of the huts, and their mother was lying down in a hammock.

The maidens with the ferocious father

"Who could that be with our sister?" they asked each other curiously.

When they saw that it was a man, they danced with joy around their sister and her new friend.

"Our sister has brought us a husband!"

They hugged the young man tenderly. They smoothed his hair and playfully caressed his arms and back. The hunter felt uneasy and said he had to leave – that people were waiting for him in another village. But the girls laughed and surrounded him. They offered him grilled fish, *gongos*, yams, Brazil nuts, and *chicha*. How could he leave?

The girls set up a hammock for their new friend. He slept by himself, but the young women's hammocks were hanging all around him: above, below, on both sides, as close to him as possible.

The next day he told them again that he had to go away.

"Just wait a few days. Our father will come home soon, with *taquaras* that don't exist on your land. Let us give you some as a present! And then you can stay here with us and be our husband!"

"But your father will want to eat me! I'm scared!"

The girls promised not to let their father harm him in any way, and so the hunter stayed and let the exquisite young women pamper him. But he was still terrified at the thought of their ferocious father.

Two days later, at the end of the afternoon, he heard the rumble of the girls' father approaching, still some distance away. He brought the strangest *taquaras*, the like of which the young man had never seen and he wished they belonged to him.

The daughters offered their father countless gourds brimming with *chicha*, but he never got full – he was a Txopokod, a spirit. He never felt stuffed as we do. He burped and belched and kept wanting more.

"My daughters, I smell people around here!" he muttered.

"You must be mistaken, Father. There's no one new around here," they said.

Hidden in a corner, the young man whispered to the girls that their terrible father was going to kill him. But the girls said they would kill their own father before they let anything happen to the young man.

The Txopokod father kept insisting that he smelled someone, but his daughters continued to deny it.

Night fell and the young women went to bed with hatchets in their hands, prepared to kill their father if necessary. As on other nights, they surrounded the hunter with their hammocks, very close, protecting him.

They expected their father to attack the hunter and knew that no one would be getting any sleep that night. Fear and all, the young man let himself be sheltered by the women and calmed down a little with the swaying of his hammock.

The father pretended to snore so everyone would think he was asleep. But the young women stayed alert – they didn't believe he was sleeping. They heard him get up and start looking in his daughters' hammocks, one by one. They kept very quiet and still, until finally one of the girls cried out:

"Our father is going to kill our husband!"

As if a single person, the girls leapt out of their hammocks to beat their father.

"Everything's fine, my daughters, I'm not going to do anything! Leave me alone!"

The daughters knocked him down on the ground and beat him until he was covered with bruises. Then they let him be.

The next day the scene repeated itself. The father snored shamelessly and pretended to be enjoying a deep sleep. When he stopped snoring and prepared to attack his invisible son-in-law, the women screamed in a single voice that it was time to kill him. This time they beat him more severely, but he didn't die because he was a Txopokod. He took his beatings and bled a lot, but he stayed alive.

The young women never got any sleep. They spent every night fighting with their father and were exhausted. No matter how much they beat him on the head and the rest of his body, he kept trying to murder the young man who was seducing his daughters.

A husband for everyone

Finally, after several days, in agony and purple with bruises, the father gave in.

"Very well then, my daughters, I can see that you are not going to give up this man – this man you met by chance in the jungle. But will you at least agree to have him make arrows for me? I want him to work for me."

The hunter spent many days making arrows and the young women stayed by his side and begged him to stay. When it was time for him to scorch the *taquara*, they kindled fires for him. They sat with him while he carved the arrows and decorated them with wild boar's fur. He painted elaborate patterns on the new arrows with genipap dye – and the girls stayed close by his side.

He had been working on the arrows for days when his friend, the first Kaledjaa-Ipeb he had met, insisted they go hunting. She said there was no food left and that they had to go find some game to eat. The two of them went into the jungle alone and the sisters stayed home and waited for them to return.

The beautiful hunting teacher

They walked and walked and walked. As they went along the hunter tried to imitate tinamous and other creatures, trying to lure them into an ambush. But not a single animal appeared while the hunter grew more and more ashamed. Didn't he know how to hunt any more? Couldn't he provide for his pretty young companion?

The two kept hunting. The hunter remembered that the Kaledjaa-Ipeb usually hunted by themselves and finally he asked:

"Do you hunt the same way I do? Do you use the same bird calls that I do?"

The young woman gently taught him a different way to hunt. She took a leaf and whistled with it. Tinamous and guans and curassows and toucans all appeared as if enchanted.

The hunter shot at the birds, but even with so many all around he missed every time and soon ran out of arrows. It was the Kaledjaa-Ipeb girl who killed the birds.

They put the dead birds – curassows, guans, toucans, and tinamous – into an enormous *marico* and headed back to the village so the sisters could pluck and roast their game. The young woman carried the *marico* on her back as if it were as light as a feather. The burden was nothing to her, even though there was so much game.

There was plenty to eat for days. There were chunks of meat on the grill as well as set aside already cooked in clay pots. Everyone ate their fill: the young women, their father, and the hunter. The young man said that now he could go away, but the young Kaledjaa-Ipeb woman wouldn't even discuss it. When the food was all gone, she asked him to go hunting again. And that's how it always was.

It was on their walks in the forest that they began to make love – until then the hunter had slept alone in his hammock, still afraid of the girls' terrible father and of their mother too – she was also very fierce. But now, in the jungle, the hunter abandoned himself to the charms of this woman who was so different: who knew how to hunt and fish better than he did, who was strong and yet so pretty, who made love with the same magical touch that she did everything else.

It was always the young woman who called the game; when the hunter tried, the animals would disappear.

One day the girl killed all the birds except the toucan.

"At least kill the toucan!" she said.

This time the hunter hit his mark. The young Kaledjaa-Ipeb woman grabbed the dead bird and sucked out its eye.

The hunter's enchanted life and longing for his mother

At night, in the village, the sisters prepared the game to be eaten. Their father had by now accepted his son-in-law and his presence no longer bothered him. He even joked good-naturedly about what had happened.

"My own daughters almost killed me! Imagine wanting a husband that much! I guess I'll let these devilish girls keep the man they found."

The hunter felt intoxicated and happy, being around so many beautiful young women all the time. But he also thought about his own people, about his mother who by now certainly must have thought he had died. He told his wife and his sisters-in-law that he was going to visit his village. They agreed to let him go, but only if he promised to come back soon. His wife, the Kaledjaa-Ipeb woman, urged him not to tell anyone about the young women and their village.

The hunter walked for several days until he came to his family's hut. His mother asked where he had been for so long, but all he would say was that he had been visiting some relatives – he respected the Kaledjaa-Ipeb woman's warning. He spent a few days with his family that he had missed so much, but soon he remembered that the Kaledjaa-Ipeb had asked him to hurry back home to them.

There was plenty of *chicha* waiting for the young hunter when he returned to the village of the Kaledjaa-Ipeb and all of the young women wanted a chance to feed him. But their father complained about his son-in-law's absence the past few days – no one had gone hunting or fishing and there had been nothing to eat.

The young man always went hunting and fishing with the same young woman, his wife. The other girls had to stay at home and keep making *chicha* for their father.

The huntress loved going to the forest with her husband. She promised to teach his people how to hunt more efficiently – she knew many secrets! She showed him that the screen he used to hide from the animals, made of palm fronds, didn't have to be solid like a wall – a few leaves would do the trick. And she said she would teach him how to call the animals, and show him which leaves to use to attract them. He would never again be without meat to eat.

His father-in-law sent him to the fields with the women to help them clear more land in the jungle for planting. The young women took him with them to the fields, and while he cut down the trees, they made *chicha*.

The young man missed his people and went to visit them a second time. He stayed a few days and returned without any problems to the Kaledjaa-Ipeb women. He arrived as he always did, at sunset, and the father called to his daughters:

"Go hunting with my son-in-law!"

The enchanted women's children and the Stubborn One

By now the young man had his own plot, and had made love to all the young women.

His wife, the first woman he'd met in the jungle, was pregnant.

"I'm pregnant!" she told her sisters, contentedly. "Now it's your turn to go out walking in the jungle with him," she said to all of them.

The other young women began to go hunting and fishing in the jungle with the young man. One by one they made love to him and it made them all very happy. The first girl had her baby while the next became pregnant. They took turns like that and only went walking in the jungle with the hunter when they weren't pregnant.

The first baby was a boy. He grew quickly because the Kaledjaa-Ipeb women bathed him with secret leaves that make a child grow as much in just a few days as we do in many years.

The hunter continued to visit his mother's village but his relatives were very curious and kept pestering him with questions. They asked him where he had been and why he stayed away so much, but he just said that he'd gone to visit distant cousins. No one was satisfied with his answer – they wanted to know everything.

There was a Stubborn One in the village who tormented the hunter all the time and wouldn't leave him in peace. The hunter thought about his son and about the baby soon to be born and he resisted – he didn't want to tell. But the Stubborn One kept insisting and kept reassuring him until finally the hunter revealed everything about his parallel life among the Kaledjaa-Ipeb women.

"I want to have a baby with one of those women, like you did. Your women are Txopokods, they're not real people! Wouldn't it be incredible to have children with Txopokod women?" the Stubborn One said over and over again.

The Stubborn One pestered and harassed the hunter so much that he ended up telling him how to get to the black women's village, just to get a little peace.

The Stubborn One went right away to try to find the Kaledjaa-Ipeb women's village. He followed the hunter's instructions and found his way without difficulty, and when he arrived he saw a very lively boy playing in the yard. It was the hunter's son, who was always very happy and excited to see his father. He always missed him so much that he would jump laughing and singing into his lap.

But when he saw the Stubborn One, the boy was indifferent. He interrupted his game but was quiet – he didn't know the strange man. Now if it had been his father, then what a warm welcome he would have given him!

The women received the stranger politely, but without pleasure or enthusiasm. It would have been different with the hunter! The Stubborn One was disappointed by his chilly reception.

The boy said to his mother, "Now they've found us! There are strange people coming here."

The Kaledjaa-Ipeb women were fearful of being discovered and captured and they told their worries to their father. They put up a hammock for the Stubborn One inside the hut near a rock. When the stranger fell asleep, they ate him. They killed him with the rock – he wasn't the father of their children! Besides, who told him to be so stubborn?

The women without men disappear
and the hunter goes looking for them

The hunter, the little boy's father, soon thought that something bad must have happened, because the Stubborn One had not returned. That was when he finally told his mother the truth. He told her about the son who was already big and about the other who was about to be born. He talked about the women and the boy with bitter longing.

The hunter felt more and more unhappy. He was miserable with longing and set out to look for his women, but when he arrived in the place where they had always been, there was nothing there – only a barren field. Everything was quiet. There wasn't even a single hut, and instead of the boy who was always so happy to see him, there were only noisy swarms of buzzing bees.

The Kaledjaa-Ipeb women had taken everything with them, even their huts. Only the Stubborn One's bones were left behind on the ground, clear evidence of what had happened.

The hunter returned to his village crying, his heart broken. His mother tried to cheer him up.

"What will I do without my son?" lamented the hunter.

"But he's not a person, he's a Txopokod," said his mother, trying to help him shake off his sadness.

But nothing could console the hunter when he thought of the charmed life he had enjoyed among his loving Kaledjaa-Ipeb women, who hunted and fished so well, who could have given him so many children. Even though they had such a scary monster for a father, they showed him only love and taught him wonderful things. And in the end, even his father-in-law had been treating him reasonably well.

The hunter wandered sadly through the jungle, until one day he happened upon his son playing among the trees. After a long time he had found himself on an enchanted path – a straight path, not winding like the other trails in the jungle – which brought him to his son, who was overjoyed to see him.

The hunter asked his Kaledjaa-Ipeb wife to let him take his son back to the other village, his mother's village. He reminded her that he had never wanted to stay with them in the first place, that little by little they had seduced him into staying. The Kaledjaa-Ipeb woman refused to be separated from the boy. The hunter wanted to kill his father-in-law, but the women wouldn't let him.

All that remained was for him to return to his village, sadder than ever. But with the feeling of vengeance fulfilled, he told his mother that all that was left of the Stubborn One was his bones – there could be nothing more just than the death of the one who had caused the end of the happiness he had enjoyed in his two separate worlds.

And so, because of the meddling of the Stubborn One, people lost the teachings of the women without men: the knowledge these women would have revealed to their husband as he grew more and more accustomed to them, as their children became his companions: the secrets of the leaves, of abundant hunting and fishing.

The great snake, awandá,
the boa constrictor

Narrators: Überiká Sapé Macurap and Iaxuí Miton Pedro Mutum Macurap
Translators: Biweiniká Atiré Macurap and Alcides Macurap
Other narrators in Portuguese: Wariteroká Rosa Macurap and Aienuiká Rosalina Aruá

The independent lover

There was a beautiful, hardworking young woman who had many suitors, but she pushed them all away. At the insistence of her mother and her family, however, the young woman ended up getting married anyway – it's not possible for our women to stay single.

She didn't want to have anything to do with her husband; she felt disgusted whenever he approached her. At night she kindled the pitch fire to light the hut and help her to avoid his advances. Even so, her husband climbed into her hammock and tried to embrace her. The girl pushed him violently onto the ground.

"I already told you I don't like you! Can't you get it through your head?"

"You've been pushing me away for too long, just like you did all the other men! But I'll find a way to get even. Just wait and see!" responded the young man, furious and humiliated.

He went to talk to a friend. He told his friend how his wife had viciously pushed him out of her hammock because he wanted to make love to her. He said he didn't know what to do, that he couldn't stand living like this – burning with desire – despised by his own wife.

"My wife doesn't want me! How can I get even with her? I want revenge!"

The friend had a plan. The two men went to cut down and draw sap from a variety of trees: rubber trees, gum trees, cabbage palms, and *paxiúba-barriguda* palms. They mixed the liquids, mashed them together thoroughly, poured the whole mixture into the hollow of a small section of bamboo, and sealed it tightly with straw and resin. Then the friend told the husband what he must do.

"When your wife pushes you out of her hammock, when she turns her back on you – so she doesn't even have to see you lying on the ground – then pour this liquid on her back!"

And that's what the husband did, that same night. He took the section of bamboo out from its hiding place in the straw wall of the hut, waited until everyone was asleep, and approached his wife. He went to lie down with her in her hammock, but she pushed him away and he fell to the ground. The young woman turned away and her husband spread the sap all over her back.

When she woke up, the young woman felt an unbearable itching all over her body. She complained to her mother, who soon guessed what had happened.

"Ah, my daughter, you didn't accept your husband, our son-in-law. He must have found some way to harm you!"

Every waking minute the young woman scratched herself against anything she could find made of wood or straw. She bathed in the river. She used leaves. But nothing helped.

Her mother tried to help her, but without success. At night she lay awake listening uneasily to her daughter's unhappy moans and groans, but eventually she drifted off to sleep. Finally the wailing stopped and the girl seemed to have calmed down and gone to sleep, but the mother woke up feeling anxious.

So she could take better care of her daughter, the mother kindled a fire and blew on it to bring up a good blaze. But when she looked in the girl's hammock, what a shock! The girl had disappeared and in her place was an *awandá*, a boa constrictor. There was no doubt, thought the mother, the rejected husband had bewitched the girl and transformed her into a snake. The girl's father and brother came and saw a boa constrictor.

The girl's brother was very upset over what had happened and cultivated an intense hatred for his brother-in-law. He wanted his sister to have an appropriate place to stay, so he made a hole in the straw wall of the hut and dug a well nearby for her to live in. He began to wander, dejected, through the jungle – how was it possible for someone to do such an evil thing to his sister?

On one of his new walks the brother encountered a genip tree. In those times, the Indians didn't have any good body paint. They used charcoal, but it came off easily with water. The brother prepared some dye made of green genipap from the genip tree (which was still unknown in the village), and decided to take it to his sister-snake, so she could paint beautiful designs all over his body.

When he arrived at the small pool where his sister lived, he called to her tenderly:

"Sister, sister! I've come to visit you!"

She hesitated at first but then she came to the surface. The boy showed her his new invention, the dye. She told him to put the dye in her mouth, and then to slip his arm inside her.

"Come enter into me slowly, in my mouth. Come slide inside so I can lick you gently with my tongue and my teeth. When you come out, you'll be painted all over – you'll be beautiful and happy!"

"I want you to paint my whole body – every inch of me! I'll go in very gently!"

Using her teeth and the genipap, the sister painted marvelous designs and motifs all over the young man's body. First one arm, then the other, then she moved on to his legs. Next, so she could paint the rest of his body up to his chest, she told him to hang from a branch and slide almost his entire body inside her.

She said, "When I'm finished, I'll give you a signal. Then you must urinate inside me – that's the only way for me to expel you out of my body."

He did everything just as she had told him to. He made the most of the
painting session: he vibrated inside the snake, and her subtle tongue caressed
him with the genipap. At the height of his bliss, he urinated and came out. He
was dazzling, ready for the *chicha* feast that was planned for that night.

The artist brother

It was a lively party and when the young man arrived, everyone was already
dancing and drinking and enjoying themselves. But who could this be?
Everyone in the village looked at the brother with admiration. (Other men's
bodies were painted too, but with charcoal; they went to wash themselves off
so they wouldn't be at too much of a disadvantage.) The young man seemed
like a spirit from the heavens. Everyone kept asking him how he had accom-
plished such a marvelous, extraordinary thing.

He went to many parties, always painted exquisitely from head to toe. But
the painting wasn't the only new thing about him: after finding the genipap,
it also happened that he knew how to hunt much better than before. He went
to set an ambush at the foot of a fruit tree, a genip tree, where lots of squirrel monkeys liked to climb. Jaguars came too, looking for the monkeys, more
jaguars than he had ever seen. He watched from his hiding place and planned
to come back the next day and kill them. When he returned to the village, he
didn't tell anyone of his plans.

He returned the next day, and so did the jaguars looking for the little monkeys. Instead of killing the most beautiful jaguar right away, he started with
a much less impressive one. The others ate the first one he had killed. Then
the hunter killed a second and a third jaguar the same way, and so he tamed
the wild beasts. Only now did he kill some of the especially beautiful ones,
and with their hides he made fantastic hats to go to parties in.

The young hunter also captured lots of macaws while they were eating fruit. He didn't attack and kill them; instead he gave them food. They also grew tame and allowed him to pluck out their feathers.

And so the brother became the most envied warrior at every party. He went with his body elaborately painted; he wore hats made from jaguar skins, such as no one had ever seen before, with headdresses of colorful macaw feathers. Other unusual feathers decorated his arms and legs. The other men, ashamed, threw away their hats and their ornaments.

The jealous husband

The brother-in-law, the one who had turned the sister into a snake, was dying of envy. He tormented the brother to find out how he had transformed his body into such a work of art – but the brother was one who knew how to keep a secret.

One day, the brother-in-law secretly followed him. He saw how the brother prepared the genipap dye and he saw the boa constrictor painting him. He carefully observed each step of the painting process and the next day the brother-in-law went alone to try to do it himself.

He went to the edge of the pool the brother had built and called the snake. She guessed it wasn't her brother calling and wouldn't come to him. But he was so persistent that finally she floated to the surface. The brother-in-law put the dye in the boa constrictor's mouth and slipped his arms and legs inside her. Finally he dangled himself from a tree and slid his entire body into the woman. He wanted every inch of his body painted, including his neck and face. He didn't urinate to be expelled – either he didn't want to, or forgot he was supposed to, or the snake's tongue and teeth didn't arouse any feeling at all . . . The snake swallowed him.

The people in the village noticed the man was missing. The brother, suspicious, said to his mother that the brother-in-law must have gone to the snake-sister's pool. He went after his sister and called gently to her for many hours. But she was gone. She had rushed away with the man in her stomach.

The men of the village went looking for the snake. They wanted to kill her. The mother cried, adding her tears to the water in the little pool. The snake kept going, and on a narrow river bank she gave birth to a baby snake. A little later she vomited up the dead man, painted all over with genipap. The villagers found him there.

The snake traveled on, hiding along the banks of the Guaporé River. The men of the village saw her, in the middle of the river. They shot their arrows but couldn't manage to hit her. She still lives there today, and in the Amazon River – in deep rivers everywhere.

Akarandek, the flying head,
or, the ravenous wife

Narrator: Iaxuí Miton Pedro Mutum Macurap
Translator: Ewiri Margarida Macurap

A man loved his wife very much. She had been his lover since childhood and he took good care of her. He was a fine hunter and he cleared and planted a large vegetable plot – the couple lived well. They always slept together in the same hammock and hugged each other tight all night long.

They were happy, in spite of the fact that the wife had a strange habit. Every night her head separated itself from her body and went searching for game meat in other huts and villages. No matter how much the husband hunted or how much food he provided, his wife always wanted to go somewhere else and eat more. It seems that the wife had a lot of lice but wouldn't let anyone pick them out, and that it was the lice that were always so hungry and cut her head off from her neck – at least that's what some people say.

Could she really be so greedy? Wasn't it enough, the game that her husband so lovingly provided? And how did the head eat? When it swallowed, why didn't the food just fall out through its neck?

The truth is that at dawn the wife's head would stick itself back onto her body, which stayed in the hammock hugging her husband. But there was nothing to see: no sign of blood on the woman's neck, no blood spattered on her husband's chest.

No one knew anything about it, not even the family. One day, however, when it was still dark out, the young woman's mother decided to go to her plot and dig up some yams for an important ritual she was planning. She had to go before dawn, or there wouldn't be time to make enough to drink, and she wanted her daughter to keep her company on the way to the field and help her carry the yams back to the hut.

The old woman called her daughter many times, but there was no answer; everything was quiet. She approached her daughter's hammock and was horrified when she saw the mutilated, headless body lying in her son-in-law's arms.

She screamed until everyone in the entire village woke up. She pointed to the blood on her daughter's neck and demanded revenge against her son-in-law.

"But I didn't kill her! I'm crazy about her!" protested the innocent husband. "Wait just a little while more. You'll see how her head comes back at sunrise and sticks itself back onto her body!"

No one believed him. They pulled the girl's body out of his desperate embrace and buried it. The husband wept inconsolably.

At dawn, the head came whistling quickly home through the air. It looked everywhere for its body. It flew and walked from one end of the village to the other, but its body was nowhere to be found. In great distress, the head went and perched itself on the husband's shoulder.

"Didn't I say she would come?" wailed the exhausted husband.

The wife's head clung to him and wouldn't leave. Now the husband had two heads. Wherever he went, there was the other head. It talked, looked around, gave him orders – it was part of him. The worst of it was that the head started to rot, now that it was separated from the rest of its body. It smelled terrible. It was unbearable. And now there was no longer the beautiful body to keep him warm in the hammock every night, while the greedy head went on its rounds!

The young man was going crazy. No one would come near him because of the smell. Even he was nauseous all the time. Now he didn't have a woman to love, just a stinking head.

After much suffering the husband resolved to kill some game for the head-woman. He hunted a lot and grilled the game. Then he walked some distance away and told the head to go back and eat the meat.

And that's how the husband got the head to let go of him. He ran away.

The bewildered head went searching for him, but she kept on falling over. Seeing that she would never find her husband's shoulder again, the head made itself a little nest by the path to the field. It stayed there most of the time, and if anyone happened to pass nearby, the head ate them. It was the shortest way to get to the fields, but everyone avoided it.

One day, a young man was in a hurry and didn't feel like going the long way around just to avoid the head — he didn't believe it was so dangerous. The brave boy was almost safe when the head started to chase hungrily after him. But he was a strong, fast runner and managed to escape to the village to tell the others — who had already noticed the stench of the decomposing head.

She came rolling along on the ground. Ever since she had become only a head she was a Txopokod, a spirit. She didn't have any blood any more, just the horrible smell.

The men beat the head to bits — but the smell persisted. They had to plug their noses to keep out the disgusting odor that invaded their nostrils like a plague. The shamans had to exorcize the stinking remains of the head and throw them away.

The unlucky hunter,
or the tree-lover

Narrator: Iaxuí Miton Pedro Mutum Macurap
Translator: Ewiri Margarida Macurap

There was once an unmarried man who was very unlucky. He couldn't manage to kill any game whatsoever and he couldn't find a lover. He was a strong, handsome young man – nothing at all wrong with him – but the young women ran away whenever they saw him. There was no apparent reason for such bad luck – but all he could do was lust after the girls from afar with a sad look on his face. He always came back from the forest empty handed, with no meat to offer them.

He was called Ateab, the Unlucky Hunter, and was good friends with Pibei, a Lucky Hunter. They always went to the jungle together looking for game.

Pibei would usually stay in an ambush while Ateab, the Unlucky One, went ahead.

Pibei would soon kill several tinamous. He would tear out the birds' innards, throw them on the ground, and walk on. As soon as Pibei was gone, the Unlucky One would circle back, skewer the bird guts on an arrow, and kindle a fire to grill them on. When the Lucky Hunter reappeared, Ateab would offer him the guts wrapped in leaves, as if they were a piece of grilled tinamou meat.

Pibei thought it tasted bitter and he started to get suspicious. One day he unwrapped his food and saw that it was just innards, not real game at all.

Now Ateab went out alone. He shot arrows at many animals but never hit his mark. He thought he would never find a lover.

One day he found a tree, a *pau-âmago* (*komabo*, in our language), that had a crevice in it lined with *orelha-de-pau* mushrooms. It looked like a pussy, like a cunt. The *pau-âmago* tree is made of very hard wood. Its bark falls off and the wood remains exposed, but covered all over by soft, moist *orelha-de-pau* mushrooms. Ateab thought the tree was like a woman – after all, aren't *orelhas-de-pau* just like a pussy? He made love to it. He entered the cleft in the tree and shamelessly rubbed his cock against the soft *orelhas-de-pau* – even more of which were growing inside the tree. Ateab stayed and had his pleasure.

The tree was becoming a person to Ateab. He spent hours with her, caressing her, flattering her, talking tenderly to her – as if she were a real woman.

Pibei started to wonder about the long walks his friend was always taking and went to see what was going on. From his hiding place he saw Ateab violently beating his tree-lover.

"You betrayed me with Pibei!" shouted Ateab, infuriated, crazy with jealousy for his lover.

He hit the tree hard and turned his back on her, with a jealous, stubborn look on his face. Then later, he made love for real, to the soft crack in the tree trunk. He cried out and moaned, making believe it was a woman making sounds of pain and pleasure, responding to his excesses.

Pibei approached his friend and watched quietly. When Ateab became aware of his presence, he wanted to disappear into the ground, dying of shame.

The Txopokod's balls,
the ashes of the invisible

Narrator: Iaxuí Miton Pedro Mutum Macurap
Translator: Alcides Macurap

Two friends went walking in the forest to gather coconuts from *tucumã* palms. They found a clearing with lots of *tucumã* palms all around and decided to spend the whole day there. The two boys were having a good time and talking about all kinds of things, when they were approached by a Txopokod, a spirit. The two boys, clever young men that they were, soon realized who they were dealing with.

The Txopokod pestered them with a million questions. He asked them for coconuts. He asked about how they lived. And he wanted everything they had. It was a real torment.

"What can we do to get rid of this pest?" whispered one of the young men to the other.

"I already know what to do. I'm going to pretend I popped one of my balls."

Without letting the Txopokod see, the boy hid a small coconut from the *tucumã* palm between his legs. When the spirit started again with the annoying questions – *poc* – the boy split the little coconut with a loud crack.

"What are you doing? What was that noise?" asked the Txopokod.

"Nothing. I'm popping one of my balls."

"I want to try it too!"

"Very well, but you have to squeeze with all your might!"

And the stupid Txopokod obeyed.

"It hurts. Am I doing it right?"

"You have to squeeze harder! That's not hard enough!" encouraged the boy.

The Txopokod squeezed even harder, burst his testicles, and died.

"And now, my friend, what are we going to do?" the two friends asked each other.

They decided to burn the Txopokod until nothing remained but his ashes.

"What are we going to do with these ashes? They must be good for something!"

The two boys made crosses on their bodies with the ashes and they disappeared. They became invisible.

The boys were delighted with their new ability and realized they could visit other villages and eat whatever they wanted without anyone seeing them – they would no longer need to hunt or work. They put the ashes in two small baskets to take with them on their walks.

Soon they found out about a big party, a *chicha* feast. Now was the time to try out their new powers. They brushed the ashes on their bodies in the shape of crosses and became invisible, just as they had on the day of the Txopokod's death.

So they went, invisible, to the neighboring village. There were enormous quantities of meat prepared for the guests of the party: peccary, armadillo, and skewers of grilled curassow. The young men ate a lot. They grabbed the young women – who didn't understand what was going on. They slept with the girls in their hammocks and the girls enjoyed themselves, but thought they must be imagining it. Stuffed with food, pleased with their mischief, the boys filled their *marico*s with as much meat as they could and went home to their own village.

When the two boys arrived at their village they offered meat to everyone. They planned to teach the others the art of making themselves invisible with the ashes. They could rob their enemies and stop having to think about how to feed themselves.

It was a long time before the villagers finished eating the meat the boys had brought home. It was an abundant feast and for a long time all the villagers did was laugh and sing and eat.

But a certain Stubborn One started to needle the others, "How did these two bring us home so much game?"

The others told him to show some respect and be more discreet and later maybe the two friends would teach them. But the Stubborn One insisted – he couldn't control his curiosity.

One day, when all the others had gone out walking, or gone to take baths, he hid and lay in wait for the masters of the Txopokod's ashes. He saw them smear the ashes on their bodies.

The instant the Stubborn One saw them and discovered their secret, the ashes lost their magic. The boys tried three times and – nothing. They were still visible.

They had to throw out the precious ashes that now were good for nothing. The Stubborn One had tried to take advantage and had ruined everything. The boys were going to teach everyone, but the Stubborn One wanted to learn before it was time. The ashes lost their power.

When children were born from their mothers' toenails

Narrator: Überiká Sapé Macurap
Translator: Biweiniká Atiré Macurap
Other Narrator: Aroteri Teresa Macurap
Translator: Sawerô Basílio Macurap

In the old days men only made love to women through their toenails. The women didn't have pussies. Women got pregnant in their feet and gave birth from their feet. They went walking through the jungle and gave birth from their toenail. Their bellies didn't grow big and they had no pain during labor.

That's how it was for a long, long time.

There was a young woman who was married to Caburé, Pygmy Owl, whom we call Popoa, and who in those times was a person. Caburé made love to the girl through her toenail. She didn't have a pussy and she didn't have any breasts.

A man named Djokaid liked Caburé's wife. He made a hole in her — a pussy — and made love to her the same way we do today. After that she started to menstruate.

Caburé would go out in the middle of the night to capture butterflies (which were his food) to bring home to his wife. While he was out, his wife would go to her lover.

Caburé always scattered ashes beneath his wife's hammock so he could follow her footprints if she went out secretly. But Djokaid came from above down a rope into his lover's hammock. He left no trace at all.

Caburé ended up knowing what was going on and was overwhelmed with jealousy and rage. Until now, he had made love to his wife through her foot, but now there was this new thing – which didn't interest him at all. All he wanted was to take revenge on Djokaid.

He invited his rival to an extravagant *chicha* feast. In secret, he told the Bat to get Djokaid drunk during the party and also told him about the outrageous insult: the invention of making love to a pussy.

No sooner said than done. They got Djokaid drunk, and when he couldn't handle any more and fell to the floor dizzy, the bats sucked his blood, leaving little puncture wounds over his entire body. It was a horrible bloodbath. There were red stains and pools of blood all over the hut.

Since then women started to give birth from their pussies and labor began to be painful. Caburé's wife's breasts grew, and all women started to have them. Toenails lost the charm they used to have.

The Pleiades, Watxuri

Narrator: Überiká Sapé Macurap
Translator: Biweiniká Atiré Macurap

Once upon a time there was an old man, a very old man. It seemed as if he was older than the world. His name was Watxuri, the Pleiades. He was all shriveled up: his face, his back, his leathery skin – he was covered all over with wrinkles.

He was a hard worker and strong, in spite of his immemorial age. He cleared great fields and chopped down huge trees all by himself. But he never worked during the day – he didn't want anyone to see him. It was only at night that he took his ax and went to clear his fields.

His nighttime activity awakened great curiosity in the village. What could he be like, this man who never showed himself in the light of day? He must be hideous. He must be a monster, a dangerous being – in spite of his fields being so beautiful. They decided they had to see his face and that the best way to go about it would be to get him drunk.

One night Mboapiped, Boariped, or chief (Boariped means chief), summoned the old man to a party and kept offering him *chicha* until he got dizzy. Watxuri wanted to go work on his field, but each time he got up to leave he was offered more to drink. It would have been rude to refuse, so he kept on drinking. The night slipped away and the sun came up. There was the old man sitting down, his eyes glazed over, without the strength to get up.

Everyone was curious and came to take a look. Watxuri was withered and shriveled like a passion fruit; there was room for not one more wrinkle in his skin. Each and every person who saw him let out a gasp of astonishment.

Strong as he was, the old man was embarrassed and ashamed of being so wizened and withered. The day passed and his intoxication passed. He went to his field to work hard and try to forget his humiliation. But his heart remained heavy. He thought it would be better to leave, to go to the sky.

Orion is Watxuri, the old man. His son is the Pleiades and this is how he appeared.

When the old man went away to the heavens, he left his son hidden in an upside-down pot.

The women passed by the pot and heard:

"Hey, lucky me, I wish I could slip inside your nice pussy, your hot *txaniá*! It would feel so good!"

Every day they heard another outrage, without knowing where the voice was coming from. He taunted them so often and with such disrespect, that the women complained:

"Who has the courage to speak like that to us?"

They followed the sound of the words and found that they came from the upside-down pot. They turned the pot over and discovered Watxuri's son. He was small but old, like his father. He acted as if he didn't see them and cried out:

"I wish I were inside your hot cunts!"

But it was not to be. Instead the boy went away and joined his father in the sky.

The prick made of *muiratinga* wood and the frog, *páapap*

Narrator: Überiká Sapé Macurap
Translator: Biweiniká Atiré Macurap

There was a girl who wasn't interested in men at all. No matter what sweet things they said, she didn't so much as look at them even when they brought her fruits and presents. When they came to her hammock she pushed them away violently. It seemed as though she found men disgusting.

The girl told her mother she didn't need men in order to make love. She had made a cock out of a *muiratinga* branch. It was beautifully made and looked just like the real thing. It was this wooden prick that she turned to and pleasured herself with every night. During the day she guarded it carefully in a straw basket hidden in the wall of her hut.

She drove all the young men crazy. What a waste, such a beautiful young woman, with such a firm, womanly body that she swayed provocatively from side to side as she went to fetch water or danced at parties. But she couldn't care less about any of them, not even the nicest and best looking. They had to find out the reason for her disdain.

One day the women all went to the fields and the girl went with them. The boys took advantage of this opportunity. They rummaged through all the women's bags and belongings to see what they might find – maybe a hidden lover or some other kind of secret. Finally they came across the prick made of *muiratinga* wood. It was perfectly sculpted, with the foreskin, glans, urethra, and everything. She had even carved testicles in the wood.

"So that's why she doesn't need our cocks, the trickster! Our dicks aren't good enough for her!" they exclaimed, enraged. "We'll show her what happens to someone who doesn't want to make love to us!"

They spread red pepper, the hottest there is, all over her precious object. Then they put it back in the corner, in its straw holder.

That night the young woman took the wooden prick and went to bed happy with anticipation. She talked jealously to her sculpture as if it were a man, whispering words of love.

"Ah my sweet one, how I missed you! I want you so much! Come quickly into my warm pussy!"

She was in such a hurry that she didn't even stroke the wood with her fingers and her tongue as she usually did. She spread her legs and slipped it into her *txaniá* – and how it burned! She bit her lips so she wouldn't scream. She put her inanimate lover in its case made of *tucumã* palm and lay quietly in her hammock, trying to bear the pain. Finally she cried out for help.

"Mother, *Nhã*! I must have sat on some pepper! My *txaniá* is on fire! I'm going to burn to death!"

"Wash yourself right away! Pour lots of water on it!"

The girl ran to the door as fast as she could. She squatted down in the cold water, scrubbing and washing herself and screaming,

"*Nhã*! Mommy! It hurts! It hurts! It hurts!"

The bath gave her no relief at all. She kept wailing with pain. She screamed so much that she turned into a frog.

The next day, the men saw the frog (*páapap* in Macurap) jumping in the courtyard, going back to her mother's hammock.

"Ah, arrogant girl, is this what you wanted?"

Menstruation,
the sibling lovers,
the moon, and genipap

Narrator: Iaxuí Miton Pedro Mutum Macurap
Translator: Ewiri Margarida Macurap

In ancient times it was the men who menstruated. They secluded themselves in small huts, sat down, and the blood flowed out of their cocks. That's how it was and the women took it easy, walking around as they pleased. One day a married woman went to make love to her boyfriend who was menstruating. He threw his blood on her pussy. Since then, it is the women who menstruate, not the men.

They also tell the story of menstruation in another way.

One night a single young woman, not much more than a girl, lay half asleep in her hammock when she felt something unusual. She opened her eyes in the dark and just barely made out the form of a strong young body embracing her. The unknown man asked her to keep quiet. He whispered beautiful words in her ears and told her that he had liked her for a long time and that she was driving him crazy with desire; he caressed her so ably and tenderly that finally she gave herself to him. But it was impossible to see her lover's face – not even a resin lamp was burning.

Time passed and the girl started to wonder who her lover might be. She told her mother and other relatives that someone was making her very happy, but she didn't know who it was. Her mother told her to paint her seducer's face – the next day she would find out who he was.

The girl had lots of annatto dye that she used to paint her waistbands. That night after making love, the girl painted her lover's face. The next day she looked at all the men's faces – but not a single face was painted. Her lover had gotten up early and washed his face in the river!

The girl thought the paint might have been washed off and decided to try another kind of dye. She filled a small drinking gourd with genipap dye (that doesn't come off for many days, even with water), and put it by the side of her hammock. The girl waited until her lover fell asleep and gently painted his face, being careful not to wake him.

The girl got up the next day at sunrise and went to warm herself by the fire with all the other villagers. She looked at the men but didn't see a single painted face. Everyone was there – except her brother. A shiver ran up her spine.

Before long her brother came and joined the rest of the villagers by the fire. He'd gone to the river and washed himself in the icy water – he didn't know his face was still painted.

"So the man I fell in love with in the dark is my own brother!" wailed the girl and burst into tears.

The brother felt deeply ashamed and withdrew sadly to the jungle. He hid there and called a friend and told him what he had planned.

"I'm going away to the sky. There's no place here for me any more. All that's left for me is to disappear! I did what I mustn't do with my sister. Now I'm going to be Uri, the Moon. Go tell our friends I'll appear within a few days and that they have to go outside their huts to see me. Tell them that when I appear in the heavens they must call me by my new name, Uri."

That's how the brother left the Earth. For three nights it was pitch dark and no one saw him. But on the third night the sky was bright.

The friend called everyone to the courtyard.

"Come see Uri, the Moon!"

The sister went too. She already knew it was her forbidden lover and took just a quick look and went back inside. Even so, she started to menstruate.

Women have menstruated ever since.

The Tapir's wife

Narrator: Überiká Sapé Macurap
Translator: Biweiniká Atiré Macurap

There was an unmarried young woman who wasn't interested in any of the men in her village. She thought they were very dull and she scorned all their advances and their flattery.

One day there was a big party with plenty of *chicha*, and visitors came from many neighboring villages. The last guest to show up was strong and rugged looking; the demanding young woman was dazzled. The stranger had a long face, a big nose, and was very hairy — much hairier than any of the men she knew.

It was love at first sight. The young woman wouldn't leave the stranger alone. She brought him *chicha* and cashews and Brazil nuts, and sat next to him on her straw mat — even though she knew he was the Tapir (in those days animals were people).

She found a shady spot and hung up the finest hammock her grandmother had ever woven for the Tapir to lie down in. Then she brought him hot toasted corn in a basket made of *tucumã* palm leaves. They sat and talked and hugged, and finally the young woman lay down in the hammock with Tapir-man. She liked him a lot. They didn't want to let each other go.

"What a terrible thing has happened to our beautiful girl! She fell in love with an ugly animal instead of one of us!" complained the young men in disgust.

The Tapir-man was happy in the girl's arms; he felt forgetful of the world, but he remembered to warn his new sweetheart that their love couldn't last.

"I want you, but you can't come live with me in my house. I'm not a person, I'm from the jungle and you wouldn't be able to put up with my way of life."

The girl didn't believe him and wept when he said he was going away. She said she wanted to go with him, no matter how difficult it might be.

"You can't come with me, my darling. I'm not of your world, I am of the forest. You won't survive!"

"I'll do anything to stay with you. I'm going with you." After that she wouldn't leave his side, clinging to him tightly all the time.

"Very well, if that's how it is, then let's go," said the Tapir-man.

The day for them to leave the village arrived and they went on their way. Shortly after they reached the far end of the village plot, the Tapir wanted to go to sleep (tapirs sleep during the day and run around at night). The girl waited while he slept the entire day.

"It serves me right – it's good he warned me," thought the girl, "but I have to stay with him anyway."

The Tapir-man slept every day and the girl walked around aimlessly, looking for fruit, thinking, longing for her mother. At night the two went out in the jungle to gather fruit. In the beginning the girl didn't eat anything, because she wasn't used to the jungle foods. But she was losing weight and had to eat something.

They had gone a long way – this way and that, sometimes in circles – and by now the girl didn't have any idea where she was. But one day she saw a planted field and recognized it as her father's; she saw the cleared space her father had made around the plot to protect it from fire.

"Look, husband, it's my father's plot!"

"No it isn't, but go look for yourself if you want to!"

The girl went to take a look and saw that indeed it was her father's plot. She recognized every detail, every little corner he had planted and harvested.

The hungry young woman took advantage of the opportunity and grabbed armfuls of yams, peanuts, and corn. She ate her fill.

By now the young woman had already had a son by the Tapir. The Tapir-man would pull his son out from inside her uterus and put him back again so he wouldn't grow too much and so that she wouldn't suffer during labor. When the baby was born it looked just like a little tapir, with a snout and thick hair all over its body. Even the girl was starting to look like a tapir from living so long following her husband's ways.

The girl's brother began to notice that someone was stealing from their plot. He warned his father and the two of them kept watch to find out what was going on.

"Ah, my sister!" said the boy, recognizing her despite the fact that she was starting to look like an animal. "And look how much hair you have on your arm! Is it you who has come to visit us, my sister?"

"It's me! I think about all of you all the time!" said the girl and showed him her snout-faced cub.

"Invite your husband to our hut so we can get to know him and honor him!" said the father and the brother. But without a doubt they were plotting to kill their jungle in-law – they knew full well the girl was married to a beast.

While the girl went to the jungle to persuade her Tapir-husband to come visit, her father and her brother called together all the men of the village to lie in wait for the couple. They dug a big hole in the ground, like a grave in a cemetery.

The sun was already coming up when the girl finally convinced her husband that it wasn't dangerous to visit her family.

"I'm dying of hunger and my family wants to feed me lots of yams and manioc!"

The girl took the little tapir cub in her lap and led the way. The Tapir-man was suspicious and followed slowly behind her, dragging his feet. He kept wanting to go back, but was so used to walking with his wife that he kept going.

As they neared the plot, the Tapir-man stabbed himself on the sharp stakes his in-laws had prepared for him. He fell into the trap they had dug in the ground. The warriors immediately shot him with their arrows and killed the Tapir-man and the little Tapir cub.

The brother called to his sister; he tried to console her and asked her to return to the village. Her mother had prepared a good, hot bath with ashes to throw on the girl's head to get rid of the ticks and the thick hair that grew all over her body (she really was turning into a tapir).

The ticks and the hair fell out; but after three days the girl died of sadness. She had grown used to living in the jungle and wept for her dead Tapir.

The Txopokod orphan

Narrated in Portuguese by: Wariteroká Rosa Macurap

There was going to be a big party in the Macurap village, a *chicha* feast. The men went hunting in the jungle every day so there would be plenty of meat to offer their guests.

The hunters stored the meat in a small hut on top of a grill, but they soon noticed that it was disappearing. Someone was stealing their game. The men grilled monkeys, pigs, tapirs – every kind of animal. Each night the meat disappeared.

The chief was fed up. At this rate there would be no meat for the party! They had to find out who was stealing from them.

"I'm going to keep watch tonight. I have to know who is coming and taking what belongs to us. Let's put out all our fires so we can hide in the dark and wait for our thief!" said the chief.

That evening the hunters gathered silently around the grill hut. In the middle of the night, a Txopokod looking just like a person arrived, carrying a great *marico* to put the game in. He approached the grill hut and grabbed all the meat. The Txopokod obviously knew the men were there, because he yelled out as if he himself were one of the hunters:

"Catch the thief! Shoot an arrow through his earring!" and he ran away laughing shamelessly. He ran to his home in the hollow of an *apuí* tree, but the hunters weren't quick enough for the wily thief and didn't see where he had gone. They decided to wait for him again the next night.

The Txopokod arrived the same time as the night before and balanced himself heavily on the roof of the grill hut. He snatched up all the grilled meat, put it in his *marico*, and ran off.

The hunters were after him in a flash. They saw him go into his hollow in the *apuí* tree, through what looked like doors in the bark. The Txopokod had a nice home there in the apuí tree; it was laden with fruit that Txopokods like to eat.

The men went back to the village and asked everyone to gather a very hot, dry pepper. The hunters took the pepper and stuffed it in the hollow of the *apuí* tree and set it on fire to kill the Txopokod and his family.

Smoke billowed from the tree and the Txopokod couldn't stand it and tried to escape (Txopokods hate pepper!). But he died and his wife died soon after. Then out of a hole in one of the highest branches came the Txopokod's daughter, alive – a strong, beautiful young woman.

The chief's son saw her and his eyes lit up. She was such a womanly woman: her skin and hair were shining as if she had just taken a bath in the river, her eyes were timid and frightened. The young man was crazy for her right away. As his father was about to shoot her with an arrow, the boy said:

"How could you kill such a beautiful woman? Give her to me – if she's dead she won't be good for anything!"

He brought the woman to the village, where they soon became lovers and were married. It seemed as if she got used to her new life and enjoyed sleeping with her new husband.

The girl's father-in-law, the chief, often asked her to make *chicha* while his people went to the field to harvest corn. The young woman obeyed, but she never drank the *chicha* she had made herself; she didn't eat the same food as the others. She asked her husband to get fruit for her from the jungle, fruit from the *apuí* tree – which is what Txopokods eat.

"Oh husband, go get me some fruit to munch on while I make your *chicha*, but bring it soon, before I chew the corn kernels to ferment the *chicha*."

Deeply in love, the boy would go looking for her food – but his wife was never satisfied.

"Is that all you brought me?" she would ask.

"We'll pick more tomorrow!" her husband would assure her.

One day she gobbled up all the fruit her husband had gathered for her, made the *chicha* as fast as she could, and went to take a bath in river. It was already growing dark when she called to her husband:

"Come, my adored, sweet husband. Go get me some more fruit! I'm still hungry!"

"But I can't! It's already getting dark and your tree is in the middle of the jungle!"

But the Txopokod girl was so insistent and gave him such a seductive look that the boy agreed to go. She had him tied around her little finger.

The two of them walked farther and farther into the jungle as the sun went down. The Txopokod wife wanted to get far away from the village. She wanted to kill her husband.

They finally arrived at a clearing in the forest where there were lots of *apuí* trees heavy with the fruit the girl adored. She ate the fruit as fast as her husband could pick it and kept asking him for more. She wanted it to get dark before they had a chance to leave.

(We don't really know what kind of fruit it is. It's like beans, but it's sharp and it really burns – but it's not pepper. It's not just food for Txopokods; we use it too today, but it burns the tongue, and you can only eat a tiny bit.)

The boy was high up in the tree while his wife peeled the fruit where she sat on the ground. She ate until the boy had picked all the fruit, and finally she let him climb down. He was in a hurry to grab her and hug her – he couldn't believe it when she told him she was going to kill him. When he saw it was true, the boy tried to climb back up the tree – but he couldn't escape. His Txopokod wife ate him whole, and ended up with an enormous belly.

It was already the middle of the night and the boy's family realized he wasn't coming home.

"I'm scared that something terrible has happened," said his father. "That young woman's not a person, she's a Txopokod!"

The boy died because he couldn't resist the young Txopokod woman. She was beautiful, like a young girl at the age to get married – and it seemed as if she liked her husband, but the men of the village had killed her father and mother. She had stored up her hatred, now she had taken her revenge.

The next day the men of the village went looking for the Txopokod girl who had murdered her own husband. First they found traces of her shit, then they found her and killed her.

But Txopokods can't really die from an arrow wound. Only pepper can kill them. And when they die, they don't stay with the spirits of those who have died, the *dowari* spirits. They wander here and there over the earth . . . just over there . . .

The offended wife,
the flight to a macaw husband,
and the height of Brazil nut trees

Narrated in Portuguese by: Wariteroká Rosa Macurap

There was a girl who was already married and had two children, but she was still very young. Her husband was always after her to go walking with him in the jungle: probably so he could make love to her.

"Shall we go out and gather Brazil nuts? They must be ripe by now," he said.

They walked in the forest until they came to a Brazil nut tree. (In those days, Brazil nut shells were soft and Brazil nut trees were low) The husband made his wife climb up the tree, pick the Brazil nuts, and throw them down to the ground.

"Hey there! Eat one and tell me if it's tasty!" she exclaimed. She was curious and she wanted to try one too.

"It's delicious! Just like your clit!" he called up to her.

The girl threw down another Brazil nut.

"Is it good?"

"Scrumptious! Like your clit!" he repeated.

Instead of enjoying it, she was irritated. It's rude to talk like that! The husband always played the same game — he liked to eat Brazil nuts and he liked to eat her pussy.

Maybe he was much older than her, or it could have been that she wasn't much interested in making love. The fact is, the girl was disgusted and said to herself, "I'm going to kill this old man!"

She threw another Brazil nut, and it hit her husband right on the head and killed him. Then she sat on her branch in the Brazil nut tree and waited for her husband to come back to life again. Someone else would have run away in fear of her husband – but she stayed and waited. He woke up and she was still sitting in the tree.

"You're going to pay for this!" threatened the husband.

The husband made the tree grow taller and taller until it towered over him. Now it would be impossible for her to get down.

Every day the husband went to take a look, waiting to see if his wife could manage to climb down. She didn't know what to do. She was exhausted from trying to think of a way to escape.

"How could he have done such a terrible thing to me?"

Every day the Parakeet, the Parrot, the Macaw – all species of birds – came to suck out the nectar from the Brazil nut tree blossoms. Mosquitoes were also attracted by the sweet scent and wouldn't leave the poor girl in peace. She itched unbearably, which made her hunger and her thirst even worse.

One day, early in the morning when Parrot always likes to eat his fruit, the girl said, "I'm hungry and I'm thirsty! I really wish this Parrot would carry me away from here! I wish they were people so they could get me out of here, maybe even marry me."

Parrot and Parakeet grew quiet as they tried to hear what the girl was saying. The Parrot chief appeared.

"What are you saying there?" he asked.

"I didn't say anything!"

"You said something! Don't deny it!"

"I admit it, it's true, I did speak. I was wishing Parrot and Macaw would turn into people and carry me away from here!"

"We are people. Here we eat like macaws, but we're people. We have a village. We have huts. I'll take you away to be my wife! You'll stay with me."

It was Macaw who wanted to marry her. He finished with his Brazil nut blossom in a hurry; he couldn't wait to take his new bride home with him. The Macaw groom and his Macaw father perched on the branch of the tall Brazil nut tree and put the girl between them. She opened her arms to hold onto their wings.

"Grab on tight, we'll carry you! But you must close your eyes and keep them closed so you won't fall. You can only open them when we arrive."

They flew away.

When they arrived at the Macaw village, the girl's fiancé said, "Now you can open your eyes!" And the girl saw that the Macaws were just like people.

Three days after the wedding, the father-in-law asked the new bride to make chicha. She went to prepare the corn and started cooking.

Meanwhile, the husband who had played the trick on his wife went to the foot of the Brazil nut tree to take a look. His wife was gone. He couldn't understand how she could have gotten down from such a tall tree. He sent his sons to look for their mother.

"Your mother went away! She disappeared!"

No one had seen Macaw fly away with his wife and no one had figured out what had happened. The husband was frustrated – he had wanted to visit her every day and watch her die slowly. Now she had disappeared.

"If you boys don't go look for your mother, I'll kill you both!"

They started on their way, singing as they went, and before long they arrived at the river bank where their mother used to fetch water to make chicha. Far away in the Macaw village their mother heard their songs, from far away.

"It's nice to hear my children singing. I wonder where they could be?" she wondered. "But I'm not going there! Suppose that shameless old man sent my sons to look for me!"

She waited and the two boys kept walking, singing as they went.

Finally they arrived at their mother's doorstep.

"Mommy, Daddy sent us to find you! He told us to tell him when we found you."

They all went inside. Their mother was very happy to see them and fed them until they couldn't eat another bite.

"Don't tell your father I'm here!"

"Don't worry, we won't tell him!"

The boys went back the way they had come. The boys' mother should never have let them return to their father!

As soon as they arrived home, the boys' father asked them about their mother. They said they didn't know anything, but they had brought home some grilled meat that their mother had given them – she wanted her children to be well fed.

"You're lying! Your mother gave you that meat, and if you don't tell where she is, I'll kill you right now!" shouted their father.

The boys were so afraid that they told their father about their mother.

"We found Mommy. She's making *chicha* in Macaw's house and she has a new husband. It's better if you don't go there."

The husband was furious and decided to go after his escaped wife. Somehow he transformed himself into an old woman. I don't know how he disguised his prick, it seems as if he used some wax. I don't think he cut it off, but he became just like a woman. I really don't know how, but he managed to disguise himself. He took an old *marico*. He really turned himself from a man into a woman.

The old woman arrived at the Macaws' hut late in the afternoon.

"Here comes an old woman! Grandmother, come in!"

She used a cane and walked just like an old woman. She went inside the hut, sat down, and the girl, wife-of-the-one-who-turned-into-an-old-woman, sat beside her.

The old woman slept there, in the Macaws' hut. The next day they all sat in the courtyard (which was just like ours). The old woman's wife sat with her other husband, the Macaw.

The first husband, who had turned into an old woman, had brought with her a cane with a very sharp point, made from the wood of the *pau-âmago* tree. She started to stand up slowly. It took her a long time and when she was finally upright, everyone invited her to sit down again. But she didn't want to sit down. She started to circle around and kept poking at the Macaw's feet with her cane (Macaws had feet like ours, not bird feet, as they have today). She poked his foot hard, but the Macaw good-naturedly withdrew his foot and acted as if nothing had happened. Suddenly the old woman stabbed the Macaw's foot and hurt him for real.

The Macaws attacked. They knocked the old-woman-husband onto the ground and ate him all up. There were no leftovers. Macaw ate the ex-husband-old-woman because she'd hurt his foot; she pierced it with the cane made of *pau-âmago* wood.

That's how the Macaw's foot became how it is today. It turned backwards.

The next day the Macaws started to think it wasn't a good idea to go on living in the same place. The husband-old-woman was dead, but now he was a Txopokod. She might come around and want to eat the Macaw people, to take revenge. She might try to kill the Macaw husband.

The Macaws thought about it a lot and decided to move away.

"We have to find another place. Who knows what might happen to us if we don't? The Txopokod came back to life – it didn't really die completely."

They moved their village the next day and brought the woman with them. She enjoyed her new life and didn't think about her old husband any more. No one stayed in the old hut.

The woman who made love to her son-in-law

Narrator: Iaxuí Miton Pedro Mutum Macurap and Wariteroká Rosa Macurap
Translator: Ewiri Margarida Macurap
Other narrators in Portuguese: Buraini Andere Macurap and Menkaiká Juraci Macurap

A hardworking Macurap boy named Iarekô and his young wife, Paiawi, were a happy, loyal couple.

The girl's mother, Katxuréu, had eyes for her son-in-law. She no longer had a husband and kept thinking about the fun the couple must be having in their hammock, right there next to her own. Her daughter always looked so contented, radiant with sensual fulfillment. If only it could be her lying there in her daughter's place.

One day she invited her daughter to go with her to the jungle to pick coconuts from the *tucumã* palm. When they passed by the corncrib in the old field, she pushed her daughter into a deep, deep hole. Then she went back to the village and pretended to be her daughter. They looked alike, and in the dark Iarekô didn't even notice it was his mother-in-law sleeping in his arms.

Now it was the old woman who chewed corn and manioc to make the *chicha*. She didn't have any teeth left, so her gums bled when she chewed and the drink was soiled with drops of red blood.

Iarekô brought her lots of game, lots of tinamous and curassows. The old woman had to pretend to eat the meat, bones and all, as her daughter could. But she was toothless and all she could do was suck on the meat. Iarekô noticed her different habits and was suspicious.

One day Iarekô went hunting as usual and waited in ambush for tinamous. He shot his arrow and it fell to the ground nearby. He went to look for it, but couldn't find it. He was puzzled – he never lost his arrows in the jungle. He shot again and missed again. He looked for his arrow among the leaves on the ground, but again he couldn't find it.

It was his wife, Paiawi, down in her hole, who was pulling the arrows down to her, to help him find her. Iarekô finally shot his last arrow and when he went to look for it, Paiawi managed to grab his arm.

"You think it's me you're making love to in our hammock every night? Well it's not me! You're sleeping with my mother!"

Iarekô was overcome with sadness when he saw his wife in such bad shape and discovered the truth. He wept to see her bitten all over, all scratched up, worms gnawing at her flesh. He couldn't manage to pull her up out of the hole – it was very deep.

Paiawi told her husband to call everyone in the village together, to have them throw a party, a *chicha* feast.

Iarekô returned to the village, and before even talking to the others, he ran after his mother-in-law and beat her until she was all bloody. His sister, who was nearby, protested.

"Don't you hurt my sister-in-law!"

Iarekô told her the truth and she stopped complaining. The old woman screamed while her son-in-law hit her. She didn't yet know she had been unmasked.

"Why are you beating me, my adored husband? Are you jealous? But I only make love to you, no one else!"

The old woman thought she should have put an end to her daughter when she had the chance. She should have eaten her, then no one would ever have known she was an impostor. But it was too late. When she went to find Paiawi in the hole, there was no one there.

It was a black wasp (that we call *cavalo-de-cão*) that pulled Paiawi out of the hole. The Rainbow, Botxatô, had been watching over the girl while she was stuck in the hole. A tiny wasp sent the black wasp to try as hard as he could to free the young woman. The black wasp used the Rainbow. He tied it around his waist and pulled the girl to safety.

The Rainbow, Botxatô, a snake, taught Paiawi exquisite songs. There, deep in her prison, Paiawi learned songs that no one in the village knew; she learned Botxatô's songs by heart.

At night, the husband returned to smear his wife with ashes, as if they were soap to wash her with. He spread the ashes on his wife's body and washed her all over. She had lost all her hair while she was stuck in the trap.

Iarekô threw his mother-in-law into the very same hole she had thrown her daughter in. He brought Paiawi home to their hut so she could recuperate, so she could gain weight and regain her strength.

Everyone drank *chicha* that same night, but Iarekô didn't want his wife to go out yet, she was too weak.

Paiawi lay stretched out in her hammock and heard the men singing in the courtyard while they drank. She said their old song was ugly, that they had it all wrong. She would teach them the real songs.

In those days no one knew how to sing real songs. They learned from Paiawi, who in turn had learned while she was a prisoner in the trap her mother had set for her.

Paiawi went to the *chicha* feast two or three days later and taught everybody. She sang with a beautiful voice and made fun of her husband, who had made love to his mother-in-law without realizing it, who lived with his lover's mother and hadn't even noticed. Paiawi's song made a fool of her husband. Everyone listened with admiration and wondered where she could have learned such beautiful music.

Wakotutxé piõ, the mutilated lover

Narrator: Aroteri Teresa Macurap
Translator: Sawerô Basílio Macurap

A young woman was engaged to one young man, but was in love with another. She refused to accept her betrothed and kept as far away from him as she could. One day the young man decided he had had enough – he was fed up.

He brought the young woman to the jungle and when they got there he made a big straw basket. Then he ran and grabbed the girl. She screamed because she thought he wanted to make love to her. The betrothed man grabbed his fiancée and cut off her vagina, her ear and her mouth, and put them in the *marico*. Then he tied the girl up tightly and put her inside the straw basket. He threw her on top of a tree and left her there, still alive. He returned to the village and delivered what he had cut off from the girl, mixed with other grilled meat, to her mother. He told her he had hunted black monkeys, and that the meats were innards, that he hadn't brought back the whole body. The girl's mother ate it – it was dark, and she couldn't see what it was.

The girl had disappeared from the village and her lover went looking for her but couldn't find her. Finally he came across the *ouricuri* palm that the betrothed man had taken the *capemba* leaves from to make the basket. The boy looked up and saw the basket hanging in the tree. He made a ladder, climbed up, and brought the basket down to the girl's father and mother who were waiting below on the ground. They opened the basket and the girl was inside, still alive.

She said she wouldn't go home with them. She said she was going to turn herself into a *wakotutx*é *piõ*, a bird that sings when summer arrives. (She could speak, even without a mouth.) Her parents wept with grief.

The girl said to her father, "On the day summer starts to be good and hot, light a fire in your field, on the day that I sing!"

Her lover was very sad.

Peniom and the winged bride

Narrator: Aroteri Teresa Macurap
Translator: Sawerô Basílio Macurap

There was a young man named Peniom who still hadn't gotten married. He saw a *tocororô* bird singing in the middle of the courtyard and had an idea.

"I wish you would turn into a woman so you could marry me!" he said to the bird.

Then he went to sleep. When he woke up, he saw a beautiful woman lying by his side in his hammock.

"What did you say yesterday?" she asked.

"I said I wished the *tocororô* bird would turn into a woman!"

"Well, that's who I am!"

The next night she untied the hammock, and carried the young man away without him noticing. She tied the hammock over the middle of the river. When Peniom wanted to get down, she didn't let him; she warned him that they were above the water.

"We're not in the hut?" he asked.

He heard the sound of the water and went back to sleep. The next night they were already back on the ground.

"So we're on land again? Weren't we just in the middle of the river?" asked Peniom.

They were in the jungle, in another village. The two went walking and came to a *tucumã* palm.

"*Omeré*! Husband! Pick some *tucumã* for me!" said the *tocororô*-woman.

Peniom tried to pull the small coconuts closer to the ground but the bird-woman asked him to climb up the trunk. The trunk of *tucumã* palms is covered with thorns and Peniom only climbed up because his new wife kept insisting. He grabbed the coconuts and came down full of thorns.

They kept walking, and farther along the way they found an *inajá* palm, which doesn't have any thorns.

"Husband, pick some of that fruit for me!"

Peniom climbed up and started to chop down the tree while his wife waited below. She said:

"Cut it down, but be careful the tree doesn't fall and kill me!"

"Eat, I'll cut it down slowly!"

The bird-woman ate and Peniom kept chopping away at the tree. Finally the trunk cracked and fell on top of the *tocororô*-woman and she died. But she didn't really die – she was a Txopokod.

Peniom came down from the tree and went home to his village. His mother had been worried, wondering if he had gone with a Txopokod, thinking it was a woman.

It took days to pull out all the thorns. They were all over the poor boy's body – in his chest, his legs . . .

Finally he recovered and went back to the jungle to hunt. Soon the *tocororô*-woman appeared and tried to get Peniom to make love to her again. But he wouldn't, so she went away.

The boy told his mother. She thought about what he could do to protect himself.

"I know what to do! Let's shave your head!" she said.

They gave Peniom a good close shave and now his head was completely bald. The next day when the *tocororô* appeared in the jungle, they made love.

"How beautiful you are!" sighed the *tocororô*-woman, admiring his bald head.

Peniom didn't like her, because she wasn't a person. He didn't want to make love to her any more. When he got home, he told his mother what had happened.

"Did she find you handsome? She wasn't scared?"

His mother told him to take an ax with him the next day and told what him what he must do.

"Tell her you shaved by sticking your head in an ant hole. She'll want to imitate you and she'll put her head inside the ant hole. That's when you can chop off her head."

The next day, when the two were alone together, Peniom did what his mother had told him to do. The girl grabbed him and hugged him and caressed his smooth, bald head. She wanted to shave too and stuck her head in the ant hole.

"It hurts!" she cried.

"That's the way, that's just how I did it!" encouraged the boy. Then he chopped off the Txopokod's head. He waited and waited, but the *tocororô-*woman never appeared again.

Piron, the Blue Tinamou

Narrators in Portuguese and Macurap: Buraini Andere Macurap and Menkaiká Macurap
Other narrators in Macurap: Amampeküb Aningui Basílio Macurap and *Iniká* Isabel Macurap
Translator: Aiawid Waldemir Macurap

A group of men went to the jungle to hunt. They came to a clearing, set up camp, and went to sleep. The next day they killed a lot of game.

One of the hunters had a recently born baby son so he couldn't eat any kind of game. He went with the others, but he didn't eat any meat. He didn't kill any game – he wasn't allowed to.

The hunters found Piron, a kind of tinamou of a deep blue color. It had more than ten eggs.

Piron, the Blue Tinamou, cast a spell on the hunters and made them go to sleep. One of the hunters wanted to kill the Blue Tinamou and lay waiting in ambush. But just when he had almost captured the bird, without wanting to he dozed off to sleep. The Tinamou flew away.

"How did I miss him?" the hunter wondered.

Again the next day he set a trap and sat down to wait. He fell asleep and the Tinamou flew away. The same thing happened several days in a row.

"Ah, I'll take the Tinamou's eggs for us to eat, since I can't manage to kill anything," he decided.

He told the others he hadn't brought back any game and that each time he was about to kill the Tinamou, he dozed off to sleep. The hunters cooked the eggs and ate them. Night fell. From far away, the hunters heard the bird whistling, "piron, piron . . ."

The Pirons, a blue tinamou couple, came and attacked the hunters in their camp. The young man with the new baby hadn't eaten the eggs, because it's forbidden to those who have just had a baby. He tried to wake the others and warn them that Piron had come to attack them – but they were all fast asleep. He decided to get to safety himself and tied his hammock far away from the others. He stayed awake.

The Piron couple came and sniffed everyone's mouths.

"That one ate our eggs, and this one over here ate some eggs . . ." they said.

Each time they smelled their eggs, the two Pirons would eat the hunters' eyes – but only the eyes of the ones who had eaten the eggs.

Only the one who hadn't eaten the eggs could still see.

"What will I do? Can I lead them all by the hand back to the village? They'd trip and stumble the whole way home!"

He spent the entire day thinking. The next day he went to take a shit and sat trying to think of a solution. He saw a tiny dung beetle walking along nearby.

"That will do the trick!" he thought.

The man picked up the little beetle and brought it back to the camp. Then he crushed the beetle and put little pieces of it into each blind man's eyes.

"Can you see now?" he asked.

"A little – very, very little. But better than before!" they said.

The man went back to the jungle again and sat down to think. He captured another beetle, brought it back, and pushed pieces of it into the sockets where the blind men's eyes had been.

"And now what will we do?" they asked one another.

"Let's turn into black monkeys, *arembô*!" And the men took their bows and attached them to themselves as tails.

"The women won't want us any more!" they said.

The men rolled up their hammocks and threw them into the jungle. They became branches for them to swing on.

"We're going to stay here. You go home to the village and make arrows and a good bow. Then come back here, tie up your hammock, put your wife in the hammock, and put your legs on top of her and hold her there. Then call us and you will have plenty of game."

The man-who-could-still-see did what the other men said. He came back with his wife, strung up his hammock, and sat solidly on top of her spread apart legs. He called to his companions.

"*Arembô, arembô*! Monkey, monkey! Come, make love to my wife!

The monkeys who had been men, the former hunters who had left their wives in the village to go hunting, wanted a woman. The hunter had brought lots of corn and he gave it to the monkeys; that was the first thing he did. The monkeys came after his wife – they wanted to make love to her. They tried to grab her pussy, but she protected herself with her hand while her husband sat steadily on top of her. Now was his chance to shoot the monkeys. He killed a lot of game.

The hunter went back to the village carrying lots of fat monkeys for everyone to eat.

And that's how it was many, many times.

But there was a Stubborn One in the village who wanted to kill monkeys too; he didn't want the hunter to be the only one. He pestered the hunter so much that the one-who-could-see finally gave in.

"Then get ready and have your wife cook some corn for you!" said the hunter.

The Stubborn One went to the jungle and hung up his hammock, put his leg on top of his wife, and called the monkeys.

The monkeys knew it was a different hunter, and instead of waiting for the monkeys to eat the corn – as the other hunter had told him to – the Stubborn One started shooting his arrows at them right away. While he was shooting, a great horde of monkeys came and grabbed the Stubborn One's wife and took her away. He couldn't do anything about it.

The Stubborn One went home crying to the village, without his wife. That's how the black monkeys found themselves a woman, who turned into a monkey.

The first hunter, the one-who-had-seen, decided to take his wife and go hunting just as he had before. But this time, however much he called the monkeys, only a little baby monkey came and ate his toasted corn.

The hunter grabbed the tiny monkey and threw him up onto the branch of a tree – and he is still there.

TUPARI

Pawatü, the headhunters

Narrator in Portuguese: Etxowe Etelvina Tupari

A woman with no husband was pregnant, but she didn't know who the father was.

During her pregnancy, the young woman had an enormous craving for lice, but she only ate the heads – lots of tiny lice heads. She picked the lice from her own head and other people's heads and ate as much as she could. Finally the baby was born. It was a strong healthy boy.

When he was two or three years old, the boy already went hunting nearby with his miniature bow and arrows. He killed grasshoppers and crickets and pulled off their heads. He brought the heads – but not the bodies – to his mother, and the two of them ate the delicacies with relish.

The boy grew a bit more and was given a bigger bow and began to shoot his arrows at little birds. He cut off the dead birds' heads and threw the bodies away. He brought the grilled meat to his mother – only the heads, nothing else. His mother adored the food her son provided and they always ate together.

Now he was becoming a young man, already full grown and armed with a real bow and real arrows. He had excellent aim and hit his mark with animals of consequence. He shot tapirs, deer, and monkeys, and proudly brought the heads home to his mother. Not only his mother, but his aunt, uncle, and grandmother all ate the heads, but his uncle was indignant and complained:

"Why do you only bring the heads?"

"Ah, the bodies aren't worth eating!"

Now he was an adult, a mature man, and became a great hunter. He killed monkeys, howler monkeys, peccaries, and wild boar, and brought home basketfuls of grilled heads for his family. They ate them with toasted corn and sweet cassava. The food he and his mother ate was different – they ate animal meat, but only from the chest up.

"This Indian is fierce! He will be ferocious in war!" people said.

The young man gave animal heads to everyone as presents – deer heads, pig heads, tapir heads, curassow heads. His mother had taught everyone to appreciate eating the heads, and not to like the bodies any more. The people ate the heads and enjoyed them – the uncle was the only one who complained.

The young man was offended by the rumors and gossip about him. He was considered strange – an outsider; his uncle had made things uncomfortable for him and he thought about leaving the village.

"Mother, I'm going away, to sleep in the jungle. I'm not sure what day I'll be back, so don't be anxious. I'll make a trail and after a few days I'll fetch you – you can come live with me."

The boy disappeared into the forest and his mother was overcome with longing for him. He came back some time later and asked his mother to go with him to prepare his food –he couldn't manage to cook his game alone in the jungle. He promised her they would return to the village later. But it was a lie – he had no intention of living with his relatives again.

The boy's mother told her brother she was going away for a while with her son.

When they arrived in the jungle, the mother heard people talking. She was frightened. Who could they be?

"It's another people who came to live with me!" explained the son (whose name was Haüwud), trying to calm his mother.

But he was lying. The ones who were speaking the strange language weren't humans like us. Haüwud had cut trunks and branches from the *laran-jinha* tree (a jungle tree that's like an orange tree but with no fruit), to make people. The trees had turned into people to become his brothers – they were all men. Shadow men, ghost men.

They spoke a different language and were strong, fat, and tall. The mother shivered with fear. Did she and her son have to stay there, so far from her brother, her mother, from her other family?

Haüwud carved a beautiful woman out of the *laranjinha* tree to be his wife. His mother saw her daughter-in-law emerge from the tree trunk and start speaking the strange language. The tree-woman cooked and she slept in Haüwud's hammock, and caressed him and went with him everywhere.

The *laranjinha* tree-people started to have children and the population grew. It was like a city, with the ceaseless murmur of conversations and children's games. But they were ghosts, not human beings.

Now Haüwud began to kill people and cut off their heads, just as he had the game animals.

One day he told his mother he was going to the village to get his uncle, her brother, and bring him back to live with them, to cheer her up. It was a lie. He wanted to kill his uncle so he could eat his head. And that's what he did. Before killing his uncle, he sprinkled drops in his eyes to turn him into a Pawatü ghost, one of the people he had created, the beings of the *laranjinha* tree. He killed his uncle, cut off his head, and brought it home for everyone to eat.

Haüwud arrived back in the Pawatü village with his uncle, who was now just a ghost, and whose head was hidden in a *marico* for dinner. His mother was suspicious and didn't fall for it. She cried out,

"That's not my brother – you killed him! That's not my brother's face, with such a sullen, gray expression – like a dead person! It's easy to see it's just his ghost, just his shadow! Now I've lost my brother!"

She cried inconsolably, torn between her love for her brother and her love for her son. She tried to hug her brother, but he was just an image with no substance, impossible to touch, with no flesh. There was no one left for her to turn to; she had to stay with her son.

The Pawatü ate the uncle's head, just as they ate the heads of the other people they killed. The village in the jungle was full of ghosts, only Haüwud and his mother were real people.

A few days later, Haüwud told his mother he was going to the village to bring his grandmother to live with them among the Pawatü. She trembled as she imagined what was going to happen. She begged him not to go, but nothing would change his mind.

Haüwud went to talk with his grandmother, who was happy to see her grandson again. The poor thing didn't know what lay in store for her. Haüwud sprinkled drops in her eyes and she became a ghost. Then he killed her and took her head with him, leaving the body behind. Haüwud's mother wept again – all that was left of her own mother was a ghost and a head that everyone was longing to eat.

From then on, Haüwud and his people lay in wait for the villagers, to cut their heads off and eat them. They preferred dishes made of human head flesh; they weren't interested in game meat. They only taught their children to kill and eat people, never to work, farm, or build houses.

When the older Pawatü made new ghosts out of trees or from the cadavers of their dead enemies, they whistled the tail feathers of red macaws through the air to give the ghosts blood. When the red feathers whirled by, the blood spattered on the ghosts, and began to circulate within their fleshless bodies.

The Pawatü set up sharpened stakes and thorns soaked in blood to kill anyone who passed by. They singed the hair on the heads of the dead in the fire, as if they were monkeys on a grill; then they roasted them. They ate their enemies' brains, which had practically no meat at all, and they also ate the men's and women's breasts. But they abandoned the corpses without burying them.

When the spirit of another people's chief turned into Pawatü, after being murdered, it also had to chase people and kill them. If the Pawatü killed a Tupari, that was his destiny.

Haüwud didn't want anything to do with the Tarupás, the white men who wanted to establish ties with the Tupari. He counseled his people to be ferocious with the strangers who came from far away. He told them not to follow the example of the Tupari who worked for the Tarupás on their rubber plantations, receiving presents from them – long knives, clothes, food – and getting sick and dying in droves. Haüwud didn't make any concessions, and he was just as terrible with the Indians. He attacked the Tupari villages, and I know for a fact that he killed my great-grandmother in the field.

With his wife from the *laranjinha* tree, his mother (frightened as she was), and the ghosts of his uncle and grandmother, Haüwud felt happy and fulfilled. There were lots of people's heads to eat and they only had to go after Tupari and other Indians to get a new supply. The Pawatü, the headhunters, always had plenty of meat to eat.

Their numbers grew, either because more were born, or because Haüwud spat on trees to turn them into people-ghosts. They all ate people's heads. They made flutes from the head bones and toe bones of their victims, and they made trumpets to call to each other from far away, in a musical language of whistles.

When the Pawatü went on warring expeditions and attacked other Indians, they cut off their enemies' heads. They came home carrying the heads on their shoulders, and when they got to the courtyard of their village they were happy and threw the heads up humming into the air, "prrrr . . . prrr . . ." The chief caught the heads in the air, and he prayed and performed rituals for them to eat the meat in good health. He cooked up a soup of the enemies they had killed. This was the food of all the Pawatü, the headhunters: only the heads.

The Pawatü massacre the Tupari

Narrator in Portuguese: Etxowe Etelvina Tupari

The Pawatü always terrorized us – they were our main enemies. Ever since I was little I heard how our great-grandparents were massacred by the Pawatü. This is how it happened:

There was a man who played the Tupari's traditional ball game – a game where you use your head and not your feet. The ball was made out of sap from the *mangaba* tree that they blew into until it grew to the right shape and size.

The man loved to play ball and that's what he did, all the time. His little daughter cried from hunger and his wife cursed him:

"My young daughter is hungry and all my good-for-nothing husband thinks about is playing ball!"

The ballplayer grabbed a club and gave his wife a thrashing. The men used to beat their wives a lot.

"You scum! Leave my daughter alone!" cried his father-in-law in defense of his daughter.

But it didn't stop the ballplayer – he beat his father-in-law too.

The father-in-law swore he would take revenge.

"You're going to pay for this! You'll see!"

He called all the men together – including his son-in-law – to go hunting in the jungle. They started out at dawn for a march of several days.

The father-in-law knew about some crazy leaves that the Pawatü used. It seems that the leaves make the owner's wishes come true. The father-in-law found a tree and tore off a fistful of the leaves to help him carry out his revenge. His head still hurt a lot from the blow his son-in-law had dealt him with the club. He mixed the leaves with the scab that was forming where he had been hit, blew on it, and applied it to his open wound.

Because of the powerful mixture of the leaves with the wound, the Tupari expedition drew near to a band of Pawatü who were camping in a clearing. The hunters couldn't quite muffle the noise they made as they moved along through the forest and the Pawatü were soon aware that there were strangers in the jungle. The headhunters were gathered around a fire, preparing to eat the head of a woman they had just killed.

The father-in-law and his men silently, cautiously, approached the Pawatü huts, camouflaged by the dense green of the jungle. But the trumpeter birds and curassows shrieked and warned the Pawatü of their enemies' presence. The father-in-law, dreaming of vengeance even at the cost of his own life, warned his people that they were about to die, that the Pawatü would spare no one and would let no one escape.

The Tupari didn't pay him much attention, however. Once the hunters found the Pawatü camp, they withdrew and set up camp at a considerable distance. They felt safe.

They hunted and slept there and felt relieved. Day after day they set traps to catch animals – howler monkeys and deer – and stuffed themselves with meat.

Their happiness was short-lived. They were gathering honey one fine day, when the Pawatü came suddenly, leaping mysteriously from the calm and quiet of the jungle. They shot everyone with their arrows, even the men high up in trees gathering honey.

They killed and killed. All the Tupari men lay stretched out on the ground. Only three people who had been far away escaped; one of them had a shaven head because he was going to become a shaman. The three heard the attack and hid under some *capemba* leaves.

The Pawatü gathered the Tupari dead together into long rows of corpses. They spat on the bodies to turn them into ghosts and they cut off their heads to take home as game. Among the dead were the father-in-law and the son-in-law.

The father-in-law was a relative of Haüwud's and that's how he had learned the secret of the leaves that make the future — like the catastrophe he had invoked to get revenge, at the price of his own life.

When the Pawatü disappeared into the dark tangle of trees, the surviving Tupari came out of their hiding place and went sadly back to their village, bringing the news of the horrible tragedy. They cried and cried.

"The Pawatü killed us . . ."

Akiã, the Tupari woman
who was mutilated by the Pawatü

Narrator in Portuguese: Etxowe Etelvina Tupari

It happened on a day that the shamans arose at daybreak and began preparing *rapé* (a mixture of tobacco and powder from the *angico* tree). The birds were singing and warned the shamans that the Pawatü were nearby.

The shamans in turn warned the women when they went to cut firewood. Among them was Akiã, my great-grandmother.

"Akiã, don't go out today! Stay home! The birds are prophesying that the Pawatü – the ones who eat heads – are nearby!"

"But I need wood to make a fire. I'll take my dog and the Pawatü won't harm me!" said Akiã.

"You're wrong not to heed our warning. First they'll kill the dog, then they'll kill you!" said the shamans.

Akiã, my great-grandmother, a stubborn young woman, took her stone hatchet and went out alone to gather firewood; her dog followed behind her. The Pawatü surrounded her, armed with bows and arrows. She didn't even have time to scream. First they killed the dog, then they shot Akiã in the stomach. She fell down right there. They cut off her head and her breast and carried them away. Akiã's body lay in a heap, covered by a *marico*.

Even though it was a day for taking *rapé* (snuff), Huari, one of the shamans, went hunting. It is not the custom for shamans to go to the jungle on the days of ritual, but Huari's daughter was hungry and he decided to hunt monkeys for her, before the *rapé* session. Huari listened for the monkeys and overheard the Pawatü yelling, teaching their children how to kill. He hid and saw Kiribô, the chief of the Pawatü, pass by carrying the recently cut-off head. With horror, the shaman recognized Akiã.

Without thinking, crazy with rage, Huari shot an arrow at Kiribô, the Pawatü, who cried out and shot an arrow at Huari as he ran away. But he missed his mark and his arrow hit a hanging vine instead. Kiribô died a short while later.

Huari arrived out of breath in the village, saying he had killed a Pawatü. But he was always joking and no one believed what he was saying.

"It's not a lie! I killed Kiribô, the chief. And I think I saw him carrying Akiã's head! Where is she? Did she return from the field with the other women?"

The frightened men ended their *rapé* session and went to see for themselves. All they found were Kiribô's remains, which the Pawatü had chopped into little pieces, leaving behind only a hammock on the ground – a different kind of hammock, similar to the ones the Tarupás use. They had taken Akiã's head.

Now the men believed Huari. The women had returned from the field and Akiã, my great-grandmother, was missing.

A little farther along, the Tupari warriors found her head, beaten, left behind by the Pawatü. Our men were now so close that they overheard Kiribô's father raging at his people.

"Cowards! You don't have arrows? You're not strong? You don't kill your enemies? You let my son die! You! You who live only by hunting heads, now you are going to have to work, like the other Indians!"

Because of Kiribô's death, the Pawatü stopped persecuting the Tupari, and that was the last we ever heard of them.

Piripidpit, the maiden whom the men devoured

Narrator in Portuguese: Naoretá Marlene Tupari

Piripidpit was a headstrong, strong-willed young girl. She had to marry Moroiá the warrior, but she couldn't stand him. Moroiá was crazy about Piripidpit and pursued her relentlessly. He dreamed of having such a beautiful, haughty young woman in his hammock. He asked her to make *chicha* and cook for him, but Piripidpit treated him with contempt, not even trying to hide how she hated her betrothed.

Moroiá couldn't contain his rage at being rejected yet another time and swore revenge. He got his friends together and planned to set a trap for her.

"Just let me call my friends and you'll see what a beating you get!" he told her.

Piripidpit had gone to take a bath and came from the river trembling with cold. It was just sunrise and she went to warm herself beside the fire, still half asleep. She looked up and saw the armed warriors surrounding the fire.

"I brought my cousins to beat you!" Moroiá cried.

Piripidpit wanted to escape, but Moroiá approached her and grabbed her tightly. He gave a signal and the arrows sang through the air – there were so many arrows that they almost hit Moroiá too.

Piripidpit made a superhuman effort and managed to escape from the circle. She flew to the sweet cassava fields, but she stumbled and lay stretched out on the ground. A single arrow had wounded her in the back.

The cruel fiancé ordered the men to kill Piripidpit by beating her on the head – so as not to spoil her body. He swore he would grill and eat the flesh of the woman who had scorned him.

The men lifted that pretty girl's dead body up off the ground – that girl who never had a chance to fall in love and have children. They cooked her. They removed her entrails and made a roast.

While they grilled her flesh, the warriors sang ferocious songs around the fire. Her flesh sizzled just as if she were a fat animal roasting slowly over the fire. She was plump, that young girl.

They grilled her slowly over the fire, singing and singing . . . like I'm singing now.

It's a sad, horrifying story. Every time I hear it, it's as if one of my favorite relatives had died. Since I was a little girl I've heard the song of Piripidpit. I tremble with fear. I cry because the girl was punished like that, just because she didn't want to marry the man her family arranged for her.

The meat was almost dry and ready to eat when Piripidpit's spirit appeared, walking, dripping with blood. She was crying and singing about her life, that she had so recently lost. Her spirit howled with pain and pointed to the arrows and wounds all over her rigid body that only a short while ago had danced and played in the courtyard.

It was already morning when they finished grilling poor Piripidpit's body. Her spirit wept and threatened revenge as she faded away in the light.

Moroiá chopped up the proud girl's smoke-dried body. He left pieces of meat on the grill and the murderers came, took a little at a time, and carried the delicacies back to the hut to eat. Everyone ate their fill, but there was still some of the special game left over.

Visitors showed up, Indians from a neighboring village.

The hosts offered game to one of the visiting warriors named Arekuiaonsin. He had never eaten human flesh before, but he thought it was very tasty and quickly learned to appreciate it.

Another guest, named Koiaküb, took part in the banquet without knowing what he was eating. The men only told him after he had already swallowed a big piece – because human flesh is not something to be eaten casually.

"Eat some more, my friend. Isn't it delicious? It tastes like monkey meat!" said Arekuiaonsin.

"You're right, friend. It's a delicacy. It's like eating white-lipped peccary."

Arekuiaonsin went back home singing a new improvised song:

"What you offer I will eat,
hot or cold, as long as it's fresh . . .
Game from the jungle I will eat,
even if it's human flesh . . ."

Now Arekuiaonsin goes around eating white people whenever he can.

Even today, when a girl doesn't want to get married, they tell her the story of Piripidpit. In the old days, if a girl didn't want to get married, they had her killed.

Independence and torture

Narrator in Portuguese: Naoretá Marlene Tupari

It is dangerous for a woman to refuse to get married.

There was another girl who resisted. The abandoned lover took revenge with unheard-of cruelty, alone, without help from anyone.

He invited the girl to gather honey in the jungle, just the two of them. The girl had no intention of giving in to him, but went anyway. Who could resist the idea of gourds full of honey?

They walked and walked. The girl didn't see any bees anywhere and began to be suspicious. At a certain point in the road, the boy told her to make a rope out of *envira* fiber, to make a *marico* for them to carry the honey gourds in later.

The poor girl willingly obeyed, without knowing she was being tricked. She took the fiber, made a rope, and gave it to the boy.

The boy was stronger than the girl and tied her to a tree with the newly made rope. He put the poor young woman in the form of a cross – her legs apart, her arms spread wide, and bound her as tightly as he could. Without mercy, he cut off her lips and her pussy. Her screams made no impression on him. He finished killing her as if she were an animal.

The evil fiancé skewered the lips and the pussy and brought them back to his village. He went to the girl's mother and threw it all in her lap.

"There you are. You should have told your daughter to stay with me! You can keep what's left of her!"

The men's menstruation

Narrator in Portuguese: Etxowe Etelvina Tupari

A long time ago it was the men who menstruated. They secluded themselves in little huts near the village and only bathed at twilight or just before dawn. They had to stay away from the others, especially the shamans, who must never touch a menstruating man.

A young warrior was menstruating, secluded in his little hut. He kept his flowing blood in a small clay pot. From time to time he would squat and dribble the blood into a small straw loincloth, *tamará*, in our language, and spill it from there into the pot.

A group of curious girls passed by not too far away, trying to spy on him. One of them teased him sarcastically:

"Lucky men! You have to stay shut up in there menstruating, with your blood flowing, envious of those of us who can come and go as we please. We're free, no one bothering us – while you men are humiliated, wiping up pools of blood!"

The boy was enraged and turned as red as the blood he was collecting in the little pot.

"Things can't stay like this, with us always locked up in here, suffering with menstruation! I am going to do something about this!" he grumbled.

A friend passed by outside his hut and the boy asked him to bring him a stalk of dried grass, *punhakam*.

The next day the girl came again and mocked him even more contemptuously.

"Eh, poor thing, how are you doing in there, with blood flowing all over, without seeing the light of day? It's nice to be like me, clean and dripping drops of sparkling water. Going wherever I want . . ."

The boy grabbed the stalk of dried grass, filled it with blood as if it were a spoon, and threw it at the girl's body. He hit his mark — right between her legs.

On that day, women all started menstruating: brides-to-be, little girls, old women, with no exceptions. Since then, women are the ones who menstruate, the ones who must stay in seclusion every month. In the beginning even young girls and old women menstruated — later on, only in the age of ripeness.

Now it's the men who make fun of the women.

Kempãi, the woman with only one breast

Narrator in Portuguese: Etxowe Etelvina Tupari

There was an old woman who had only one breast, the left one – she was just born that way.

She used to call to little girls as they passed by, one by one. She pretended to have a splinter in her breast and would ask the girls to help her pull it out.

"My granddaughter! Will you come do me a favor and help me take this splinter out of my breast?"

"Where is it, Grandma?"

The girl would approach, lift up the old woman's breast, and look for the splinter. While the girl was absorbed in her task, the old woman squirted her milk into the child's eyes and she died. The old woman used her breast to kill young girls so she could eat them.

The old woman would carry the dead girl to the river bank and fetch water to cook the fresh meat. She chopped it up and cooked it and ate every bit. When she was finished and was hungry again, she would call to another young girl.

The girls were gullible fools – they always believed the old woman and came to help her.

Another naïve young girl was examining the breast, expecting to find the splinter.

"Where is it, Granny?"

"It's right here, look carefully, my little granddaughter!"

Another squirt of milk and this girl died too.

One day the old woman carried her human game to the riverside and climbed down to fetch some water. She left the little girl's corpse on the river bank; she would cut it up after she lit the fire. The Big Snake, Kenkat, swam by and saw the girl's body before the old woman had had a chance to chop it up and boil it.

"That one-breasted woman kills so many pretty young girls! This one was very pretty, with strong legs, breasts not yet fully grown, such a smooth face! She should have been my wife, but once again that horrible old woman decided to eat a sweet young thing!"

Kenkat, the Big Snake, brought the girl back to life and took her with him to be his wife.

The Woman-with-only-one-breast came back from the river and found that her game had disappeared.

"Where is my food? Where is the game I killed today, my human flesh? Who took it? I want to eat my dinner! Could it be that I carried this heavy water for nothing? That I'll go hungry?"

The birds the old woman raised – the woodpecker, reddish-bellied parakeet, and *cao-cao* – were watching and thought it was quite funny.

"Ah, you scoundrels, it was you who told the villagers I killed a girl, just so you could rob me!" The old woman was so furious that she killed her own birds.

Meanwhile, the Big Snake, Kenkat, was in the river with his bride.

"You have a father and a mother, you have a family. If you miss them I'll take you back to see them!"

The Big Snake felt bad for the girl, seeing her cry, not understanding where she was.

"Don't cry. It was I who brought you back from the dead. It's thanks to me you're alive and I won't mistreat you. I'll bring you to your father's house," promised the generous Snake.

He kept his promise. He asked the girl to tell her father and mother that she had been saved by the Big Snake after being put to death by the Evil-old-woman-with-only-one-breast. He took her almost to the door of her hut.

Her father and mother were crying, certain they would never see their daughter again.

"I was really dead! I died from a drop of milk from the Old-woman-with-only-one-breast. She asked me to help her get a splinter out of her breast, but then the Big Snake swam by and felt sorry for me. He brought me back to life! But, he decided not to marry me and brought me back to you!"

That's how the Big Snake warned the little girls to stay away from the Old-woman-with-only-one-breast, who liked to eat young girls, not ripe women or old women.

The clay woman

Narrator in Portuguese: Etxowe Etelvina Tupari

In those days women didn't yet have pots to cook with.

A young married woman complained that she didn't have anything to cook the *chicha* in. Her mother felt sorry for her and promised to find a way.

"My daughter, I don't want you to be unhappy because there are no pots. I'm going to turn into clay for you to make a pot. Just turn me upside down and my pussy will be the mouth of the pot. Clean my insides well and then put me on the fire to cook the *chicha*. When the water evaporates I'll tell you and you must put more in, so that my heart won't burn."

The girl did just as her mother said. She turned her mother upside down and she became a clay pot. The girl washed the mouth of the pot thoroughly, knowing it was her mother's pussy. She gathered firewood, kindled the fire, and put the mother-pot on it to cook the *chicha*. Each time the soup boiled, she added more water – she was afraid to heat her mother's body too much and burn her heart. And so it went . . . whenever the *chicha* was done, cooked just right, the young woman took it off the fire and put it up in the loft to cool down.

The girl emptied the pot, rinsed it out well, and her mother became a person again – exactly as she had been before.

"Oh, little daughter, I'm a tired woman from boiling so much water in the fire!" she said as she sat and strained the *chicha* for her daughter.

The girl's husband, the mother-of-clay's son-in-law, adored the new *chicha*. He thought it was delicious. He asked for it all the time and when he went to the fields, the mother and daughter repeated their routine of turning into a pot and cooking the *chicha*.

"Do you want to make *chicha* again, my daughter?" offered the mother. "Turn me upside down so I'll become clay. Then wash me well and cook with lots of water!"

As it happened, the girl's husband had a girlfriend, a lover. The girlfriend hid and spied on the mother and daughter. She found out how they made the tastiest *chicha* in the village. She felt spiteful and decided to do something about it; she ran to the field to see her lover, the mother-of-clay's son-in-law.

"You like your wife's *chicha* more than you like mine, but she cooks it inside your mother-in-law's cunt!"

The boy was doubtful. How could it be?

"You don't believe it, but you'll see! Doesn't it make you sick to eat what comes out of your mother-in-law's pussy, out of her cunt?"

The young man kept brooding over it and grew suspicious. He ended up believing what his lover had told him and was furious. He ran to the hut and screamed at his wife and accused her of giving him disgusting food.

"I thought your *chicha* tasted good! I thought it was made in a clean, well-washed pot! Meanwhile you're cooking inside your own mother's cunt? How can you eat something so filthy?"

The pot was on the fire, brimming with *chicha*. The husband kicked the mother-in-law-pot and it broke into many pieces – poor mother-in-law.

In tears, the girl gathered up the shards. She tried to glue them back together, to make her mother whole again. Her mother moaned with pain.

"My daughter, I can't live here any more. Your husband shattered me to pieces. Just thinking about it hurts as much as does my broken body. I want to go away to where there's clay, to keep making pots for you."

They say the clay-mother went away to live on the river bank. Now she really turned into clay and from the clay she made all kinds of pots and pans, everything we need to cook with.

The women of the village found out and took the prettiest clay to make pots themselves. They kept taking the clay, but they forgot about the girl, the clay-mother's own daughter.

The girl was pregnant and had a huge belly. She was always crying. She felt sorry for her mother and she missed her.

"You're all taking the clay and you don't give me even a little," she complained, "but the clay is my mother. I'm going to have much more beautiful pots than you do!"

The others went to the river bank and the girl stayed alone, crying for hours on end. Then her mother came to her, in the form of a person. She tried to console her daughter and told her that the clay the others took was only the ashes from her oven, that she would give her daughter the most beautiful pottery in the world. And the mother said the others would come to see the pottery, and they would be jealous and ask for it, but that the daughter wouldn't have to give it to anyone.

The mother turned back into clay and the daughter went into the muck and pulled out all shapes and sizes of beautiful, ready-made pots. She put them all in her *marico*, said her farewells to her mother — who again warned her not to give any of the pots away to anyone — and took the road back to her hut. Before she reached the village, she hid her clay presents in the jungle.

When she got to the village, the women asked the girl where she had been, but she just cried. She knew that after giving her so much pottery, her mother would go far away and they would never see each other again. As for clay, all that was left were the ashes from the oven and that's what the women used to make their pots. And as for the girl, little by little she brought her magnificent pots home from the jungle. They were true works of art and the others were jealous and coveted them for themselves.

The ghost baby's nanny

Narrator in Portuguese: Etxowe Etelvina Tupari

The warrior Paküa was married to Tereü and the two were deeply in love. Tereü became ill and died and a shaman sent her spirit to the other side. Her husband died soon afterwards from grief. They had few relatives, and they also soon died; their family disappeared.

The ghosts of Paküa and Tereü stayed together; they were still married. They lived in an old abandoned hut and their daily lives were similar to those of the living, but they ate rotten fish, or the flesh of dead people. That is what ghosts eat.

In those times, there was a Tupari woman who wanted very much to have children but couldn't get pregnant – her period came every month. But still she kept hoping her period would not come and she might finally be able to have a child.

One day she started menstruating and on her way out to the little house where she would stay secluded, her husband, full of rage at having a sick wife who bled every month, exploded and threw her out of the house.

Crying and crying, she walked until she came to the abandoned hut where the ghost couple lived. The young woman entered the hut, never imagining its strange inhabitants. She was shocked at how dirty it was; it smelled bad, broken pots lay on the ground and rotting game was everywhere. But since she had to stay there, she set about cleaning and putting things in order. She

swept the courtyard and the path down to the river bank. The hut was transformed; it looked as if it had been lived in for a long time by a big, proper
family.

When she finished her work the young woman was exhausted and sat in
the courtyard spinning cotton. It was growing dark.

As soon as night fell, the ghosts, Paküa and Tereü, arrived. They were
shocked and furious to see that someone had cleaned their hut. They ran to
see if the intruder had disturbed their little ghost child, who they had left safe
in an old pot. They felt better when they saw it was still there sleeping peacefully, but they were still very angry.

"Who threw so many thorns on the floor for us to pierce our feet?" they
complained – because for ghosts, cleanliness is dirtiness: a nicely swept house
leaves them with a floor full of sharp stakes; everything that for us is messy
and foul, for them is cleanliness. "We'll kill whoever messed up our house,
whoever laid out branches for us to hurt ourselves on, whoever spoiled our
floor and our courtyard and the path to the river!"

They saw the girl trembling with fear in a corner, now aware of the danger
she had put herself in.

Luckily for her, just when Tereü was going to attack her, she recognized
her as an old friend, with whom she used to take walks and play when she was
alive.

"Was it you who came into our hut, and turned everything upside down?"
asked Tereü, already calming down.

"Yes it was me. I'm an unhappy woman. My husband wanted to have a
son, but I always got my period and never became pregnant – so he sent me
away. I didn't know this was your hut. I didn't even know there was a child
sleeping here while I was cleaning."

"If that's how it is, then you can stay here with us. You'll take care of our
little child while we go to the jungle to find dead fish. I'll nurse her when I
come home at night."

Tereü had her living friend watch over her ghost child – who was a little girl – every day, while she and her husband, Paküa, went out looking for dead people so they could bring home the rotting flesh for their dinner.

The living girl stayed alone with the girl ghost, who, because she was a spirit, had hair all over her body. Even so, the young woman grew fond of the child.

She was frightened when the ghost couple came home, bringing dead people's flesh. They always offered her some, which she accepted, but even though she was hungry, the meat made her nauseous and she buried it.

She saw the couple cook the dead people's earrings. Some were made of mother-of-pearl, which is very hard for us, but is a delicacy for ghosts. The earrings turned blue and the ghosts devoured them.

During the night, the living girl heard the Tupari weeping for their relatives who had died. She was sad and frightened, but the ghosts tried to console her.

"It's okay, it's just the frogs croaking. We'll go find them and bring back some food!"

For ghosts, the cry of people in their graves is the sound of frogs croaking. When they hear it, they feel happy and go out looking for the corpses.

The living girl didn't have a minute's peace; she was always terrified, hearing the wailing of the mourning, seeing the rotting flesh of her own relatives. She decided to return to her husband and see if she was cured, if she could get pregnant.

She dressed up the little ghost girl, who was like a daughter to her. She painted her, put little earrings and necklaces on her – like people wear – and took the little girl with her to the village. She hoped her husband would want her back now that she was, even if in a very peculiar way, a mother.

Tereü's ghost was hysterical when she returned and couldn't find her daughter. Tereü went after the living nanny and, arriving in the door of the hut, she warned the kidnapper to give back the child. How could she have made her suffer, so far from her child? How could she have betrayed her after having been treated so well? How had she dared to steal a ghost child?

Tereü threatened to kill everyone in the village if she didn't get her child back. But the living husband told his wife to give the child back. The little ghost girl was all cleaned up and painted with genipap, wearing little necklaces, already looking like a living child, no longer with hair all over her body. But the girl's adoptive mother had no choice but to give her back to her ghost mother.

Tereü's ghost threw the child onto the floor to burst her apart, to kill her so she would turn back into a ghost like before. She complained about the bad smell her child had in the hut of the living – but now she was a ghost again, without genipap, with the body paint of the dead.

From that day, Tereü's husband would allow no more living guests. He promised he would kill any who showed up.

The young woman who took a ghost/*epaitsit* lover

Narrator in Portuguese: Etxowe Etelvina Tupari

There are ghosts that wander at night through the jungle and the villages — they are the *epaitsit*. They don't stay with the other spirits, the *pabit*, in Patopkiã, the land of the dead. We are very afraid of the *epaitsit*. When we're alone in a deserted area, we make a fire so they won't come around — they're scared of smoke and fire. They also detest clean places, which, for them, are dirty. Messy, foul places are perfect for them.

There was once a woman who was menstruating and went to an old hut to stay in isolation, which is the Tupari custom. She didn't know that an *epaitsit* was living there.

The girl was setting up her hammock when the *epaitsit* appeared. He was a man. He asked the girl what she was doing there and she explained that she had only come to spend a few days in seclusion, while she was menstruating. The *epaitsit* was very pleased and asked her to marry him; she accepted. When her period was over, she didn't return to her village.

The ghost went hunting, but all he brought home for his new wife to eat was dead people's flesh and rotting fish or frogs. Even so, she liked being with him and so she stayed.

One day the husband invited the girl to go meet his family, in the land of spirits.

"It is time for you to get to know my father and mother!"

"But I'm scared! They're going to eat me!"

"There's no danger, you're my wife. Don't worry."

He was so insistent that she decided to go. She was curious to see what the country of spirits was like. They started walking and she kept asking if they had arrived yet, if they were almost there, anxious to know what lies on the other side.

The *epaitsit*'s mother was alarmed.

"This is your wife? Nobody alive has ever come here before!" she cried.

The girl trembled with fear – ghosts were circling all around them! She told her husband that this time she wouldn't escape, she would get eaten up for sure.

"There are so many Tarupás! They want to eat me!" she wailed.

"Don't worry, this isn't the land of the Tarupás – the land of red earth is their land. And you're my wife, I'll protect you," responded the *epaitsit*.

But the ghosts were excited by the smell of a living person and wanted to eat the girl. Her husband tried to protect his wife and fend them off, but he did not succeed. The ghosts ended up devouring the poor girl. Finally the husband helped eat his young wife, who was very beautiful.

The living people in the girl's village continued to wait for her, but never saw her again. She too turned into an *epaitsit*. She started going around in the dark with the other ghosts, searching for the flesh of human cadavers to eat. Like the others, she stayed alert, listening for our people weeping – for the *epaitsit* it's the sound of frogs croaking – hunting for the bodies of those who have just died.

The old woman who ate young boys

Narrator in Portuguese: Etxowe Etelvina Tupari

There was an old woman who adored eating handsome young men. She told them she was looking for a son-in-law, that she had a beautiful daughter who was dying to have a lover. One by one, the boys got very excited and almost always accepted the old woman's proposition.

She would tell a boy to get inside her *marico*; then she killed and ate him.

The boys noticed they were disappearing and began talking among themselves to figure out what to do. One of them, a brave young man, said he wouldn't be fooled like the others. He would shoot her with an arrow and take revenge on the old woman.

One day the young man met the old woman on the road and, as was her habit, she offered the boy her enticing daughter in marriage. Pretending to believe her, the boy crawled into the old woman's *marico*, but he had his arrow and everything.

The old woman walked along the path carrying the heavy *marico* — she planned to kill the boy and eat him when she got home. But the boy was slowly cutting through the straw of the *marico* with his arrow.

The old woman heard the scraping of the straw being cut and talked to the *marico*:

"Shhhh, tantantitantanti, shhhh . . .," telling it to quieten down, as she thought the noise was just the *marico* bouncing around while she walked.

"Don't fall, my grandson," she said when a noise came from the straw.

They went along like that and the brave boy almost had cut all the way through the *marico* when they came to a bridge that crossed a big river. Halfway over, the boy finished cutting the hole in the *marico* and fell in the water. He came up hidden, well down river.

The old woman tried to find him in the water, grabbing at the fish that swam by.

"Come, my grandson, come suck on my breasts!" she offered, thinking that the fish were people. After a while she captured a *traíra* fish.

The boy was watching from his hiding place in among some *sapopemba* roots. A second time he saw the old woman invite the *traíra* to suck on her breasts, thinking it was the runaway boy.

The *traíra* obeyed and bit her. The old woman fell down, dying of pain, and the young man finished her off. Then he went running to tell the others how clever and brave he had been.

The *Cobra-cega*'s lover

Narrator in Portuguese: Etxowe Etelvina Tupari

A young girl had her period and went into seclusion in a little hut. She went by herself to take a bath in the river and spread clay on her hair to wash it.

Sitting in the mud, she felt something tickling her between her legs. It was the *Cobra-cega*, hidden among the pebbles in the river. The girl would sit down and the *Cobra-cega* would come and tickle her; she liked it a lot and started going there every day.

That's how the young girl became the *Cobra-cega*'s lover and got pregnant with his child. Her belly was growing but she didn't understand what had happened. She told her mother she hadn't been with any men at all.

The shamans prayed for her, blessed her meat, and pulled and scraped off her hair. Her belly kept growing and the girl was worried and unhappy – could it be that she would give birth?

The tiny *cobra-cega* embryos were growing, making a rumpus, wanting to poke their way out of her belly. They went climbing up to her heart. They finally reached the girl's heart and she died.

Lots of little *cobra-cega*s came out of her dead body: from her nose, her ears, her asshole, and her pussy – from everywhere. The girl's mother buried her daughter and her worm children – they can be dangerous.

There is a worm that comes down from the sky, called Alerokat, which is very dangerous. It enters underneath the fingernail, then it climbs and climbs until it reaches the heart. It must come from the girl's *cobra-cega* children.

The clay pecker

Narrator in Portuguese: Moam Luís Tupari

An unmarried girl made herself a prick out of clay. It was just like a man's — but hollow inside. She made love to her new friend and talked to it as if it were a real person. Whenever she felt like it, she inserted the clay pecker into her pussy: she didn't need a boy at all.

It happened that one day, without her noticing, an *emboá*, a dangerous little insect with many legs, similar to a centipede, slipped itself into the hollow of the girl's clay lover. The tiny, shameless creature entered the girl too. It went way up inside the girl and sucked at her entrails. It stayed there where it was nice and warm.

For no apparent reason, the girl's belly started to grow. It grew and grew, but the girl didn't know why, because thanks to her clay artifact she had never had a single man. There were lots of *emboás* growing inside her and now they wanted to get out.

When the girl saw some *orelha-de-pau* mushrooms (which grow along tree trunks), she sat down and crowds of *emboás* went out to nibble on them. Once they escaped, they didn't return.

"Could it be that I got rid of all of them?" the girl wondered, and she wandered through the forest in search of more *orelha-de-pau* mushrooms, not to eat, but as bait for her *emboás*. She couldn't wait to get rid of the disgusting things.

But there seemed to be no end to the little worms, and day after day the girl hunted for *orelha-de-pau* mushrooms. Finally the *emboás* were all gone and the girl swore to herself:

"What a relief, I'm free of them! I'll never use my clay prick again!"

The king vulture's rival,
or the crazy horny girl

Narrator in Portuguese: Etxowe Etelvina Tupari

A man was setting traps in the jungle. His dog had died, and the hunter left its rotting carcass as bait and waited to see if vultures would come to devour it; he wanted to pluck the vulture feathers to put on his arrows. *Tapuru* worms were growing in the pustules of the dog's spoiling flesh.

Hordes of vultures flew down to eat the dead dog. They talked and gossiped among themselves like people. They asked each other when their female companion would show up: a beautiful, fat woman who could make them a nice dinner from the spoiled meat.

"Ah, she's late!" one of them explained. "She didn't finish baking our manioc cake, but she'll be here any minute!"

The hunter couldn't wait to see the king vultures' beautiful woman. He thought if she was nice and white and pretty, he would want to marry her.

More king vultures kept arriving to peck at the *tapuru* worms, but still no white woman vulture. The hunter hoped she might still appear and decided not to kill the vultures.

The king vulture girl took her own sweet time making her manioc cake, but finally she came. She was enchanting, just like the talking vultures had said: she was white and yellow, and had a brilliant, glossy coat. She ate the *tapuru* worms with her cake — she ate so much that the others went back to the sky and left her by herself.

The hunter gathered his courage and asked, "I've been single for a long time. I can't find anyone to marry me. How about you come to my hut to be my wife and cook *chicha* for me?"

"But I'm a king vulture! Won't your family want to kill me?" said the girl.

The hunter talked her into it. He reassured her and flattered her and talked to her so sweetly and tenderly that she decided to go with him. She liked the village and she liked her husband. Everyone was full of admiration at the sight of such an attractive woman. How had the hunter found such a beauty?

He set up their two hammocks right next to each other. He killed a lot of game for her, but she wouldn't eat it – she said that freshly killed meat smelled bad. She only liked rotting flesh, full of *tapurus* and other worms. The hunter had to set aside some pieces of meat so they could rot – then she liked it. He always reserved some of the game and put it safely away to spoil.

The vulture-wife was a hard worker and made lots of *chicha*, but no one liked it – they thought it tasted spoiled. Everything that she liked smelled bad to the others, and vice versa.

The husband, who previously couldn't even find a woman to marry, now had a lover – who came to him right in front of his vulture-wife. His wife was beside herself.

"Ah, shameless girl, making love to my husband right in my face. I'll have to cast a spell on you."

The lover tried to create problems between the hunter and his wife. She told the husband that the stranger's *chicha* was no good, that it had a putrid smell. But the husband said he liked it like that, that it was he who had brought the king vulture woman to the village.

Tired of seeing the other woman with her husband, the king vulture woman gathered roots and leaves from the jungle to cast a spell with. She called her rival and offered her what she had picked, saying that it made people beautiful and white. The other believed her and spread it all over her body.

The girl had hardly finished applying the medicine when she went crazy. She wanted to make love to every man who passed by. She was even aroused by the sight of her own father and her own brother. She lost all modesty. The magic spell had taken its effect! The girl was without shame; she chased after all the men and offered herself to them.

The vulture-wife saw that her revenge had taken effect and flew back to the sky. From there she looked for her husband, trying to shit on his head. She chased him for several days until she succeeded. He died.

The crazy lover girl's mother was ashamed of her daughter and didn't know what to do to hide her. Finally she took her away to an old house to keep her from her father – the girl was always begging her own father to lie down with her. The mother cleaned and tidied up the old hut and stayed there with her daughters, hoping for some peace and quiet and for her daughter to get better.

One day the mother sent the girl to fetch water from the river. She sang as she went, calling to all the men, aroused, always wanting to make love.

Tianoá, the nighthawk, was high up in a tree eating fruit. The girl saw his reflection in the river and got excited.

"Oh handsome man! Come to my hammock and I'll make you very happy! You've never had a woman like me!" she cried.

The sister looked up and saw Tianoá, the nighthawk, on a branch sucking on hog-plums. She begged him to come make love to her.

Tianoá is a disgusting bird. He's hideous, but she wanted him anyway – she was already spreading her legs and begging him to take her. Tianoá came down to make love to her and he liked it. The girl's sister ran away terrified.

The girl went back to the old hut and told her mother what had happened. They decided they'd better hide up in the corn loft that night so they wouldn't get eaten – Tianoá is dangerous.

When the sex-crazed girl came home, she kept yelling for Tianoá to come make love to her again. The mother was afraid and went up to the loft with the sister. The sex-crazed girl was lying down alone, calling to Tianoá, saying how she wanted him, that she couldn't stand it any more.

Finally Tianoá came and entered the old hut, with a little lamp on his head. He approached the girl's hammock.

"Hurry, my lover man! I'm lying here waiting for you! Come see how delicious, come make love to me now!" moaned the girl.

The ugly bird lay down in the girl's hammock and made love to her again while the mother watched, dying of fright. She knew that Tianoá is dangerous. As he made love to the poor girl he started to eat her.

"Don't eat me. No! Make love the right way, come inside me, that's what I want!" she wailed.

Tianoá started to eat one of the girl's legs. The mother heard and kept quiet – she didn't want the bird to find her and her other daughter.

The love-banquet continued, Tianoá eating pieces of the crazy girl who, even so, didn't get tired of making love.

In the middle of the night, the sister pissed up there in the loft, and it dripped onto the hammock. Tianoá felt it and realized someone was there. He got up and left his lover at the waist – he had already eaten her legs and arms, almost everything.

The devoured girl, already in pieces, said, "Tukutudu! Tukutudu!" making the noise of a bird beating its wings, of a pigeon when it flies. "I want to do it again! I want to make love! I want this man to fuck me!"

The mother said "I'm going to throw you into the air!"

The mother threw her and the girl started turning into a bird, into a pigeon. While she sang, she called to her mother and sister.

"When I find the way I'll tell you which way to go, vrrr, vrrr . . . with my wings . . . you can walk in the jungle, vrrr, vrrr, go for walks, gather firewood . . . you won't get lost, I'll advise you . . . vrrr, vrrr . . ."

She was turning into a pigeon; the pieces of her became a bird. She went away singing, beating her wings, always wanting to make love. That's why the pigeon sounds like that. The mother went back to the hut with the other sister. She was very, very sad.

The *Caburé* and the Musician Wren,
or the deceived bride

Narrator in Portuguese: Moam Luís Tupari

The *Caburé*, a small owl, was a very ugly man. He wanted the Cat's (the Jaguar's) daughter for a lover, but the girl was interested in Amsiküb, the Musician Wren. The three of them were at a party, a *chicha* feast.

The *Caburé* heard the girl and Amsiküb talking and – just like I, Moam, am singing right now – cried out, "I heard you, I heard you!" But the two didn't notice.

The Musician Wren whispered to the Cat's daughter, "I don't like my wife, I'd much rather have you instead. I'll leave the party first and mark the road so you can find your way to my house. I'll wait for you there!" The *Caburé* had been listening.

The Musician Wren left the party and went home, plucking out his feathers and leaving them along the path so the Cat's daughter would know where to go. The *Caburé*, shameless person, secretly followed behind and moved all the feathers so they led to his own house instead.

The Cat's daughter followed the Musician Wren's feathers, just as the two had agreed – but ended up at the *Caburé*'s house. He was asleep when she arrived, but his mother was awake spinning cotton and knew that her future daughter-in-law would be coming. She offered the Cat's daughter some *chicha*.

"Ah, here comes my daughter-in-law. I'm glad my son told me you were coming! Come in and welcome! Wake up, son, you invited your woman and now she's here, she followed you here."

The Cat's daughter thought it would be the Musician Wren, and was disappointed to see the *Caburé*. She was furious. But there was nothing she could do about it – she would just have to make the best of it.

"Ah, shameless man!" she fumed silently. She hated the *Caburé*.

The next day, the *Caburé* went hunting and promised to bring back meat for everybody. He came back happy and tired.

"I killed a monkey and left it in the middle of the road! Mother, send someone to get it. It's a big monkey with a little baby monkey and everything – you can hear the little monkey crying on top of its mother's body!"

The mother-in-law sent the Cat's daughter to get the monkey. The girl went, but it was just a rat! She came back and asked the *Caburé*:

"Maybe you said you were hunting a rat?"

"It's a monkey. Go back and take a closer look!" said the *Caburé*.

The girl went back one more time to the path, but all she saw was a rat.

"Go get it yourself! There's nothing there but rats!" she cried.

The *Caburé* sent his mother to get it. She went and brought back the game – a big rat.

"We don't eat monkey, we only eat fish at home!" said the Cat's daughter when she saw the nauseating rat.

"Tomorrow we'll go fishing!" promised the *Caburé*. "For now, we'll eat this monkey I killed for you."

"What monkey? That's not a monkey, it's a rat!" complained the Cat's daughter.

Even so, *Caburé*'s mother seared and grilled the meat so they could eat it.

"Have some monkey, my daughter-in-law!" said the mother-in-law.

"In my village we don't eat monkey, we only eat fish!" replied the Cat's daughter.

The next day, instead of fishing, *Caburé* went out looking for worms. He didn't find any and came home empty handed.

"I didn't find any fish, my wife, but I saw honeycombs and bees. I'll get you some honey!" said the *Caburé*. Honey is the sweetest dish of all!

The *Caburé* put his ax on his back and went to the jungle to carry out his promise. He walked and walked and walked, but there was no honey: he chopped down trees for nothing. Alone in the forest, he pierced his own eyes with a thorn from a rasp palm and filled a gourd with his tears. He brought it home to his wife and told her it was honey. But it was a lie. It was only the ugly little owl's tears.

The Cat's daughter drank it all up, thinking it was honey. She asked him for the honeycombs to suck on:

"Where is the rest, where are the honeycombs?" she asked.

"All I took was the honey. I left the honeycombs there. But I saw other bees, so let's go get some honeycombs!" he lied.

They walked and walked and walked, looking for the honey. The *Caburé* pointed to a tree and said,

"I'm going to climb this tree looking for honey. You wait for me here on the ground."

He chopped at the tree, to pretend he was cutting it, tapping the honey — but he secretly pierced his eyes once again. He filled a small gourd and brought it to his wife. She drank it and asked him for the honeycombs too.

"I forgot them up there in the tree!"

The Cat's daughter said, "Go get them for me. In my village we like to eat them! And how about the beeswax?"

"I didn't see any! Now go get another gourd for me to fill," said the *Caburé*.

The Cat's daughter started to get suspicious.

"What can this man be doing?" she thought.

It seems that the Cat's daughter's sister appeared and told her about the honey, and showed her it was fake. The two girls ran away and escaped from the *Caburé*. They left their spit to talk to him as he called to them from high up in his tree. The saliva turned into fungus and talked to the *Caburé* while the two sisters went far, far away.

Caburé climbed down from the tree and couldn't find his wife. He ran home crying to his mother's house.

"My wife ran away!" he wailed.

"Did you hit my daughter-in-law?" asked his mother.

"I didn't hit her, no! I don't know why she ran away! Mother, I'm going to walk around the world and take revenge on whoever stole my wife. I'll be away for a long time."

"Be careful, my son!"

"I'll be careful. I have the courage to go walking!"

Caburé went walking and walking, asking in every village if anyone had seen his wife.

"Have you seen my wife? Tell me the truth, if not I'll kill you!" he would ask.

He would hit the person with his club and crack their head open.

The dead husband

Narrator in Portuguese: Etxowe Etelvina Tupari

A man died and his body decomposed, leaving only the bones. They buried the man, but he came back up from under the ground.

While the villagers went to the work in the fields, the dead man got up out of his grave to gather food and drink *chicha*. He stuck his hands into pots and rummaged around in people's belongings. He ate *tacacá* and corn cooked with peanuts. He drank some *chicha*, and filled a little bowl to take back and drink in his grave – he took lots of things to enjoy in his home underground. When his provisions ran out, he returned for more – but only when no one was around. He was nothing but bones – white, white bones – but even so he went out looking for food.

We lived in a large, round hut, and the deceased man circled around smelling out *tacacá*, cooked chicken, and roasted corn – anything he might want. All the flesh had rotted off his body, his bones walked on their own. When his relatives were about to come home, he took the food to his grave. That's what happened, every day.

"Who could be messing around with our food? I didn't take the grilled meats, or *chicha*, or roasted corn – there were leftovers for us to eat tonight!" they complained. "Let's keep an eye out. Let's ask a child to find out who's stealing from us!"

Everyone was angry, especially the chief's wife, suspecting there must be a thief. The next day when they went to the fields, they left behind a little girl, who stayed as quiet and still as she could manage.

The dead man got up out his grave and there was a terrible rumbling and cracking as the ground broke open. The little girl trembled with fear.

"It's the dead rotted man who's walking around and taking our food!" thought the girl and ran to find her mother.

"The dead man who was buried just a little while ago didn't die! No! If he were dead, he wouldn't be able to come out of the ground and eat our food. He was white, only white bones! I don't understand how he could drink *chicha* and eat, but it's true!" she cried.

The villagers asked the dead man's wife to kill him, as maybe he wasn't really dead.

It was the season for *tanajura* ants. When we lived in the jungle, in the village, we always got up at dawn to go wait for the *tanajura* – we all loved to eat them. The dead man's wife went to the jungle with her brother, bringing along her young son and daughter. The brother made a little hut and left the others in their new camp, while he went out after the *tanajura*.

They soon heard the sound of a horn, coming from far away. "Tum . . . tum . . . tum." It sounded just like a living person.

"Your uncle is already returning with *tanajura*!" exclaimed the widow, thinking it was her brother.

They waited quietly, but they were uneasy; they were suspicious of the sound of the trumpet.

It was the dead man coming with a little pitch lamp on top of his head to light the road. He was nothing but bones, coming along, blowing his horn.

"Your uncle is almost here!" repeated the widow.

When he was almost there, the deceased man put out his little lamp – he did it on purpose, so his family wouldn't escape. He came slowly and quietly, his wife still thinking it was her brother calling.

But it was the corpse. He lay down with his wife in her hammock. I don't know how she could stand it. He spent the whole night on top of the poor woman, smearing her beautiful body with the rotting fluids of the dead.

"She was my wife, my love and happiness, the one I used to sleep with every night! Now I want to fuck her again!" he said in a loud voice.

He spoke a different language from ours, the language of the dead. He spread his sticky stuff all over the woman's body. The smell was horrible.

"Go kill frogs for our children to eat!" said the woman.

In those days we ate frogs. The woman imitated the sound of frogs croaking so the dead man would go get them. She wanted to be free of the offal that was embracing her, of the lover with rotting flesh. The dead man brought back some frogs.

"Go get more, I want to eat lots of them and so do the children. This isn't much at all!" insisted the woman.

While the deceased man went out to get more frogs, the mother called her children and they went to hide under a waterfall.

"What will happen to my brother when he comes to meet us? The creature will kill your uncle!" she said, frightened to death. "How can I warn him?"

The rotted man sat on top of a tree to wait for his living brother-in-law. The brother-in-law came along carrying a club in his hand. He gave the dead man a final blow.

"Ah, this creature ate my sister!" thought the brother, starting to cry, not knowing that she was hiding behind a waterfall with her children.

The woman scrubbed and scoured her body with sand to get rid of the rotting flesh. But there was no way to get it off or to get rid of the foul odor.

The brother wept and returned to the village.

"That monster ate my sister!" he cried to his wife.

He was deeply unhappy, but a little while later his sister arrived. Together, they dug up her husband and buried him again. This time they did it right. The dead man's bones never came out of their grave again.

The man with the long cock

Narrator: Kabátoa Tupari
Translator: Isaías Tarimã Tupari

There was a man named Tampot who had an extremely long cock, a pecker that could reach over two hundred yards. From far away, he slipped his cock into women whose minds were on other things: when they thought they were alone and opened their legs as they bathed by the riverbank, or crouched in the fields to harvest manioc.

Tampot never left his hut. He watched the lovely young women; he watched where they went from afar. And then, if they went to the river bank . . . it was one of the best places, with their husbands far away, suspecting nothing.

Wherever a pretty girl might be, there went Tampot's long cock, trying to find its way inside her pussy. A beautiful woman had no peace. If she didn't want to play with Tampot's cock, if she went somewhere else, if she went farther away — it didn't help, the cock reached her; it showed no mercy. Married or single, it didn't matter; the husband wouldn't even know: he would always be far away.

The woman would run away to the river bank, think she had escaped, and there would be the big cock. And Tampot wouldn't even have gotten up from his seat in his hut. The only thing to do was to give in and let him have what he wanted for a while — until he got tired or took a liking to someone else. Because if the girl ran away to the middle of the trees, to the thick forest, the cock would burrow under the ground until it reached her, no matter where she went. He was completely shameless, this man, with his clever prick.

Ah, if Tampot were here, you women who are listening to me – you are so pretty, and just the kind of shape that Tampot always lusted after: round and plump, what he adored – you wouldn't have any peace at all! You'd have to do a lot of lovemaking. He would have his eye on you, licking his lips, already aroused, until he slipped inside you . . .

AJURU

The moon

Narrator: Galib Pororoca Gurib Ajuru
Translators: Pacoré Marina Jabuti, *into Jabuti*; Sérgio Ajuru, *from Jabuti to Portuguese*

A family lived in an isolated place, just the parents, two sisters and a brother.

A lover came to the sisters every night, in the dark, but they didn't know who it could be. They wondered:

"Who could our lover be? There are no men around here, only our brother! Could he be tricking us?"

They went to get a dye from the jungle to paint the unknown man's face with while he slept. They found a fruit, made a juice from it, and painted the man's face. But in the morning, they didn't see any dye on their brother's face. What happened was that he had washed his face early in the morning and all the dye had come off.

One of the sisters came across a genip tree (in those days genip trees were very low). When they tried to pick the fruit, the genip tree grew. It turned into a very tall tree, just as it is today. Now when they climbed up to pick the fruit, the genip tree's owner appeared. He was called Sírio.

The sisters asked him to give them fruit so they could make some dye. Sírio gave one to each of them. They wanted more; they each asked for two and each of them got two. The two girls ran to prepare the dye and painted each other to test it out. They took a bath in the river and the paint remained on their skin – genipap takes a long time to come off.

One said to the other:

"Tonight, while he's hugging you in your hammock, spread dye on our lover's face. Tomorrow we'll know for certain whether it's our brother or not!"

The other sister, in the dark, grabbed a gourd full of the dye and painted it on her lover's face. His eyes burned.

"Mommy, help me!" yelled the brother, walking around the hut. "My eyes are burning up!"

"My daughters, your brother's eyes are burning! Run to fetch water for him to wash himself with!" called the mother.

"I told you it was our own brother making love to us! What a disgrace!" wailed the two sisters.

The brother left the house without speaking to anyone. While it was still early in the morning, he took a *capemba* leaf full of water – that's what Indians use for a mirror – and looked at his face. It was completely black from the genipap. He felt he would die of shame and went to live by himself in the jungle and didn't go back to the hut.

He thought about climbing to the sky and tried to make a ladder from pieces of wood, but it fell down. He tried again, but it wouldn't hold his weight.

Sírio arrived, the master of the genip tree.

"Go at night to ask your mother for a pot of corn *chicha* and a chicken. I'll make you a ladder to climb up."

The boy returned with some warm *chicha*, a roasted chicken, and eggs, and gave them to Sírio. Then Sírio told the boy to gather lots of long sticks to make a ladder from. While the boy climbed up a tree to cut down some branches, Sírio, planning to trick the boy, pulled a thread from his own belly button and made a string to climb up to the sky, without using the branches the boy had already cut down. Finally, Sírio called the boy.

"Your ladder is ready! Climb up!"

The brother obeyed.

"Are you there yet?" asked Sírio, still on the ground.

"Not yet!"

Sírio was a Wainkô, an evil spirit. He wanted to eat the brother and planned to knock down the ladder when the boy had almost reached the sky.

Sírio kept asking and asking, but still the boy hadn't quite reached the sky. Finally the boy got to the sky, but waited a little before he told Sírio.

"I'm here!" he called down.

Sírio cut down the ladder, but it was too late.

"You knew all along! I was going to eat you!" he bellowed furiously.

Before long, the Jaguar, Amekô, grabbed the boy and bit him. He ate him all up; only the boy's blood was left over. The Master of Wax, Pibiro, a being of the heavens, licked up the brother's blood and he came back to life. He hid the boy under his fingernail. But the Jaguar came back and ate the boy once again. And so it happened several times: the Jaguar kept eating the boy, and the Master of Wax would lick up the blood, bring him back to life and hide him under his fingernail.

The sixth time, the Master of Wax secretly gathered the boy's shit that he used to bring him back to life. He smeared him all over with the shit and it made him very bitter tasting. When the Jaguar came to eat the boy one more time, he found him to be very bitter and couldn't eat him.

And so the Jaguar ate the brother six times but the last time he left him untouched. The boy turned into Pacuri, the Moon, that appears in the heavens.

The brother and sister raised by
the Jaguar

Narrators: Galib Pororoca Gurib Ajuru and Aperadjakob Antonio
Ajuru
Translators: Pacoré Marina Jabuti, *into Jabuti*; Sérgio Ajuru, *from
Jabuti to Portuguese*

The spirit Wainkô kidnapped a brother and a sister and stuck their hands in
a hole in a little mound of earth. The girl was the older, almost ready to
menstruate for the first time.

The children remained prisoners for days and Wainkô urinated on them.

One day the Jaguar found them. It was a male Jaguar. He tried to pull the
children's hands out of the hole, but couldn't. The Jaguar wore a hat on his
head, which he slipped inside the hole. Then he tickled the children, which
freed their hands. The Jaguar took them away to raise them.

When they got to his hut, the Jaguar gave the children a bath. He soaped
them all over with his soap, which is ashes from the fire, and washed them
well until they were nice and white. Then he washed their hammock and
made it white as well.

The Jaguar started sleeping with the girl and became her husband, even
though she was still a child and had never even menstruated. The Jaguar hid
the boy high up in the corn loft so the other jaguars wouldn't eat him. He
couldn't come down, no way!

Every day the girl took her brother's urine, in a chamber pot or little bowl
that he used, and threw it out so that no one would know he was there.

One day she forgot and went out with her Jaguar-Husband and didn't come back in time. The boy pissed too much and the bowl overflowed and drops started to fall on top of another jaguar. The Old-Jaguar, the girl's father-in-law, father of the Jaguar who had saved the children, felt the urine dripping on his back.

"Ah, there's some game around here!" he said, as he smelled the drops of urine.

The Old-Jaguar tried to imitate the girl and asked for the chamber pot so he could throw out the urine. But the boy was suspicious, he knew it was a jaguar speaking and wouldn't give him the chamber pot.

A few hours later, the Old-Jaguar filled his *marico* with straw mats and threw it into the main room of the hut. It made a lot of noise, as if it were the sister returning from the jungle. This time the boy thought it really was his sister and brought down his chamber pot. The Old-Jaguar grabbed the boy's arm and killed him.

When the girl finally arrived, she called her brother in vain. There was no answer. She climbed up into the loft and didn't see anyone and knew that her brother was already dead. She cried and cried; she was brokenhearted.

At midnight she stopped crying. She kept quiet and pretended to sleep. She heard her Jaguar-Husband ask his father if he had killed the boy. The old father said that he had indeed.

"Have a piece, my son!" offered the Old-Jaguar. "Your wife is asleep!"

And thinking that the girl was asleep, the Jaguar-Husband accepted.

"Ah, Poppa, it's delicious!" he exclaimed. He picked up the *marico* with his brother-in-law's head inside to see how heavy it was.

The sister started to cry again. Her weeping was a song – like I'm singing now, repeating the father-in-law's name, *Amekotxewé*. The father-in-law taught her this song, so she would learn his name.

Time passed and the girl asked her husband for all kinds of baby animals to raise as pets, to console her for her brother's death. She wanted baby tapirs, deer, macaws, parrots, parakeets, black monkeys, and many other kinds of animals. The jaguars did what she asked them to. There was a whole horde of animals all around her, birds flying around in the air, animals running along on the ground. The girl was a mother to all these animals.

They played with the grandfather, the girl's father-in-law who had eaten her brother. They played with the Old-Jaguar so they could tame him – the girl was teaching them how to take revenge for her brother's death.

When the little animals had been properly brought up, their mother had them kill the grandfather.

There were two types of *japó* birds. One pierced the Old-Jaguar's head, the other stuck his beak inside the wound and killed the Old-Jaguar grandfather.

The large *japó* has a red beak – they say it's the Old-Jaguar's blood. The *japó* birds killed the Old-Jaguar and went away; the other animals that walk on the ground, like deer and tapirs, stomped all over him and finished him off.

The Jaguar-Husband appeared and wanted to kill all the animals. The girl lied to him and told him she would go after the animals and bring them back so he could take revenge for his father. She went to the forest and escaped with the animals.

The Jaguar-Husband went and buried his father.

The enchanted girl

Narrators: Galib Pororoca Gurib Ajuru and Aperadjakob Antonio Ajuru
Translators: Pacoré Marina Jabuti, *into Jabuti*; Sérgio Ajuru, *from Jabuti to Portuguese*

My father's people are called the Ajuru and this story is about something that happened to their neighbors. These neighbors lived in an open field and were called Eriá, Iguá, Iguariá, which means, "The ones who live in the field." The Iguá and the Ajuru often drank *chicha* and went out walking together.

In the village of the people of the field there was a snake that started to eat everybody. If a person went to the river bank, the snake ate him. The Iguá were disappearing.

One day, the chief's son went to take a bath, as if the snake had called him. The others went running after him to keep him from falling. Thanks to the help of his friends, the boy didn't die; they knew that it was from this part of the river that people were disappearing.

They called together people from many villages, from five big huts, to throw the snake's water away. Men, women, children, and old people all came with clay pots; they filled the pots and threw away the water.

The snake kept urinating, however, and the pool where he lived kept filling up again. Finally, after the people had worked a very long time, the water ran out and the snake stopped pissing.

It was a huge boa constrictor. The people shot at her with arrows and she defecated. The smell was unbearable; it was so bad that everyone trembled just from smelling it. They finished killing the snake with an ax made of stone.

"Let us take our revenge for each one of us that he ate. Let's eat the snake!" they shouted excitedly.

They cut the enormous snake into many pieces. It was really huge and fat, but there were lots of people to do the eating. They divided it up fairly.

They put pieces of the snake meat to cook in a great clay pot, but it shattered. They tried roasting the meat on the coals, wrapped in leaves — but the leaves spoiled. The meat fell off the grill. No one could figure out what do with this snake meat.

And so no one managed to eat the boa constrictor. Those who had come from far away took pieces of the snake meat home to eat in their villages, but instead they threw them into a bay called Karuê (the name of a river). They say that today, in the place where they threw the pieces of meat, there is no end to the snakes, and that from that day, the snakes started to eat the Ajuru people.

When the two of us, Pororoca and Antonio, became shamans, we knew this story. It was like this:

A girl was having her first period. She was in seclusion and couldn't even lift her head while the people threw the pieces of snake meat in the water. She kept quiet, with her head bowed.

The people who killed the snake all died. The only one from the village to escape was this girl. I think the snake was the one who harmed all the others, but not her, because she hadn't done anything.

She stayed alone. She ran away and lived in a house made of stone. She was bewitched. They say that when someone went fishing nearby, she would ask for fish. She would take her fish and then she would disappear.

Our family, the Ajuru, decided to go get the girl. When she shouted and asked for fish, they grabbed her.

She lived with them, but the shamans had to bless everything she ate, they had to bless all her food before she could eat it.

One day, the Ajuru man she had married in the village got annoyed.

"You only eat food if it has been blessed!" he said.

After her husband's complaint, the girl ate food that hadn't been cured. She just ate it and disappeared; she went away. She went back to her own place – she was enchanted.

The snake-husband

Narrator: Galib Pororoca Gurib Ajuru

Translators: Pacoré Marina Jabuti, *into Jabuti*; Sérgio Ajuru, *from Jabuti to Portuguese*

A family built a new hut and moved in. Only an unmarried woman stayed in the old hut. She liked a snake that we call Two-heads and they were lovers.

The snake turned into a person at night, but during the day he was a snake. When day came, the girl protected her husband so no one would see him.

One day the girl's mother was going through her daughter's belongings and saw the big snake lying on the ground. She killed him.

The girl, already with a large belly, was out gathering firewood. She came home and saw her husband dead on the ground. She laid the snake's dead body across her legs and wept with despair.

"Why are you crying, my daughter? Because we killed the snake? That ugly animal was your husband? I didn't know – that's why I killed it!"

Another month passed and the girl lay went into labor. She gave birth to all kinds of snakes: rattlesnakes, *pico-de-jaca*, anacondas, *jararaca*. In the middle of all the baby snakes a child was born, a little girl, then one more snake that was just like its father, the snake that was killed by his mother-in-law.

A few days after giving birth, the young woman told her mother she was going out to gather special medicinal leaves for her children (Indians know how to use leaves for many things).

She warned her mother, "When the baby cries, mother, don't take care of her. Let her cry until I get back!"

The snake-boy cried, the one who looked the like snake-father. The grandmother felt sorry for her grandson. She heard the snakes making a big racket (rattlesnakes have rattles and make a lot of noise) and wanted to take care of her grandchildren. She opened the door and the baby-snake bit the old woman and plucked out both her eyes. The old woman fell down and died. Then the baby-snake went after his sister, who was a person, and killed her too. Then he escaped, with all the other recently born snakes.

The girl arrived home and saw her mother and daughter dead. She ran after the snakes and found them a little while later. She gave the snakes a medicine from the jungle – the leaves that she had gone to get – so they would not be poisonous.

The girl went back to the hut and buried her mother and her daughter. The she went back after her snake-children.

Dáb is the snake's name. Mekahon is the *pico-de-jaca*. Gáptara is the rattlesnake.

The gluttonous wife

Narrator: Aperadjakob Antonio Ajuru
Translator: Alberto Ajuru

This is the story of the gluttonous wife.

She had the habit of going into other people's houses, into relatives' houses, to get more meat to eat.

One day, the people who lived in another hut were eating a deer that they had just hunted and killed. It was the Indians' custom to eat in the afternoon, outside in the courtyard.

The woman's husband went to visit the hunters' hut in the late afternoon and they gave him a piece of meat. He ate it and returned home, but his wife smelled the meat and complained:

"You ate meat and didn't bring back any for me!"

"I didn't bring any back because I only had a small piece!"

She started to cry. She cried and cried.

"Don't cry! I didn't bring any back because there wasn't enough. It was just a little bit!"

The husband went to lie down and the glutton sat there crying. She cried so much that a fox heard her and came and put its paw through a gap in the straw.

The people in the village are afraid of foxes, because they attract ghosts, foretell many things, and make fun of people. The glutton grabbed the fox's paw tightly and didn't let go.

"Here is some game, come kill it!" she shouted to the others.

The boys are always ready for anything and they ran up and killed the fox. The glutton had already gone to get a clay pot. Then she started cooking the fox's innards and ate them. She bothered her mother all night, asking for salt.

Her mother said she should leave it for the next day — her husband had already gone to bed. But the glutton insisted.

The sun was already coming up when she finally stopped eating — it was a very big fox. She only stopped eating because it was all gone.

Her husband was ashamed and went to the fields. He was ashamed to know that his wife had been eating the whole night long. Another man saw how ashamed he was and offered him his daughter in marriage so he could change wives. The husband accepted.

When he came back from the fields he was ready to marry the other woman.

The relatives tied the fox's bones to the gluttonous wife's hammock while she was in the field. When she came home and wanted to lie down, there were only bones.

The husband went to live with the other woman.

Tororõi, the frog

Narrator: Galib Pororoca Gurib Ajuru
Translators: Pacoré Marina Jabuti, *into Jabuti*; Sérgio Ajuru, *from Jabuti to Portuguese*

In the season of the sauba ants, the Indians would go out at night and dig a hole to trap them and eat them.

During this time of year a man went to capture the sauba ants, and brought with him a club and a machete. He heard *Tororõi*, the frog, crying just nearby and had an idea.

He said, "You, that are there crying, why not turn into a woman, a person, and be my wife!"

He took his club and hit the spot where the frog was sitting and crying. It jumped away and turned into a woman. The man was delighted and took her with him – she followed behind him.

They went every night to get more sauba ants, but the frog-wife only captured the *tanajura*, the queen – that bites.

The man and the frog-woman lived together. The woman who had been a frog didn't eat meat: she only liked sauba ants. While her husband ate meat, all she wanted was toasted corn with sauba ants.

The frog-wife was a hard worker and prepared *chicha* and *tacacá*. She prepared food, but she didn't need to put much in the pot: she said the food would grow by itself.

It was a mystery! She would start the *chicha* and only fill the gourd halfway, but when night came, the *chicha* overflowed and there was plenty to drink.

Even so, her husband grew tired of going to get sauba ants every day. They kept biting his hands and he was sick of it.

"You don't eat meat, you only eat sauba ants!" he complained.

Enraged from getting so many ant bites, the husband took *tacacá* that was full of hot pepper and put it on his wife's tongue. It burnt so much that she started to cry.

She cried a lot. She took a clay pot and went down to the river bank. She threw the pot into the water and it floated away on the current. Then she turned back into a frog in the water, crying and crying.

The husband repented and went after his wife and called to her by the river. But she didn't want him any more. She never returned.

Nangueretá, the flying head

Narrator: Galib Pororoca Gurib Ajuru
Translator: Alberto Ajuru

While the chief's young wife lay in the hammock next to her husband, her head went out by itself to fly around. The head went to other huts and stole *tacacá* and meat from the neighbors' pots and brought it home.

It seems she had a lot of lice on her head and that it was the lice that cut off her head every night. She cultivated the lice; she popped them with her teeth and ate their heads.

"Wake up husband, bats and lice are sucking our blood!" she cried to her husband in the middle of the night. But the husband didn't pay any attention – he didn't even hear her; he didn't know his wife's head went flying around every night separate from her body – by the morning she was always whole again.

"Wake up, husband! You sleep too much! There's a lot of lice and you don't wake up!"

The girl yelled like that every night, but the husband kept quiet and the head went out alone.

One day a friend of the husband found out what was going on and told him. The two men decided to stay awake and see for themselves.

The next night, when the head went out to go around to the other huts, the friends grabbed the girl's body and threw it onto a big bonfire.

The head returned at dawn, spinning around and screaming in pain. It threw itself in the fire and stuck itself back to the almost burnt-up body. The girl, howling from the heat of the burns, knocked over the pot of *chicha* and put out the fire.

She had lost her skin and her hair. She cried, cried, cried, and killed rats. Then she picked up a pile of rats and brought them to the forest. The rats turned into people; they became her people. And that's how the chief became a widower.

One day, in the planting season, the chief (he was a shaman, just like his father) went to the field and saw a nighthawk. But it wasn't a nighthawk, it was Wainkô, his wife's spirit, come to lure the young man into a trap.

The chief told his father he would shoot the nighthawk with his bow and arrow.

"Be careful, it's not a nighthawk!" warned the father.

But the boy kept on hunting the bird. The shamans had gathered to take *rapé* and the boy's father said he would wait for him to return; he didn't go with the boy.

The young chief shot an arrow at the nighthawk but he missed. He went to get the arrow and shot again, and he missed again. He kept missing his target and following the bird farther and farther into the forest. Suddenly, in the middle of the forest, the chief saw a beautiful girl hiding in the leaves.

"My sister wants you to come and drink *chicha* with her!" said the girl (who was really the nighthawk). "Come!"

The boy hesitated, but ended up going to the nighthawk's hut. There was plenty of *chicha* and they gave him a bowl of it right away.

They had set a trap to kill him (his wife with the flying head was the one who had prepared it). There were arrows hanging from the roof of the hut and three small parrots cut them down so they fell and killed the chief.

The moment he died, blood fell on the shamans who were taking *rapé* in the village. They soon guessed that the chief had died.

"Let's go look for your brother!" said the chief's father to his other son. When they arrived at the nighthawk's hut it was all fenced in and had turned to stone, with the rats who had turned into people still inside. It seemed impossible to get in. But the chief's father was a shaman; he made a spell and broke down the fence. He entered the stone house and transformed the rat people into wild pigs, into game. Then he escaped.

Before this there weren't any wild pigs; there wasn't any game. It was the rats that became pigs; Nanguéretá, the chief's wife, escaped and didn't turn into a pig.

The shaman, the chief's father, became the pigs' master. He kept them prisoners and only ate one once in a while. He always told his grandson not to eat the pig meat in front of anyone else.

But one day the boy forgot and ate some of the meat in front of the other villagers. They asked for a piece and they tasted it; that's how they found out about the old shaman's secret pigsty.

They asked the boy to open the pigsty door and he foolishly obeyed. The boy opened the door wide and all the pigs ran out and trampled him to death and ate him up. Then the pigs ran away and scattered themselves across the whole world.

The old shaman wept inconsolably and sent his grandson's bones to be buried. His forefinger and middle finger gave birth to the manioc root, which didn't exist before.

The greedy wife

Narrator: Galib Pororoca Gurib Ajuru

Translators: Pacoré Marina Jabuti, *into Jabuti*; Sérgio Ajuru, *from Jabuti to Portuguese*

There was a greedy woman who was also very pretty. There was never enough meat to satisfy her, so her husband had to keep hunting all the time.

The husband finally got sick of so much hunting. He went to the jungle and, instead of hunting, he cut off pieces of his own flesh. He brought home the pieces and said he had cut them off some game that a jaguar had killed and left behind in the jungle.

Time passed and the husband grew thinner. His friend (*wirá* in Jabuti, *waiküb* in Ajuru) said to him:

"You, *waiküb*, are getting thin from stealing so much game from the jaguar!"

The husband continued to bring home his own grilled flesh and say it was the jaguar's game. He said he stole the meat from the jaguar.

"Bring back some bones so I can suck out the marrow!" said his friend, suspicious of what was going on.

The hunter agreed and went with his friend to the fields, but there he disappeared. He said he was going hunting and went off by himself.

The friend wondered where the hunter had gone and went to look for him. He followed the hunter's tracks until he arrived where his friend sat cutting off his own flesh.

When the hunter saw his friend coming, he wanted to close his wound as he always did – but this time the wound stayed open.

"So that's what you are doing!" cried his friend, horrified.

"Yes, that's exactly what I've been doing – for some time now, because of my gluttonous wife!"

"But why do you put up with such a greedy wife?" protested the friend.

The husband, deeply in love with his greedy wife, took his own flesh, which was already wrapped in leaves, and blew on it. His flesh turned into rats, lots of rats that came out running.

"This new animal will finish off your crops, all of your corn!"

Soon he talked to his friend and asked him to shoot him with his own arrows.

"Not I!" resisted the friend, feeling very upset.

The greedy woman's husband climbed up in a tree and insisted that his friend shoot him with arrows; he wanted to die. The friend had no choice but to shoot the husband, but because he liked him very much he didn't shoot very hard. He didn't have the nerve to kill his friend. The glutton's husband had to push the arrows in himself.

Since the hunter hadn't died, he kept asking his friend to shoot him again. The friend finished all the hunter's arrows and started to use his own. Now he shot with more force and the glutton's husband fell down screaming and started running along the ground.

Dying of fear, the friend went home to the village without even stopping to bathe in the river, as Indians usually do every time they return from any outing. As soon as he arrived, he asked the shaman to bless his bath water. He told his wife and the shaman what had happened and didn't spare them any of the details.

They took *rapé* and the friend vomited up a lot of blood – blood of the man he had shot down with arrows.

The greedy woman's husband had arranged a time to meet the friend again in the jungle. The friend had a lot of *chicha* made and brought a bowl of it with him on the appointed day.

The glutton's husband was at the top of a tree with the arrows stuck into his flesh. But the arrows had turned into a beautiful light. The husband's body was all lit up.

"Come see what you did to your husband!" said the friend to the wife of the man who had disappeared.

Kubiotxi, the greedy wife, looked up into the tree, petrified with fear.

The husband didn't come down from up high in the trees. He even drank the *chicha* they had brought him up there.

"Don't be frightened, my friend!" reassured the man from way up high.

When he had finished drinking, he went away into space. It thundered so loudly that the earth shook.

Until today there is this thunder and this light — they foretell someone's death, a war, or a catastrophe.

JABUTI

Watirinoti, the fox of olden times, or the revenge

Narrator: Abobai Paturi Jabuti
Translator: Armando Moero Jabuti

The false friend

Watirinoti, the fox of olden times, had learned our language. He prowled around our huts and stole the animals we were raising: trumpeters, guans (in those times chickens didn't exist), macaws, parrots, and orange-cheeked parrots.

One day, Watirinoti, the fox of olden times, overheard a girl invite her friend to go pick little fruits called *tarumã*. He immediately decided to trick them. He went to one of the girls' houses in the middle of the night and, in a voice that sounded exactly like the girl's friend, said,

"My friend! Playmate! Sister! *Henon*! Come with me to gather *tarumã*!"

The girl got ready to go out, even though it was still dark out and her parents didn't want to let her go. The false friend pestered the girl so much that in the end she went, and not only that, she brought along her little baby brother.

When daylight came, the girl's real friend came to the house.

"*Henon*! Let's go gather fruit!" she called.

"Why are you here again? Didn't you just call her a little while ago?" asked the girl's parents, alarmed. "She already left!"

"No, it wasn't me!" she cried.

The friend was frightened and went to try and find the other girl, but there were no tracks near any of the *tarumã* trees.

The fox's den and the helpful first wife

The fox had already taken the girl to its den, which was covered by a big rock. The fox smoked some tobacco, and when he exhaled on the stone it moved aside. The fox, the girl, and the little brother all went inside. He was a male fox, a man.

"Where has this man taken us?" said the girl to her baby brother. She was terrified — by now she had discovered that it wasn't her friend she was dealing with.

A blind woman lived in the fox's den and she overheard the girl talking to her brother. She warned her,

"Who is that speaking? Watirinoti is a bad man! If you knew what a horror it is to live here, you wouldn't have come! You want to suffer like me? If you want to continue to see, you need to know just how to conduct yourself with this Fox-Man! I'm going to teach you what you need to do. He's going to ask you to take a thorn out of his foot and you must prick his foot and break off the tip of a thorn that you will have in your hand. Pretend there really is a thorn and he will be grateful to you; if you say there is no thorn, he'll stab you in the eye! And when he wants to make love to you, don't let him, no matter what! Tell him that you're menstruating, *heté*!"

When the Fox asked the girl to take a thorn out of his foot, the girl did as the old woman had told her and everything happened just as she had said it would.

That night and the days following, when the Fox wanted to sleep with her, she told him she was menstruating.

Watirinoti kept saying:

"I saw so many rainbows in the sky!"

In the olden days, when a woman was menstruating, a rainbow would appear in the sky. Except that, since it was a lie, and she wasn't menstruating, there was no rainbow. The girl put a piece of brightly colored cloth on the ground and the Fox thought it was a boa constrictor, a rainbow.

That's how the girl avoided him every day.

"Well, then, at least give me your arm to warm my body and pretend that I'm making love!" begged Watirinoti, the Fox. The girl gave him her arm a little, but didn't like it. When the Fox fell asleep, she took pulp from a tree called *pente-de-macaco*, *kunonhonká* – that we use to beat bananas, manioc, and corn – and put it in place of her arm. He hugged the fake arm while he slept and thought it was the girl.

The escape

At night, the Fox went out hunting for his wife, but only brought back animals and birds that her father had raised – trumpeters, parrots, orange-cheeked parrots – and she wouldn't eat them, they were her father's. The girl and her brother were always hungry.

Time passed and the brother had already grown quite a bit. One day the girl heard noises on the other side of the rock that held them prisoner and decided to send her brother to see who it was.

"Run away outside to see if it's our father, go take a look!"

Where the Fox lived, beneath the stone, was filthy and covered with thorns, *pfupfujukunin*, *watirikunin* in our language. The brother had to clear away the thorns in order to get out. Watirinoti was woken by noise the little brother made cutting the thorns.

"Where are you sending your brother? A thorn is going to puncture his knee!" said the Fox.

In those ancient times, what was said happened. The Fox only had to speak and the thorn pierced the boy's flesh and he screamed with pain.

"It's easy to pull out our thorns, *watirikunin*, there's nothing to it! You just have to give it a little poke and it will fall out," advised the Fox.

And in fact, the girl gave her brother a poke and the thorn came out.

"Didn't I tell you our thorns come out easily?" said the Fox happily.

Watirinoti went back to sleep and the boy went back to clearing away the thorns so he could escape. He followed the sound of the voices they had heard and ended up in the village of the Wanoti, the jaguar people of olden times. They were digging yams.

One of the Fox's daughters lived with the Wanoti and was married to one of the jaguars. She had already told the jaguars that her father had captured a beautiful young woman and her little baby brother. When the brother arrived at the jaguars' hut, they already knew who he was.

"This must be the little boy, the brother of the Fox's pretty wife!"

The jaguars gave the boy some baked yams to eat right then and more uncooked ones to take back with him. They wanted to give him lots of food to show him that in the land of the jaguars he wouldn't go hungry, as he did in the Fox's den. The boy returned to the Fox's den loaded down with food, carrying yams for his sister.

The two ate eagerly and the noise the boy made chewing the yams woke the Fox.

"And so here I am eating, making all this noise?" asked the Fox, in a mocking way, talking in the form of a riddle as if he himself were the little boy.

"My brother is eating yams that he got from someone else! Here in this village we go hungry because the only one here is a lazy man who doesn't provide for us and doesn't feed us!"

"Ah! The Old Fox isn't lazy, not at all! I see plenty to eat around here! Moldy yams from last year! Baskets full of year-old spoiled yams! Corn that's been moldy for over a year! Baskets of old potatoes! Baskets of spoiled beans and peanuts! So much food, why don't you two eat old moldy food? You go hungry because you want to!"

"Yes, I'm going to eat that old food, just so I can get indigestion and have a sour stomach! No, I'm not going to eat it! No, I won't!" protested the girl.

"If fox food smells bad, then don't eat it!" he replied.

"If it was from my father's field then I would be happy to eat it!" she retorted.

"Then leave it! The food stinks like the Old Fox? Is that how it is? Then don't eat it!" cried the Fox.

The Fox was furious, and when night fell he went hunting. He went to steal animals the girl's father had raised and peanuts he had planted, to bring back to the girl and her brother.

While Watirinoti, the Fox, was away, the older wife, whose eyes the Fox had poked out when she had arrived in his den, gave some tobacco to the brother and sister.

The old woman was all ruined inside: her stomach and her uterus were destroyed. When she married the Fox, there had been no one to warn her about his wickedness. The Fox's cock had a hook on it and it had ripped the old woman all up inside; her and the other wife the Fox had had. Her uterus and vagina were shredded to pieces.

The old woman always helped the girl. Thanks to her advice, the girl was able not to make love to the Fox, otherwise she would have been badly mutilated. Now the older wife gave the girl a cigarette so she could get away and save herself.

The girl lit the cigarette butt and blew on the rock that covered the entrance to the Fox's hut. The rock moved and the girl went away with her little brother to the village of the jaguars of olden times (in those days, the jaguars were people).

Marrying the Jaguar and being raped by his relatives

The jaguars were hard workers. It was harvest time and they were in the fields digging up yams.

They were overjoyed when they saw the young woman, and the chief of the jaguars soon said:

"You are going to be my wife! No one will take you away from me!"

The chief sent his youngest brother for gourds full of *chicha* to offer to the newcomers. The women jaguars were jealous.

"We've never seen your brother ask for *chicha* while he's working! We already know who it's for! It's for that pretty girl that everyone's been talking about!"

"No, it's really for my oldest brother. He likes his yams nice and sweet!" replied the young man.

Wanoti, the chief, the Old Jaguar, the Jaguar-of-olden-times, married the girl. He told her how to find his house.

"You pass this hut, then the next, at the fourth one you can go inside. That's where we will live."

The girl did what her new husband told her. When she passed by the first hut, she heard the jaguar-women cursing.

"It's her. There she goes, that worthless woman!"

They were making *chicha* and started throwing pepper in the fire to hurt the girl. The Jaguar, the one who would be her father-in-law, said a prayer for her, so she wouldn't feel the pepper burning and wouldn't suffocate.

The girl was protected, but her brother couldn't bear it. He choked on the smoke from the pepper and was about to die. One of the girl's future jaguar in-laws helped him and gave him water. The boy revived; he didn't die.

The girl went inside the hut where she was going to live and started helping the women.

That night the chief Jaguar-of-olden-times slept with the girl. She had never made love before. It was the first time. The Jaguar was her first man.

Morning came and the chief ordered all the male jaguars to make straw mats. They would lie down with the girl on their mats and make love to her one by one.

There were lots of males to lie with her. The chief ordered them all to come. They made lots of straw mats.

Only the men who would become the girl's uncles, grandparents, parents, and brothers when she married the chief Jaguar didn't want to lie with her – they were ashamed. When she married the chief, the girl would have to call these jaguars Uncle, Grandfather, Father, and Brother. These jaguars didn't make love to her.

The chief, the husband, told everyone to make straw mats, to bleach the straw well, to make the mats carefully and well, so that the next day they could lie down with his wife. The Jaguar-husband woke his wife very early in the morning. He put her on the straw mat in the middle of the courtyard and the jaguars started to make love to her.

For a while she was able to bear it, but there were many jaguars, endless jaguars pushing into her vagina. She was dying, she was all torn up, her body was falling apart. She begged her husband:

"I already knew that wives lie down with their husband, with only one man, but like this, with so many – no, that I didn't know. It's horrible, I can't bear the pain! I'm thirsty, I want water, and if you don't make them stop this terrible punishment, I'm going to die! I'm at the end!"

The chief ordered the jaguars to stop. He was the chief in place of his father, the Old Jaguar, who until then had been a great chief.

Each time a jaguar raped the girl, the father-in-law took some pepper and mixed it with the semen that had spilled into her vagina and on her legs. He licked it up and ate it. It was the sperm, the seeds of her children, the blood of the jaguars' grandchildren.

When the jaguars stopped fucking her, the girl couldn't stand up; it was as if she had died. The chief's father took care of her. He prayed and carried the girl to take a bath and her husband also helped carry her. The father-in-law had not made love to his daughter-in-law.

The father-in-law, who was a shaman, prayed and exorcized the girl and took her home. As soon as she returned from the bath, she started to menstruate. She was already pregnant by so many jaguars.

When he found out his wife was pregnant, the husband asked all the male jaguars that had raped her on the straw mat to go gather *gongos* from the *ouri-curi* palm — because they all were her husbands, fathers of her child. They all had to get *gongos* and make a feast and offer her *chicha*.

The ones who had been ashamed didn't go, they weren't her husbands.

They said, "She's my aunt! She's my cousin! She's my grandmother!"

These jaguars hadn't fucked her. The ones who hadn't been ashamed went to harvest the *gongos*. Those who weren't the fathers of her child didn't go work; they didn't suck out *gongos* and weren't the child's fathers.

Crime and Vengeance

Gongos were needed for the birth ceremony. *Gongos* are one of the Indians' favorite foods and must be offered with *chicha*, game meat, and other kinds of food.

Ouricuri is a palm tree. When you drill into the trunk, it makes a hole. The mother gongo, an insect that makes the larvae, lays an egg inside, the little worm's egg. Then you have to stop up the hole to keep the jungle animals away, to keep the coatis away so they don't eat the *tapurus*.

The chief, the Jaguar-husband, called his pregnant wife to go with him to cover the *tapuru* hole in the trunk of the *ouricuri* palm so the coatis wouldn't steal the *gongos*.

The pregnant girl's brother wanted to go too, but the Jaguar-father-in-law didn't want to let him.

"Her belly is already very big! She'll have to carry her brother and won't be able to bear the weight!" said the father-in-law.

"I'm going to bring my brother!" said the girl.

The Jaguar-husband knew that his father had already eaten many children and was frightened, but the father-in-law promised to take care of the boy.

"Leave the boy here so your wife doesn't have to carry him. Her belly is huge!" he said.

"Then take good care of him and don't harm him!" said Wanoti, the husband.

As soon as the two left, the Jaguar-father-in-law grabbed the boy, who was crying, and tore him up alive with his teeth. Then he cut him into pieces to share with the other jaguars. He gutted the boy, threw out his shit, separated out the liver and the lungs, then divided him up and cooked him for the women. He gave a piece to each one. He gave a little to everyone, to eat before the girl returned.

When she got back to the hut, the young woman looked for the boy.

"He went after you!" lied the father-in-law. "Didn't you see him?"

"You were supposed to take care of him! Why didn't you keep a better eye on him?" complained the Jaguar-husband.

"Ah, he just wouldn't listen to me!" said the Jaguar-father-in-law.

The sister wept and wept without stopping. The next morning, as the sun came up, she pretended to be asleep. The Jaguar-husband asked his father what had happened (the boy was cooked, hidden in a corner).

The Jaguar-father revealed the truth, "The boy is right here, nicely roasted! And you, why should you cry? Have a piece!"

The sister heard everything (by now she understood the jaguars' language), and started to cry desperately. As she wept she thought about how to take revenge.

Later in the morning she said to her husband,

"I want baby animals, one of every kind there is in the jungle. I want you to send your people out to gather them for me."

He was the chief and he gave orders to his men. Just as the Indians used to do, he decided at dawn what everyone would do during the day. He ordered them to bring baby animals of every species home to his wife. It seems that the first animal they brought back was a baby monkey.

"Is this what you want?" the Jaguar-husband asked his wife.

"No, that's not it," she said.

Then came the guan.

"Is this what you want?" asked the Jaguar-husband.

"No, that's not the one either."

And so it went. Baby animals of all kinds were brought to the girl, *cuatipuru* (a kind of tropical squirrel), trumpeters – every kind of bird and animal – but the girl was quiet and full of rage. The only baby animal left was the purple deer. The jaguars found and killed a *veado-roxo* deer. They put their hands on its belly and felt a baby deer moving around inside.

"It has a baby! Let's take it out and give it to the chief's wife, maybe this is what she wants," cried the jaguars.

They cut open the mother deer's belly and pulled out the baby, which had been just about to be born.

"Is this the one you want? There aren't any other kinds of animals left!" asked the husband.

"Yes, this is just the one I want!" said the girl.

She took the baby deer to her shaman father-in-law and asked him to say a blessing.

"I want you to bless this animal. I want to raise it in place of my brother!" said the girl.

They say that all jaguars are shamans; the father-in-law blessed the baby. The girl took the baby home with her and slept with him in her hammock, as if he were a person.

When the little deer grew, the girl took some very hard wood from the *pau-âmago* tree, fashioned it into horns, and attached them to his head – she had tried before with the *capoeirão* deer, but it had died – now she tried with the *veado-roxo* deer. She talked to him and told him as if he were a person,

"When you grow up, you will take revenge for your uncle!"

The little deer grew up.

"Now, my son, let's gather firewood for me to make *chicha*. You will try to chop the wood," said the girl.

She took the deer to chop dry wood, then green wood (which is good for firewood). The little deer went to work with his horns and chopped down the whole tree. The effort caused a great shudder to pass through his body like lightning.

"That's just how I want you to do it tomorrow! For now, I want you to experiment with this green wood. But tomorrow, while I'm making *chicha* with the corn that takes so long to cook, you will go harass my father-in-law. He will be afraid of you, but you must keep threatening him. Only go away when I come to get you."

The next day the girl made the *chicha*, crushing the corn with a mortar and pestle. The young deer went to see the Jaguar-father-in-law, his grandfather. He lit up suddenly with bright light, his body quivered, and lightning came out of him. The father-in-law was terrified.

"Come, grab my grandson, or else he's going to rip me apart!" he cried to his daughter-in-law.

"He's not going to hurt you, he just wants to please you, to eat the mosquitoes off your back!" she lied. She gave her son some *chicha* and he kept harassing the old man.

His mother told the deer to attack the old Jaguar where he sat in the courtyard. The young deer's body trembled, and he stuck his horns into his grandfather and split open the old Jaguar's body up to the head; half of his body fell on one side, half on the other. Wanoti, the Jaguar-husband, said:

"Didn't I say that animal would kill my father? Now I'm going to kill him!"

But the young deer ran away. He knew what to do, because he had eaten manioc leaves that his Jaguar-grandfather, who was a shaman, had given him.

"Don't go near him or he'll kill you too!" said the girl to her husband. "Let me call him, I'll give him food."

She took food to the deer and the two of them ran away to her father's field. The deer ate leaves from his man-grandfather's plot. They met the girl's father, who asked about his son.

"They ate my brother, but your grandson already took revenge!" said the girl.

The old man started to cry.

The young woman was pregnant by the jaguars. When the baby was born, the girl's other brother took care of him and gave him tamarin meat and grilled *gongos*. The young woman asked her brother to gather all the foods that are prepared for a newborn baby.

The baby boy was born, but it didn't wake up. It was the jaguars' baby and animal young don't wake up right away; they sleep for a long time after they're born.

The uncle asked, "Where is my nephew?"

"He's sleeping!" said the girl.

"This baby just sleeps and sleeps. I'm going to kill it, to take revenge on the jaguars for killing my brother. He's the jaguars' son."

The uncle killed his nephew, the jaguars' son, and the baby's mother was upset.

"You killed him! You don't even know how many fathers there are to take revenge on you! They're going to eat you! There are many of them . . ."

They buried the baby. The next day the girl called the little deer and mounted him as if he were a horse. Lightning appeared in the sky and the little deer carried his mother away.

"Mommy, you're not going to die. Grandpa, Uncle, everyone will die – the jaguars are going to kill them! But we will stay alive!"

Even today, they say that this is lightning. The two disappeared to the fields; the mother and son went away, hugging, happy with each other, running free.

Kero-opeho, the castrated man, the man who turned into a woman

Narrators: Erowé Alonso Jabuti and Abobai Paturi Jabuti
Translator: Armando Moero Jabuti

One day a hunter named Kero-opeho went to the river to take a bath. He laid down his arrows and game on the ground and dove into the water.

He swam under the water and didn't even notice when someone – he never found out who – ripped out his cock and his balls and put a frog, that was exactly like a woman's pussy, in the place where his manhood had been. The same underwater someone also gave the man a uterus, the part of a woman's body that gets pregnant. There was no blood and he didn't feel anything. It didn't hurt. But when he finally saw what had happened, the hunter was desperate.

He started looking under the water for his lost cock, but he couldn't find it. He looked around on the ground; he even looked for his cock and his balls in the sky. The hunter's wife was devastated – her husband had become a woman!

The hunter walked all around; he looked everywhere for his missing parts. While he was talking to Erowei, the water spirits, he met the *japó* bird. It was Hibonoti, the spirit of Japó, the Old Japó. Kero-opeho asked the spirit for some kind – any kind – of cock. He didn't want to be a woman!

Hibonoti, the Old Japó, pulled out Kero-opeho's frog-pussy and gave him a man's cock, except that it was tiny, the size of a young boy's. The hunter wouldn't be able to please his wife with this!

Still, feeling a little better, Kero-opeho went back to his hut. He tried to make love to his wife, but it was no good, he couldn't satisfy her desire.

"Why did they rip out my cock?" he moaned to his wife. "It won't satisfy you, your passion, your fire! You'll go looking for another husband!"

His wife was afraid of him, however, because he was a shaman, and she continued to prepare his food and his *chicha* just as before. But when she had to have a man, she went elsewhere. Kero-opeho did as his wife did: he provided food for himself and his wife, but went and found himself new lovers.

Kero-opeho found a very young wife who had never made love, just a girl, who didn't even have breasts yet. She was very small and had a very tight pussy – with her the hunter was okay. But soon the girl became pregnant and had a baby. Her pussy got too big for Kero-opeho and she no longer wanted to have anything to do with him. She went away and left Kero-opeho to bring up the baby.

Kero-opeho had to find another young girl who was still almost a child. But each new young wife left him after she had a baby. Each girl's pussy grew too large for him and each one went to marry another man, with a big cock. That's how it was with each young girl; they all abandoned him. Only his oldest wife stayed with him, cooking for him and making love to others.

Kero-opeho and his oldest wife had a daughter who died. Deeply saddened, the hunter went looking for the girl's spirit under water and in the sky. A heavy rain fell while he was searching, and with the rain came thunder. But it wasn't real rain, it was the spirit's power.

Kero-opeho found the girl's spirit and brought it back home. He asked her to wait at the edge of the river while he asked her mother to bring food. They gave the girl lots of *chicha*, then the father sent the spirit away again.

Kero-opeho died and was buried. But because he was a powerful shaman, his grave filled with water and his body disappeared, and he came back to life. They say he went away, that he didn't die.

Djikontxerô, the flying head

Narrator: Abobai Paturi Jabuti
Translator: Armando Moero Jabuti

There was a very young, very beautiful, young woman who had a young husband.

In the daytime, everything was perfect. Her only defect was that her head went out at night – just her head. Her body stayed in the hammock with her husband. The boy slept while his wife's head went out looking for game in other huts. The head would come back before sunrise and attach itself back to its body again.

Only the head went out hunting. It went to other villages and stole meat right off their grills. She brought the meat back to the hut but didn't show her husband. He went out to work while she stayed home eating in secret.

One day, her father-in-law, the boy's father, got up in the middle of the night to take a piss, and discovered his daughter-in-law's body with no head. He saw blood dripping from her neck onto the ground (in the early morning, after she returned, the blood would disappear).

"Could it be a jaguar that tore off my daughter-in-law's head while she lay in her hammock?" he wondered.

The father-in-law thought it was strange and he stayed awake. He lay in his hammock and waited to see what would happen. While it was still dark he

heard a rustling that sounded just like people walking along a path. He saw
the head open the straw curtain to get in the house and stick itself back on its
neck. And before it reattached itself to its body, he saw the head hide the meat
it had carried home. Next it jumped onto its neck and stayed put. Already
stuck to its body, the head, awake, said to the husband:

"You didn't make a fire, didn't put on more wood?"

"No, I didn't," said the boy.

The father-in-law didn't say anything to his son at the time. He waited
until the next day when the two men were alone in the field.

"Now you know what my daughter-in-law does! Send her to get firewood
to cook with, then at night, when the head goes out, throw her body on the
fire to burn!"

The husband told his wife to go get lots of firewood. She obeyed. At
night, she always called her husband to bed and made sure to flatter and
please him, so that he would go to sleep and she could go out.

The husband and the father-in-law kept very quiet and pretended to be
asleep. They heard the head humming as it flew out of the hut. The husband
got up, built a fire, and threw his wife's body onto the flames. It didn't feel
any pain, but it got very badly burned, and even from far away the head
knew that her body was on fire. She flew back and her body was already all
shriveled up. The head leaped onto its neck and screamed:

"Why did you do this to me?"

She wept, just like I'm singing now – I'm trying to imitate the girl. She
cried when she put her head back on its body, because now she could feel
the pain. Still weeping from the pain, the girl burned a leaf from a tree
(that doesn't exist here, only near the Jabuti village), to help her body to
heal – her body was all black and burnt to a crisp. She got better after a
few days.

After she had recuperated a little, the girl started to gather husks left over
from when the women made *chicha*. Rats were attracted by the smell, and
came to nibble at the corn and manioc husks. The girl killed the rats. She

killed and killed. She kept on killing them. There were already three piles of big dead rats.

The girl commanded the dead rats to come back to life and become people. And so it happened. The rats turned into people, her people.

The girl was the rat's leader. She sent the rats to build a house, and to clear and plant a field. She cried and the rats were happy. The rats were her people. They joined in the girl's crying and were happy.

Now the husband was alone and his wife lived in another village, with the rats.

The burnt woman took a rat and transformed it into a girl, then she made the girl turn into a nighthawk. She sent the Rat-girl to the man who had burned her. She told her to go to her husband's field and be a nighthawk. The Rat-girl took two little balls of cotton thread and left them on the road. She turned into a nighthawk, and this girl-rat-nighthawk sat on the cotton balls as if they were eggs.

The one who had been a husband was planting his field. He was digging in the ground to sow seeds for grain. At first he didn't see the grayish-colored nighthawk, but the Rat-girl-nighthawk flapped her wings and tried to get his attention. The man shot an arrow at her, but he missed. He decided he would kill her later.

"The nighthawk is hatching her eggs here? I'll come back this afternoon and kill her," he thought.

When he got home, the young man told his father he had seen a *curau* (in Jabuti, nighthawk is *curau*). But in those times *curau* didn't yet exist.

"I'm going to kill the *curau*!" said the boy.

His father, who was a shaman, said, "My son, the *curau* doesn't exist. How are you going to kill a creature that no one has ever seen?"

But the young man insisted. He even said he would name the bird "nighthawk".

The head, Djikontxerô, (that means "aunt charcoal"), spoke to the rat-girl from where she was. She treated the rat-girl like a younger sister. She told her,

"Just let the arrow graze you, so you won't die!"

When the young man shot his arrow, it knocked off one feather, but didn't kill the bird. When he shot again, the nighthawk turned into a woman.

"Hey, brother-in-law, you want to kill me?" she cried.

"Huh! You're not a bird, how did you turn into a person?"

"I came to talk to you because my older sister is calling you!"

"Not me! Your sister is worthless. If she wanted to stay with me, her head wouldn't have gone around stealing meat!"

"She wants to talk to you, she's fine now. She wants you to come and taste the *chicha* she made!"

The young man went with the rat-girl reluctantly as she pulled him along by the arm. He didn't want to go into the rats' hut and stayed in the courtyard. Djikontxerô, the head, brought him some *chicha*. He kept drinking and drinking until midnight.

Djikontxerô's sister came again. She said,

"Brother-in-law, my sister wants you to come sleep with her!"

Djikontxerô had set a trap in the door of the hut: she put two stone axes opposite each other like scissors, to slice her husband in two when he came in the hut, without anyone having to handle them – it was a magic spell. The boy entered the hut and the two axes fell together and chopped off his head. His head fell and only stayed attached to his body by a strip of flesh. The rats covered the boy's body with straw mats and put it in a corner.

The boy's father, who was a shaman, slept and followed his son in his dream. He saw the trap of the axes and saw his son dead. Early the next morning, he called his younger son.

"Come, my son. Let's go see your older brother – his wife has killed him!"

They went to the rats' village. When Djikontxerô saw her father-in-law, she invited him into her hut.

"Oh, my father-in-law, come in. Your son just went to sleep – he's drunk! Come, brother-in-law and father-in-law, come see my husband sleeping!"

In his dreams, the old man had already seen the trap and the death of his son. He told his younger son to run in quickly and he cast a spell so the axes wouldn't harm him. When the axes crashed together, the boy was already safe, protected by his shaman father. The axes missed and smashed into each other instead and broke. Djikontxerô made the axes move by themselves and get ready to strike again.

The old man entered the hut too and didn't die.

The axes broke again and Djikontxerô fixed them again. The two men escaped as the axes got ready to strike again. When the boy went out, the axes tried to cut him, but they broke again — and so it went: the old man came out and the axes broke again.

The father and the younger brother ran into the jungle, and the father said a powerful prayer. He prayed for the house and the rats to fall into the ground, and for the earth to cover them up. The shaman wanted to destroy the hut, with all the rats. The house went under the ground.

The shaman said his prayer; he threw it, and finished off all the rats. They turned back into rats, just animals, just as they were before. The shaman turned his dead son, the one who had burned his wife's body, into a fox. The wife, the head, also turned into a fox, Watiri-Kokoré. The rat-girl-nighthawk died because she had been sent by Djikontxerô — but nighthawks continued to exist.

It's the skin that remains. One thing turns into another, like the caterpillar into a butterfly. The shell stays. It transforms itself. The skin falls off. That's how it is. That's how this story is.

Tiwawá, the evening star, and Kurawatin-ine, the morning star, or the brother-in-law's lover

Narrator: Abobai Paturi Jabuti
Translator: Armando Moero Jabuti

Tiwawá and Kurawatin-ine were brothers. Tiwawá is the evening star; Kurawatin-ine is the morning star, which appears at dawn. Kurawatin-ine was always red, as if he had been painted with annatto dye – his skin was very red indeed. He was the older brother; Tiwawá was the younger brother.

One day, Tiwawá wanted to have red skin too. He thought Kurawatin had been painted by his wife, so he went to his sister-in-law to ask her for the red paint.

"I want you to paint me, just like you paint my brother!"

"No, I can't! The paint is in my pussy, it's not annatto!"

"But I still want you to paint me!"

Finally, after he kept insisting, the young woman agreed.

"Then let's go to the jungle!" she said.

The red paint was a liquid that came out from inside of the young woman. She invited her brother-in-law to the jungle and let him lie on top of her and make love to her. She warned him to go very slowly so he wouldn't break the pot of paint she had inside her. But Tiwawá was excited and went too fast. He was so aroused that he didn't even hear the girl's warning – he moved too fast and broke the pot inside her. The dye flowed like water in a stream and covered the boy's whole body with red.

"I told you to go slowly! You didn't listen to me and now you have broken the pot that holds your brother's paint!" cried the girl.

Tiwawá was ashamed and didn't go home. He went to the river to take a bath and scrub himself with sand. "That should take off the red paint," he thought. But his sister-in-law warned him that it wasn't easy to get the paint off, and just as she had said the color wouldn't come off – so it didn't (in those days, everything that was said really happened).

Tiwawá was so embarrassed that he only returned to his hut at night, in the dark, so no one would see his red body. His brother, Kurawatin, arrived and went to make love to his wife. He noticed that red paint no longer came out.

"You let my pot of paint get broken!" he cried.

His wife didn't even try to hide what had happened.

"It was your brother!" she said.

"But I told you! When you fool around with someone – when you let a man enter you – it has to be very slowly, so the pot doesn't break! You let it break, you went too fast! It was alright for you to make love, but it has to be nice and slow, like me – I know how to do it!"

Kurawatin was upset. He went to draw sap from lots of different trees: white sap from the rubber tree, and from other trees whose names I don't know how to translate. He turned the sap into a sticky liquid that we use to hunt birds, that sticks to their wings. He used the glue on his younger brother. (We spread this paste on a piece of wood and the game sticks to it – it's a very good glue.)

Tiwawá, the younger brother, came home with the glue all over him. He was furious. Tiwawá was sticky all over.

The next day, Tiwawá got some paste that looked the same as his brother had used on him, and he planned his revenge.

Kurawatin and his wife came back from the jungle where they had been gathering firewood. Tiwawá had put the glue in their hammock so they would get all sticky. But they just laughed at him.

"The glue he made doesn't stick to anyone!" they said, and threw the paste away.

Tiwawá was embarrassed and went away for good. He appears as night starts to fall, in the late afternoon, on the side where the sun sets. Kurawatin appears at dawn, on the side where sun rises.

Nerutë Upahë

Narrators in Portuguese: Wadjidjika Nazaré Arikapu and Kubahi Raimundo Jabuti

There were three girls, one was a virgin and two were not. They went looking for *nerutë*, baby boa constrictors. They found *mussu*, which looks like a fish, but is a snake — a lungfish. The virgin girl didn't want *mussu*, she thought it wouldn't do.

The girls looked and looked. They found a small lake, and when the girl found *mussu*, she didn't take them. The girls started to pull leaves out of the water, and one of the girls who wasn't a virgin found some little boa constrictors.

"This must be what you want!" said the girl.

The virgin girl looked at the baby snakes and recognized the markings (snakes are painted all over).

"That's just what I'm looking for!" she said.

The virgin girl put one of the little snakes in a gourd and started for home. She didn't want *mussu* (*otore* in Jabuti), she wanted a baby boa constrictor so she could be its mother. The girls had walked a little way when it started to rain and to thunder (*dekëkëtã*). The storm came because the girl was carrying a real snake, a real boa constrictor. The girls had not gone very far when the little snake burst through the gourd and shattered it to pieces.

The girls had brought lots of gourds. They put the snake into another one, but the little snake was as strong as lightning and broke this one too. Each time they put him in another gourd, he broke it.

The little snake sang on the way home to the girls' village. It sang, as I'm singing now, asking the girls to give him a pot full of water to live in. The girl did what the snake asked: she put water in a pot and put the little snake inside, but the snake broke all the pots too. The baby snake started to sing other songs, asking the girls to dig a hole in the ground and fill it with water.

The little snake's mother, the girl, dug a hole right in the middle of the hut – near the pole that holds up the hut – and put the snake in it. The rain eased up and the little snake was quiet. At night the snake's mother lay down (the mother was the virgin girl), put out the light, and the little snake came out of its pool – it looked just like lightning. It lay down with the girl, still in the form of a snake, and started to suckle at the girl's breast. At daybreak, it went back to its place as a snake.

The second night, it came out of the pool as a person, as a child. He crawled over to his mother's hammock and sucked on her breasts, which were already growing. That's just what his mother had been wanting.

On the third night, the little snake also came out of his pool as a child and lay down with his mother. She called to her father.

"Come look at your grandson!"

Her father came, and by the light of his cigarette, he saw the snake that was now a perfectly normal-looking child. The old man wanted to take care of his grandchild.

He said, "Tomorrow I'm going to send your brothers out hunting, so that later I can bless your son's food." (In the village, for children to grow up and have good luck, the shaman has to bless their food.)

The snake painted his mother, using just his tongue – a dye came out from it. In the morning, one of the other girls who had helped find the snake saw how beautifully the snake had painted his mother. She asked the mother if she could have her snake-son paint her body too.

"No! Stay away from him!" said the snake's mother.

But her friend was stubborn. When the mother went to the fields to burn stalks of *ouricuri* to make salt, to season the game – to bless the meat, to make the snake turn into a real person – the other young woman went to the snake and insisted. She thought the snake used genipap dye and she brought along some genipap paste for him to paint her with. The snake had been sleeping, but the young woman called to him:

"You're going to paint me, it was me who helped your mother bring you here."

The snake wanted nothing to do with the genipap paste, but the young woman stood right there and insisted. Finally the snake came out of the water with his tongue sticking out and painted the girl. He painted and painted. When he started to paint around the girl's vagina, he slipped his tongue inside her (he slipped his tongue inside her because she was not a virgin; but he didn't slip his tongue inside his mother, because she *was* a virgin). His tongue reached inside the girl and cut her in two, as if his tongue were a knife. The snake-boy swallowed the lower half of the girl's body. The boy's father, who was a snake that lived in the heavens, dropped down to earth from the sky and ate the upper half of the girl's body. The first snake swallowed the lower part and his father ate the upper part.

There was a sprinkling of rain and the snake's mother, the girl, from where she was in the field, knew that someone had disturbed her son. She came running, saying she didn't want her son to leave her.

The song she and her son sang is like this, like I'm singing:

"My beloved son is leaving me,
I want him to return
And stay with me."

He answered:

"I won't return, my mother.

I'm dying of shame,

I want you to come with me."

The girl hugged the snake around its middle (the snake had gotten fatter after eating the part of the woman). The snake pierced through the roof of the hut, right in the middle, by the center pole and by his little pool, and started to climb. His mother tried to pull him back, but her snake-son asked her to go with him. He climbed up to the sky, then curved back around and fell into the water, pulling his mother along with him.

As she was falling into the water, his mother asked:

"Aren't we going to drown?"

"No, no one is going to drown," said the snake.

They went down into the water and the girl turned into a snake too.

The boy told his mother that at a certain time of the year the sky would turn yellow, and that would be his birthday. This day should be noted, celebrated, and remembered as Nerutë's birthday. Now, since the contact (with white people), Nerutë's birthday isn't celebrated in the same way, it's different.

Nekohon, the *Pico-de-jaca* snake husband

Narrator in Portuguese: Kubahi Raimundo Jabuti

A tall young woman was of marrying age and didn't want a short husband. Whenever her brother brought home a suitor, she would stand back to back with him to see who was taller. If the boy was shorter, she sent him away.

The brother was tired of bringing home so many potential brothers-in-law. He decided to go to the village of the snakes – maybe there he would find someone who would be acceptable to his sister. He returned with a snake, a *Pico-de-jaca*, Nekohon, who was a man. He played happily on his bamboo flute as he approached the girl's hut. The girl was waiting and fell in love as soon as she saw him.

"Ah, this one is handsome! This is the boy I want!" she cried.

The girl went dancing up to the Boy-Snake and took him by the arm. She invited him into her hut to drink *chicha*. They drank and they danced, and that night the Man-Snake took the girl to lie down with him. They made love, but it was her first time and she couldn't bear it. She was a virgin and cried out in pain. The Snake was frightened when the girl screamed. He got up from on top of her and slipped to the ground, now in the form of a real snake.

The girl saw the big frightening snake coiled on the ground. She was scared and didn't want to have anything else to do with him. But it was too late: they had already made love and now he was her husband. When daylight came, the girl rejected her *Pico-de-jaca* husband. But her brother said:

"I brought you real men to be your husband, but you didn't want them. Not one of them would do. Now you must stay with this one."

The girl wept as she rolled up her hammock and followed her husband to the village of the snakes. They had hardly left her village behind when they came across another *pico-de-jaca*, her husband Nekohon's father. She met her father-in-law.

In those times, when a woman stepped over a snake's tail, it would let loose its sperm, which would enter the girl's body and impregnate her belly with baby snakes. She only had to walk over a snake's tail to make it spurt out its semen. The girl walked over her father-in-law's tail, then later her husband's uncle's tail; she walked over many, many snakes' tails – all kinds of snakes, big and little. Each snake's sperm shot out of its tail and into the girl's body, fathering snakes in her womb. By the time she reached the snakes' village, the girl was already pregnant, with room for nothing more in her belly.

When it was time to give birth the girl was in a lot of pain. Her Snake-Husband called his Snake-Mother, the girl's mother-in-law, to come help with her labor. She came as a snake, shed her skin, and came out half person, half *pico-de-jaca*. The top half was a woman and the bottom half was a snake.

The girl began to give birth to snakes. They came and came and came . . . the last was *Me*, the snake. The girl was exhausted from giving birth to so many snakes and told her mother-in-law she couldn't stand it any more. The *jararaca*, *merebiri*, was about to be born, but the girl closed her legs together.

The unborn snake bit the girl's vagina and she died. She died, but she came back to life. Today she is a spirit and gives advice, even though she doesn't heal people. The spirit of the snakes' mother told the *jararaca* not to do what the snakes' uncle did, not to go on paths where human beings walk, not to kill people. The snakes that bite us are the ones that were stubborn with their mother, that didn't obey her. When we kill snakes with a stick, they go back to their mother with a fever. When we kill them with arrows, they are dead already when they go to her.

Pakuredjerui aoné,
the men who ate their own shit,
or the men without women

Narrator: Wadjidjika Nazaré Arikapu
Translator: Armando Moero Jabuti

In olden times, the men went to the jungle to take a shit and took *pamonha* (a kind of pancake made from corn) along with them. Some of the women were suspicious of this strange habit the men had of taking food with them when they went to have a shit. The women went to spy on the men: they discovered that the men were eating their own shit with the *pamonha*. They went back to the village and told everyone about the disgusting thing the men were doing.

The women decided to take *rapé* like the men, to follow the shamans' diet, as if they were men, so they could become shamans. The women got thinner and thinner – they weren't eating, just smoking. They wanted to fly.

The men decided to go hunting to bring back food for the women. They wanted to see if the women would eat and stop losing so much weight. While the men hunted, the women kept taking *rapé*. They took stalks of *ouricuri* and made soap from its ashes, to wash their bodies so they could fly. They took *rapé* and called to the spirit of Bidjidji, a little spider that spins webs in the road.

It was the chief of the spiders, the master of the spiders, who taught the women how to grow feathers so they could fly. The women turned into birds, the bird we call *oné*, a little bird with a tail like a pair of scissors. It's called *tesoureiro* in Portuguese; it's white and half black. The women sprouted wings and were ready to fly.

The men were hunting when the women became birds, already rising into the sky. The men watched from the ground. From their ambush in the jungle they saw the birds soar higher and higher into the sky.

They said, "It looks like the women are going away. They told us they were going away to the sky!"

They told the others and went back to the village. All they saw was the women's empty places, the leftover soap, and the feathers that had already grown and fallen out. The men were very sad . . . their women were gone.

Luckily, one of the chief's daughters hadn't wanted to leave her father. The women had left her hidden up in the corn loft, surrounded and covered by straw mats. Her mother told her:

"If you want to stay, then stay. But you will have to marry your brother!"

The men arrived, brokenhearted.

The chief's son tried to console them. "Why should we be sad? Let's make ourselves some *chicha*!" he said.

The men took turns making the *chicha*, but it never came out right – it had no taste. The chief's son was the only one who knew the secret of the hidden girl. When it was his turn to make the *chicha* he had the girl chew it for him to sweeten and ferment it. His *chicha* was always the best.

"Ah, you have a woman, your *chicha* is too good!" said the others.

"No I don't, you just don't chew it the right way!"

The two still weren't lovers, the brother didn't yet know that they were supposed to be married. Some days passed, and a friend of the brother, his buddy, his *compadre* (his *wirá*, as we say in Jabuti language), was lying down in the brother's hammock, right below the loft where the sister was hiding. She was chewing corn for the *chicha*, hidden in the loft above. Suddenly, without wanting to, the girl dropped a little piece of what she was chewing, and it fell right onto her brother's *wirá*.

"I think my *wirá* is hiding a woman!" cried the brother's friend.

"It's no woman! It's just a rat that dropped a little piece of food!" lied the brother, trying to protect his secret.

"No way! It's a woman!" retorted his *wirá*. He climbed up into the loft, pulled away the straw mats, and saw the chief's daughter. He was enchanted.

The girl climbed down – now she had been seen! She said to her brother: "Mommy told me to live with you!"

"It cannot be! We're brother and sister, it would be shameful!"

They stayed together but didn't become lovers, and other men gave her children.

There began to be women again; the population started to grow again. When girls were born, the men treated them well and waited for them to grow up so they could marry them. And so our people grew once more – if not, we would have disappeared.

Bedjabziá, the master of the wasps

Narrator: Abobai Paturi Jabuti
Translator: Armando Moero Jabuti

Bedjabziá was an evil spirit, *hipopsihi*. He was the master of the wasps. He had wasps around his neck, in his armpits, on his belly, his testicles, everywhere.

One day, Bedjabziá saw a pretty young girl in a village and liked her. He started to go there every day; he wanted to make love to her.

It was the season of the peanut harvest and the girl's mother asked her to go to the field to help with the picking. But the girl just wanted to stay in the hut and came up with an excuse not to go: she stayed in the village and took care of her little baby brother.

Bedjabziá came and grabbed the girl's pussy and played with her clit. And he grabbed her little brother's balls (her brother was no more than a year old).

The girl was already a young woman and was really enjoying the game Bedjabziá was teaching her.

When Bedjabziá was about to arrive, the girl started to sing. She put on her finest necklaces and bracelets, and painted her body with pitch. She sang:

"Here comes Grandpa, bringing grilled paca!
Here comes Grandpa, bringing grilled guan!"

She took Bedjabziá by the arm and danced with him. Then they went inside the hut and roasted the game Bedjabziá had brought. But the wasp mis-treated the baby, the girl's brother – he was the master of the wasps!

The mother noticed that the baby boy's balls were growing. She spoke to her older son:

"You take care of your sister. I don't know what's going on with her, but she doesn't want to leave the house to do any work. And not only that, the baby's balls are growing!"

The older brother hid in the corn loft. He saw the old man coming, his sister all dressed up, singing her song. The old man arrived and entered the hut and they prepared and roasted the game he had brought. Then Bedjabziá went to take a bath with the girl. She would only put on her jewelry and dress up just before the old man arrived, so her mother wouldn't notice (she kept her jewelry by the river bank).

While the girl was taking her bath, her brother went to warn their mother.

"My sister is eating the *hipopsihi*'s game and my little brother is suffering. He got stung all over by wasps!"

Bedjabziá only stung the baby brother, he didn't sting the girl. The big brother told his mother the girl was having lots of fun and making love to someone who wasn't even a person, and who on top of that was abusing their baby brother.

"Go make arrows and kill the *hipopsihi*!" ordered the mother.

The older brother brought home lots of *ouricuri* stalks to make arrows with. He told his sister he was going hunting the next day, and she believed him.

In the middle of the night he and two others climbed up and hid in the corn loft. The old man soon came along and the girl dressed up and started singing:

"Here comes Grandpa, bringing grilled paca!
Here comes Grandpa, bringing grilled guan!"

Bedjabziá was suspicious. He sensed there was someone lying in wait for him.

"I have the feeling there's someone here!" he said.

"No way! It's just like it was yesterday, come on in!"

The girl insisted and brought the old man into the house. They started to dance, hugging, burning for each other, when the men in the loft started to shoot their arrows at the old man.

He tried to run to the door but his body was so full of arrows that he fell dead to the ground. The wasps scattered in every direction.

They burned Bedjabziá's body and the girl was left alone without him. She cried because she missed him, but her father and mother still gave her a beating.

Berewekoronti, the cruel husband, and the unfaithful wives

Narrator: Erowé Alonso Jabuti
Translator: Armando Moero Jabuti

Berewekoronti was married to a woman who never got pregnant, so he found himself another woman. Now he had two wives. His second wife had a baby.

One day, there was a party, a *chicha* feast, and the second wife drank a lot of *chicha*. Her baby cried and cried, but she didn't want to stop drinking *chicha*. She couldn't drink just a little.

Berewekoronti, the father, was irritated and took the child on his lap. His first wife was resentful and gave him a lecture:

"A woman who has a child has to nurse him! She should be taking care of her baby, not getting drunk!"

This made Berewekoronti even angrier. He called to his wife, but she didn't come – she said she would come when she was through drinking.

Berewekoronti was fierce. He gave the baby to his first wife and killed the one who was drinking. The barren woman brought up the child.

Time passed and Berewekoronti found another wife.

The third wife liked another man. She went to the jungle to make salt from the *ouricuri* palm; she invited her lover to go with her to cut down *capemba* to burn the *ouricuri* and make salt. The two were alone in the jungle. They made love and were happy.

His wife went to the jungle so often that Berewekoronti grew suspicious.

He sent his boy, the son of the dead wife, to see what was going on. The boy hid himself among the leaves and lay in wait for his stepmother.

The young woman kindled the first pieces of *capemba* to start making salt. Her lover arrived and complained:

"You should ask your husband to cut all this *capemba*! I'm helping you make the salt, but your husband is the one who will use it on his meat – I won't get any!"

"Don't be silly, I'm going to give you meat with salt and we'll eat it together! I don't want anything to do with my husband!"

The lover helped reluctantly, annoyed to be making salt for someone else. But after they worked, they jumped into each other's arms and made love.

The boy ran to his first stepmother, the one who had raised him.

"Mommy, I have a fever," cried the boy, "so my father told me to come home!"

The boy's mother made a fire under his hammock (that's what mothers did when someone had a fever). The boy pretended to be asleep, bravely bearing the heat of the fire – in the middle of a hot day. His father arrived.

"Is he feeling better?" asked the father.

"No, he's really sick!" said his wife.

The next day the father asked his son what he had seen. The boy told him everything. The father made arrows for himself and the boy and they pretended to go hunting; they hid by the clearing where his wife always went to make salt – she soon arrived, singing happily. The young woman picked some leaves to make salt with and her lover arrived a short while later. She invited him to lie down with her, but he hesitated.

"I think your husband is going to kill me today! I dreamed that a bowstring broke across my body!"

The girl insisted there was nothing to worry about, that her husband was hunting far away. She hugged her lover and led him to where they always made love. The lovers lay down, the man on top. Then the husband came with his arrows and the lover started running and yelled:

"Didn't I tell you I would die? Now I'm finished and you'll still be alive!" But the boy shot his stepmother, even as she begged him not to:

"Don't shoot me, my son!" she cried.

The husband shot his rival and his wife, and the two died. He dragged them back to the place where they always made love. He spread his wife's legs and put the man between them, on top of her. Then he went hunting as if nothing had happened. The husband was really an evil man.

He killed some birds for his son, then he killed a monkey and some other animals. When he got home, Berewekoronti gave the game to his first wife, as if it had been a normal day of hunting. He even brought some meat home for his other wife – the one he had just killed – as if everything were fine. The older wife roasted the meat.

The dead wife's mother thought it was strange that her daughter hadn't come home. It was getting dark out and the girl still hadn't arrived. Suddenly the girl's hammock fell down. And her lover's hammock, his bundle of *taquaras* for making arrows, and the feathers that he kept in a straw basket, all fell down. In the middle of the night, their ghosts cried underneath their fathers' and mothers' hammocks. Everyone knew they were dead.

The girl's mother got up very early the next morning and went looking for her daughter. She found the murdered couple. Their bodies were swollen and full of arrows. The mother struck the dead man.

"Because of you, my daughter is dead!" she cried.

She pulled her daughter away and dug her a grave and buried her. (For Indians, someone who dies from arrow wounds cannot be buried with everyone else.) She went home weeping.

No one took revenge on the husband. He wanted another wife, a very attractive young girl from a big family. But no one wanted to give him his daughter; everyone said he shouldn't have killed his wife, just the lover. Even so, Berewekoronti ended up with another wife.

Time passed and his fourth wife got pregnant. She made *chicha* from corn and kept the husks, as we always do, to raise *tapuru*, a kind of larva (*ori*, in Jabuti language). The girl was always going to the jungle to leave food for the larvae.

A man followed her. He wanted to seduce the pretty young wife, but she said no. She pleaded with him and said her husband was very mean and had already killed two of his other wives.

"It's not only he who is a man! I'm a man too! If he comes to kill me, I will kill him!" boasted the girl's suitor.

And so, wanting to and not wanting to, the girl was tempted and gave in to the man. They became lovers.

Berewekoronti, her husband, was a shaman and a great hunter. But from the day his wife took a lover, all the game ran away from him. Berewekoronti complained to his son:

"There must be something wrong! Your mother must be betraying me! I want you to go spy on her!"

The boy went to the jungle and hid where he could see what was going on.

His stepmother was making *chicha*, leaving the cornhusks for the *tapuru*. Her lover came along and started to caress and fondle her body. He pulled her to him; he wanted to make love to her. She tried to get away – her husband was already complaining about his bad luck hunting and was capable of killing them. But her lover wouldn't take no for an answer. They made love.

Meanwhile, the boy went back to tell his father. He lied to his stepmother, the first wife, and said he had a fever. She made a fire under the boy's hammock and took care of him. Then his father arrived and cooked for his two wives and his son.

The next day, Berewekoronti asked his son what he knew and so found out the truth. He set about planning his revenge. He and his son went hunting and hid so they could spy on the lovers.

His beautiful wife was there making *chicha*, but she wasn't singing – she was in a hurry to get back: she was afraid of her husband. Her lover came and she was scared and tried to resist him, but she didn't know how to say no. She kept saying her husband was going to kill them that very same day.

"If he kills us, I'll kill him too!" swore her lover.

He put his arrows aside and they made love and the husband shot them both.

They weren't far from the village, and many people heard the screaming and came to see what was going on. The husband defended his wickedness, saying that all he had done was kill a woman who flirted too much.

The girl's family told Berewekoronti he was too fast for them, and that they wouldn't even try to kill him. But the truth is that they wanted to mislead him; they didn't accept their daughter's death so lightly.

Four days later, the husband went hunting. (The husband's whole life was hunting. He didn't much care for working or tending the crops.) He asked his son to go with him, because he had a premonition that he would be attacked: he was upset the whole night before, ticks were biting him and he itched all over his body – omens that he was going to be attacked by fierce warriors.

The dead girl's family got ready and went out after the husband. They lay in ambush.

Berewekoronti was returning to the village and there was a kind of wind around him. It was the souls of the people he had killed, accompanying him, surrounding him.

"Here he comes! But that's not wind we hear, it's the spirits of the people he killed!" cried his enemies.

Berewekoronti came along carrying the game meat and his son carried the liver.

His enemies cried out, "I'm going to kill the old man!" "I'm going to kill his son!"

The men shot their arrows: two arrows hit the son and two arrows hit the father. But Berewekoronti threw down his game and fought back. Before he died, his body riddled with arrows, he managed to kill ten people. Finally he died.

The survivors buried their dead. They wanted to see why Berewekoronti had been so hard to kill. They saw that his heart was very big.

The Tapir

Narrator: Erowé Alonso Jabuti
Translator: Armando Moero Jabuti

It was the season of the fresh corn harvest. Each day on the way home from the fields, it happened that a certain young woman always found a way to go back to the cornfield alone. She told the other women she had left some corn behind, but instead of picking corn she went to make love to the Tapir.

The Tapir came running out of the jungle and pulled off his hide – as if it were a cape or a costume – and hung it on the branch of a tree. He appeared like a man: painted, handsome, and happy. The young woman was singing. She was aroused and happy and ran to hug the Tapir. He took her to a secret hiding place and they made love, oblivious to the outside world.

Each day the young woman wanted to go back to the cornfield to pick more corn, telling her companions there was some left over. She had a baby son and a husband, but she was always late coming home – she was busy making love. After a while, the girl's friends started to think it was strange that she always went back to the cornfield alone.

"Don't you want someone to help you?" asked her friends.

"It's okay, there's just a little bit of corn!" she would say.

A man went to spy on her, and he saw the Tapir run out of the jungle, arrange his hide on a tree branch and lie down on top of the woman, grunting with pleasure. In the twinkle of an eye the man ran home and brought the news to the betrayed husband.

The husband and his friend, his *wirá*, made lots of arrows, and went to hide out and wait patiently for the Tapir. They were almost ready to give up when the Tapir finally appeared. He turned into a man as usual and started making love to the girl. The two men shot their arrows at the lovers, who didn't have time to run. The Tapir, still in the form of a man, tried to grab his hide from the branch, but he was already wounded and fell to the ground.

The husband wanted to kill his wife, but she ran to her son and gave him her breast. The husband's friend wouldn't let him kill her.

In the village, they attended to the Tapir and prepared the meat for the grill. He was a big man and everyone ate a little piece. Only his lover refused.

While they prepared the flesh of the man who had been a Tapir, a young boy saw its hide in the tree and wanted to try it on. The others warned him not to:

"Don't do it! That's not a person's skin and you'll end up suffering! You'll end up riddled with arrows!" they cried.

But the boy said, "I just want to try it a little bit and then I'll put it back!"

He took down the Tapir's hide and draped it around his body. No sooner had he put it on than he ran away in the form of a tapir and disappeared into the jungle.

The boy arrived at the house of the dead Tapir's wife. She was sad, but quietly she put the boy's arrows away where her husband Tapir had always put them, in a quiver that hung on the straw wall. The boy became the female Tapir's husband in place of the one who had been killed.

The boy heard the uproar of the tapirs making love to their women and thought it was a party, a *chicha* feast.

"So many people making *chicha*! Let's go get some soup to drink!"

But the dead Tapir's wife explained:

"It's not *chicha*, it's the tapirs making love to their women! Don't you want to make love too?"

The boy lay down with the Tapir woman, but his prick was too little and the Tapir-wife was disappointed. Tapirs have big cocks – and the boy was young and had never made love when he turned into a tapir. (In the village, a fifteen-year-old boy might not know women yet.)

The Tapir-wife was suspicious:

"One day you have a big cock, the next day you have a little cock! You can't satisfy me with that!"

The boy remained a tapir for ever, but of the species of tapir that has a little prick.

ARIKAPU

Pakukawa Djeparia, the *Macucau* bird

Narrator: Wadjidjika Nazaré Arikapu
Translator: Armando Moero Jabuti

Once there was a man who resented his mother-in-law because she was always stealing corn from his plot. Not only that, but the old woman took nothing but the largest ears.

And so it went, day after day: the greedy mother-in-law always took the best of the harvest while the son-in-law grew angrier and angrier. Finally the old woman went too far and the man decided to teach her a lesson. He made the field of corn start to grow, and it grew and grew until it had no end. No one knows how the son-in-law cast such a spell – maybe he was a shaman.

The mother-in-law went to the field and started to circle around looking here and there for the biggest ears of corn. The old woman was so absorbed in her search, and the field had grown so large, that she ended up getting lost. Meanwhile, the son-in-law followed behind, concealed among the leaves, and transformed his mother-in-law into a *macucau*, a type of small tinamou (*pakukawá*, in the Arikapu language).

When the daughter went to the plot, she was frightened by the crazy size it had become. She heard an unknown bird whistling. (She couldn't have known what had happened to her mother – her husband had cast the spell on his mother-in-law in secret.) The girl followed the unfamiliar whistle until she found the bird, who was her mother, the top half woman, the bottom half *macucau*. The old woman wept and complained bitterly to her daughter:

"Just so I wouldn't meddle with your crop, so that I wouldn't pick even a few ears to ease my hunger, my son-in-law cast a spell on me and turned me into a bird! And now here I am, half woman, half bird, prisoner in this form for ever. My daughter, you must leave this man who did such a terrible thing to your mother!"

The girl went home crying in despair. She left her husband, and the mother still chirps like a bird, the tinamou *macucau*, to this day.

The object of dispute, the plot of corn, turned into a meadow. That's why, even today, there are meadows without end on this earth.

The woman-pot

Narrator: Wadjidjika Nazaré Arikapu
Translator: Armando Moero Jabuti

In olden times there were no clay pots.

A girl wanted to make *chicha* and didn't have a pot. Her mother turned into a pot for her daughter to cook with.

A man spied the woman turning into a pot and went right away to tell the girl's husband:

"Your wife is making *chicha* with your mother-in-law's body! The old woman smells bad. The *chicha* you're drinking stinks of the old woman's skin!"

The husband grew nauseous when he heard this. But doubting it was true, he asked his wife to make some more *chicha*; he hid and watched. The mother-in-law was already in the fire for her daughter to cook with.

The husband was furious. He approached the fire and broke the pot. The corn spilled all over and the *chicha* was ruined. The old woman never turned back into a person.

The daughter flew into a rage:

"What you broke should never have been broken! No! Never broken!" she screamed.

She wept as she gathered together all the shards of clay. Then she took all the pieces of the pot and put it back together again. She cried two nights and two days without stopping, but on the third night she couldn't stand it any more and slept a little.

The girl's mother appeared in her dream, asking her to compose herself and dry her tears. She promised to make some kind of vessel for her daughter to cook *chicha* in.

"A bubble of clay will appear where the fire was, the fire that I heated myself in when I was a pot, cooking your *chicha*. Open the clay at the top and pull out the insides. You will be able to make yourself a pot."

The girl woke up and started crying again. In the place where the fire had been, a bubble of clay appeared, like a fresh water spring. The girl opened the top of the bubble a little bit, took out the insides, and made a big pot. After she made it, she let it dry and baked it well. It was done. That was when clay appeared to make pots and until today women know how to make pots.

The woman who made love to a stick, and the land turtle husband

Narrator: Wadjidjika Nazaré Arikapu
Translator: Armando Moero Jabuti

A girl smoothed a piece of wood to play with, to make love to. The men were jealous and spread pepper on it. When the girl went to use it — as if it were a real man! — it burned, and how! She almost died. The pain was driving her crazy so she went to the river to wash herself. She washed and washed, but it didn't help, her pussy kept burning. She decided to take along a girl friend and go from village to village asking for help.

She arrived at the Land Turtle man's hut.

"I'm going to live with this guy, I don't have a husband!" she said.

"You'll be my daughters-in-law!" said the Land Turtle's old mother happily as she sat in the courtyard.

The Land Turtle came along singing, playing his bamboo flute.

"What a handsome boy! Let's live with him, the two of us!" said the two travelers.

The Land Turtle man came home carrying *orelha-de-pau* mushrooms to eat in his hut.

"Where did these girls come from, Mother?" he asked.

"They don't have anywhere to live, they'll stay with you!" she said.

The girl-lover-of-the-stick soon became pregnant and had a baby.

One day, the Land Turtle went hunting. He saw a small Brazil nut tree and brought home a basket full of Brazil nuts for his wives. But he wasn't the one who picked them – he couldn't climb trees. It was the Macaw who picked the green Brazil nuts and dropped them on the ground. The Land Turtle gathered them and brought them to his wives.

"I found Brazil nuts in the jungle! Let's go there again!" he lied, pretending to his wives that he had picked them himself.

The Land Turtle climbed up the tree – and fell. He climbed up again – and fell down again.

"How could it be you that picked the Brazil nuts? You can't even climb the tree!" said his wife.

"It's because you keep watching me! I can't climb up while you're watching!" said the Land Turtle.

"Then take the baby and I'll climb up myself!" said his wife.

The two women climbed up the tree: the one who had been burned by the pepper and her friend. The Land Turtle stayed on the ground and made fun of them.

"You're so hot your clits are dripping on me!"

The girls didn't like their husband's comments and threw some Brazil nuts at him to get even.

"Be careful, you'll hit the baby!" shouted the Land Turtle.

And indeed they hit the baby.

"I knew you would kill the baby!" cried the frightened Land Turtle father. He cursed them. "I hope this tree grows!" he said.

That's how the Brazil nut tree grew. It grew thicker and it grew much taller. Before that it was very small, little more than a bush.

The baby boy didn't die after all, and the Land Turtle took him home. But the two women were stuck high up in the tree and couldn't get down.

The Land Turtle came to look at the women every day.

"Let us come down!" they pleaded.

But he didn't pay any attention. He let them go hungry and thirsty.

The Macaw came flying.

"Ah, if only you could turn into a person and take us away from here and be our husband!" said the young women.

The Macaw heard them and brought lots of other macaws to help carry the two girls away.

They flew, and the two girls married the Macaw.

The Land Turtle went to spy on the women, but they had gone. He started looking for them; he was worried about his son, who missed his mother and was always crying. The boy went to look for his mother and finally found her. The Land Turtle went with his son to see his onetime wives.

The Macaw prepared a wonderful *chicha* feast and the Land Turtle snuck into the party.

"Here comes Grandpa, give Grandpa some *chicha*!" said the macaws when they saw the Land Turtle arrive.

The Land Turtle was a person, but had turned into an animal with a shell. The macaws thought he would be good to eat. They beat him and put him in the loft, planning to cook him later. But the macaws got drunk from so much *chicha* and the Land Turtle picked himself up and went away.

The next day, the Land Turtle returned and killed the Macaw. But then he couldn't escape and the other macaws killed him.

The Tapir, *Namwü Hoa*, or the men without women

Narrator: Wadjidjika Nazaré Arikapu
Translator: Armando Moero Jabuti

The chief's wife was still a girl; she had never menstruated. One day, she went to the field and met the Tapir and they made love. The girl liked it a lot and started going to see the Tapir as often as she could. The chief grew suspicious — who could be making love to his young wife? She was still so young!

Time passed and the girl became pregnant and the chief had still not made love to her — the father could only be someone from another village. The chief asked a man to go see what was going on.

The man went to lay in wait and spy on the girl. He saw the Tapir making love to the chief's wife and killed him. He divided up the Tapir meat and prepared it as we do any other game. He called the others to come and eat it.

The young man castrated the Tapir. He cut off the Tapir's balls and cock. He showed the women.

"This is what you were putting inside you!" he said.

The Tapir had been making love to all the women, not just the girl. The men hated him; they thought the Tapir was disgusting.

Night fell. In the middle of the night the women started playing their bamboo flutes. They played and played without stopping. They went down to the river, left their flutes on the cliff by the water, and started to walk away along the river bank.

They disappeared into the world. The woman who was pregnant by the Tapir was the only one who stayed behind – she couldn't walk very far. The other women left her in a little lake and then they disappeared.

The men didn't wake up when the women left; it was already morning before they noticed all the women were gone. They were without women. A little boy started to get hungry and missed his mother. He went out to look for her (she was another of the chief's wives). The boy found his mother's trail and followed her tracks.

His grandmother, the mother of the chief's wife, saw him.

"That's my grandson!" she cried.

She called to him.

The women of the women's village were out tending the fields. The grandmother gave her little grandson some food and hid him in a loft, so his mother and the other women wouldn't kill him. His mother arrived from the field and said:

"Where's the boy? I heard he was around here somewhere! Let me see him! I won't let him go without punishing him – his father was so angry at us!"

"Don't talk that way, my daughter! Isn't he your son? How could you hurt him?" said the grandmother.

The mother calmed down and stopped wanting to kill her son. She gave him some food. She spoiled him for a few days, but then she sent him away, brandishing an arrow, making him run.

"You will go to a tiny lake. That's where you'll find your other mother!" she said.

She wanted her son to go to the woman who was pregnant by the Tapir, the chief's other wife, who now lived alone underwater.

"Chew this peanut and throw it to her and ask her to return to your father," said the boy's mother.

The boy went looking and found the little round lake. He chewed the peanut and threw it into the water three times. On the third time, the woman emerged from the water, her belly huge, almost ready to go into labor.

"My mother said you have to go back to my father and cook for us!" cried the boy.

And so the woman returned to the village. The Tapir's baby was born a little while later. It was a girl. Later another girl was born, then another. That's how women came to exist again – if not, it would have been the end of mankind.

ARUÁ

Wãnẓei warandé,
the women who went away

Narrator in Portuguese: Awünaru Odete Aruá

The Tapir-lover

Every day the women went to a small lake to catch fish called *tamboatá* (*awasá*, in Aruá language). But it wasn't really the fish that attracted them – they went to make love to the Tapir. They would make *chicha* very early in the morning, leave food prepared for their families, and go have their fun.

When the women arrived at the lake, the "chief" of the women, the chief's wife, the *cacica*, beat on a sapopemba root and called out,

"*Wasa, emapiwa ongoro*! Tapir, come eat the *sapopemba*'s liver!"

The Tapir came running out of the jungle, pulled off his hide and hung it on a tree. Then he turned into a handsome man and started making love to all the women. First the woman "chief", then the woman "subchief" – the only ones he didn't touch were women who had young children. When he finished, the Tapir gathered together the mingled liquids – his own and the women's – and turned them into fish: the sperm became fish, *tamboatá* that the women were catching.

Their orgy was a daily affair, and the women always arrived in the village satisfied and exhausted. The women would say they were preparing *chicha* while the men hunted in the jungle, gathering game for a party. But the men were suspicious.

"Could this really be fish we are eating?" the men asked each other.

And it was the Tapir's sperm!

The men chose a little boy to find out what was going on. They gave him a root that burns the mouth and makes you sleepy. The boy left the men with his tongue on fire, went to find the women, and asked for help.

"Mommy, I have a fever!" he cried, and his mother lit a fire and put the boy in his hammock. Then the women made the *chicha* as quickly as they could, so they wouldn't be late. They shut the door tightly and went off to their pleasant work.

The boy climbed up to the corn loft, made a hole in the straw, and watched the line of women as they disappeared noisily along the shortcut to the lake. Then he climbed down and went to hide and spy on the women. He saw the woman "chief" beat the *sapopemba* root and call their pleasure-loving friend. The Tapir came and hung up his hide, but he sensed danger and was suspicious. Even so, the beast shamelessly made love to all the women, even the boy's mother. The boy ran away in horror.

Before long, the boy's mother returned to the village with a pile of fish – a lot of fish. The women roasted and grilled the fish, and the men – the fathers – arrived home. The boy told his father every detail of what he had seen.

The death and resurrection of the women, the bamboo flutes, and the ants that came from blood

"Today we will only hunt close to the river bank. No one will hunt far away. Today is the last hunt," said the chief. (It is the Indians' custom for the chief to give orders to the people at sunrise.)

The women went out and the men followed.

The chief grabbed the stick the women used to beat the *sapopemba* and beat it the same way they did. The men drew their arrows as the suspicious Tapir slowly and cautiously approached. He had hardly appeared when the men shot him full of arrows and killed him. The men cut off the Tapir's cock. All they brought home was his cock.

The chief hung the Tapir's cock in the doorway.

"We are going to kill the women, but not with arrows, and not by beating them, and not with clubs. We will kill them with thorns."

The men laid thorns all around the hut (thorns from the *tucum* and *marajá* palms). They had come home without any game – they hadn't gone hunting. The *tuxaua* said:

"Wife, come here and pull out this thorn for me. It hurts!"

The chief's wife sat down underneath the Tapir's hanging cock and started to look for the thorn. The cock dripped on her.

"What's that dripping on my back?" she asked and looked up.

"What is dripping is what you betrayed me with! Now you'll see what is what!" shouted the chief.

The men took the thorns and killed all the women. They spared only two little girls and a woman with a small child – because they hadn't made love to the Tapir. Then the chief ordered:

"Now that we have killed our wives, let's go away toward where the sun sets. Let's go!"

The men left the village and slept in the clearing by their fields.

The women's singing began in the late afternoon. They had come back to life. The men heard the drum beating; it was beautiful. The women played and played.

"Our women have come back to life!" cried the men.

There were two boys who adored their mother and went back to the village to see what was going on. They waited close by, just listening to the sound of the bamboo flute and the beating of the drum. (Prior to this, people didn't have bamboo flutes, or arrows, or clubs. But now they appeared, no one knows from where.)

The women played their music and danced the whole night; the young women played the bamboo flutes while the older ones danced. Just as the sun started to come up, the women saw a dung beetle arriving from where the sun rises. It came under the ground, cutting a wide path in the jungle. The women's blood, from the thorn wounds that killed them, turned into ants — little ants — in the middle of the courtyard and inside the houses.

The dung beetle said, "My granddaughters, it is time to go away!"

The women went with the beetle. They went with him.

The men went to see, but the place was bare and they couldn't find the women's trail. They were angry and upset, and went away, toward where the sun sets.

The master of the pigs

In their anger, the men killed every living creature they came across as they traveled. Each day they walked, and each night they set up camp in a new place. The men traveled five days. They traveled a long way. Finally they came upon a group of wild boars — a herd of pigs.

"Let's kill all of these pigs, to take revenge for what was done to our women!" said the chief.

The men surrounded the pigs — they didn't want to let a single one escape. They shot their arrows and killed all the pigs. Only one little one got away.

The men walked a little way and set up camp, each one with his own grill. Only the man with a small child — whose wife had not been killed, because she hadn't made love to the Tapir — hadn't killed a wild boar. He couldn't eat pig meat because he was a new father and had to follow a special diet.

The baby's grandfather spoke to his son, in the late afternoon, when the tinamou hen started to sing nearby.

"Go kill the tinamou hen! That you can eat!"

The young man kept looking for the tinamou hen, but it was already getting dark. The master of the pigs appeared.

"What are you looking for?" he asked.

"I'm looking for a white-throated tinamou hen!" said the young man.

"Did you kill our pigs, my grandson?" asked the master of the pigs.

"Not me. I can't, because I have a baby son! I didn't touch the pigs, I can only eat tinamou – that's why I'm out here looking for one!"

The master of the pigs held the little pig that had escaped, and on his arms were perched every kind of tinamou: white-throated tinamou hens, gray tinamous, curassows, guans . . . Membé Aiai, the master of the pigs, told the young man to take the birds and eat them, and he accepted.

"Pluck them and marinate them, and tell your wife to roast them. After they are cooked, call your family, your father, brothers, and uncles, to eat tinamou with you. Tell your family to sleep in your campground tonight. Tonight the ones who murdered my pigs will trade places with the ones they killed!" said the master of the pigs.

The boy did what he was told. He roasted the tinamous and called his family. But they didn't want to come, they said their bellies were already full. He called his sisters, but they didn't want to come either. In the end, he went without them to set up camp a small distance away from the others.

The master of the pigs put a spell on the men that made them all fall asleep on their bellies. (The pigs the men had killed were on the grill.) Then the master of the pigs came with some hot rubber and dripped it right on the men's backs – first was the boy's father (who hadn't wanted to go to the other campground). The father cried out, grunting like a pig; he jumped out of his hammock in the form of a pig. The master of the pigs did the same to the others: he went along dripping the hot rubber on the men's backs and they all turned into pigs. It made a huge racket.

The men who had turned into pigs ate up all the other pigs that were roasting on the grills, the game they themselves had captured the day before.

The man, his wife, and their baby were the only ones who survived, safe in their separate campground. They climbed up a coconut palm.

The master of the pigs affectionately called the boy his grandson and sent him to make lots of arrows. He told him to shoot and kill only two or three pigs at a time. He taught the boy the right way to hunt, to cover himself with a particular kind of strong vine to protect himself from the pigs.

The young man returned to the village. Now it was just him, his wife, and their little boy. Later on a girl was born, who became her brother's wife when she grew up. Another girl was born, then another boy – and when they grew up they also became man and wife. When there were five sons and five daughters, the father said:

"You will make arrows for us to hunt with!"

The population was growing, the nephews marrying, the uncles marrying. The first hunter organized a hunting party (there hadn't been one for a long time). The hunters returned to the place where the pigs had been killed, where the men had turned into pigs. The hunter and his family covered themselves with the special vine so they wouldn't be attacked by the pigs. They told the master of the pigs they were ready.

The master of the pigs let the pigs loose. They started to eat one of their own, one of the pigs from their own herd. When the people said to the master of the pigs, "That one is mine!", the pigs stopped eating each other and each hunter shot a pig.

The population kept growing, and now there were so many people that they built a big hut to live in. The chief ordered another hunting party, and that's how it was – three times. They did the same thing each time: they killed the pigs, prepared the meat, and returned to the hut. But on the fourth time, the Stubborn One went with them. (It's not only here that we have the Stubborn One.)

He cried, "I'm going! I have to kill game for my wife to eat . . ."

"No, my friend, it's not good for you to go . . ." said the chief.

But he went anyway. The Stubborn One went out with a group of other inexperienced hunters and arrived at the place where they always hunted. They made mats out of the vine to protect themselves from the pigs, but the mats were no good – they weren't like the mats the first hunters had made.

The pigs came and the Stubborn One started shooting at them before they had a chance to eat one of their own. The pigs were furious. They attacked and ate all the hunters.

The master of the pigs called the first man to him, the man he had taught, the only one who had not turned into a pig. He said:

"I taught the ones who will come, the ones who are yet to be born. But because a Stubborn One appeared, from now on men will suffer to hunt and kill game. They will have to run after the game, finding it where they can. If it hadn't been for the Stubborn One, your descendants would have had plenty of game to eat, and it would have been easy to kill it. But now it will be different. There will be little black pigs, like this one."

And the master of the pigs let loose a little black pig that he had been holding on his lap. Those are the ones we hunt. The real ones stay with the master of the pigs and he is the only one who knows where they are. Not even the white people know.

When the hunters returned to the hut, the Stubborn One was not among them.

"Your husband didn't return because he was very stubborn. And now it will no longer be easy to hunt game," they said.

The grandson's visit, and women without men

The women who had come back to life had gone very far away and built a village just for themselves. They cleared fields and went hunting themselves, without husbands. They wouldn't let any men come near them.

The first hunter who killed pigs, the son of the master of the pigs, said:

"I'm going to visit Grandma!"

His father showed him which way to go and he managed to find the women's village. He found his grandmother.

"My grandson, I'll only let you stay for two days, because no men are allowed here! After what the men did to us, we don't want them!" she said.

He stayed two days and then his grandmother sent him away. But first she wanted to find out if her grandson was an expert with arrows.

I don't know if the women are still there. It's a village that really only has women. The ones who make babies with them are from the Ako-son tribe. Poá of the Mamão (Papaya) tribe also father their children.

These men arrive when the women are in the fields. They cut the women's bowstrings and hide their arrows. When they finish making love, the women run to get their arrows to kill the men, but find that the weapons are out of their reach.

That's how they get pregnant. If a girl is born, they keep her. If it's a boy, they only keep him until he is ten years old, then they send him to his father. Before they send him away, they test him to see if he is clever and fast, if he knows how to shoot and how to run. If the father was agile and could run fast, the son is like his father was. If the father was not fast and agile, the mother kills the son – because he is like his father, who wasn't agile.

That's how it is – the tribe of women.

The white anthill

Narrator in Portuguese: Awünaru Odete Aruá

A young woman was forced to marry a young man against her will – she didn't like him at all. At night, when he came to lie down and tried to hug her, she got out of the hammock and turned her back. Every night it was the same thing.

To see if little by little she might get used to it, the girl's father invited his son-in-law to go hunting in the jungle, and invited his daughter to go along too. But she still didn't want to sleep with her husband.

Her father had an idea. He gathered lots of fireflies (*bagapbagawa man*, in our language). During the day, without his daughter noticing, the father attached lots of fireflies to an anthill (that we call *txapô*). He set up his daughter's hammock right by the anthill, and tied her husband's hammock next to hers. It was like a little hut.

Night came, they had their dinner, and the girl lay down in her hammock and went to sleep. In the middle of the night she woke up and saw the anthill all lit up. She was terrified by the sight and lay down with her husband. She never again ignored her husband, and even today there is light on the white ant hills.

The severed head

Narrator in Portuguese: Awünaru Odete Aruá

There was a young woman who was crazy about her husband. She never left his side – she went everywhere with him. If he went to set traps, she went with him; if he went hunting, she also went with him. She never stayed home to make his food.

Her mother-in-law and her mother both grew tired of seeing her spend so much time with her husband. She should be staying at home and cooking! They stopped fetching water for her.

The girl returned from the hunt with her husband, they cooked *moqueca* and ate. The girl went to sleep thirsty. The others drank, but hid the water.

"Go fetch some water!" suggested her husband.

"Not me! I want to stay here with you!" said the girl.

She went to sleep, still thirsty. Now it seems that while she was still asleep, the girl slipped off the edge of the hammock, fell on the ground, and severed her head from her body. The head kept saying it wanted to lie down. It talked so much that the husband woke up and saw the head on the ground chattering away.

Morning came.

"Throw it out, bury it!" said the family.

Only the head was alive. The husband said that now he would walk alone and he went out hunting – but the head went with him.

The man was sick of the head by now. It followed him like a ball wherever he went: to set traps, on the hunt. There was no way to leave it behind. The head even stuck itself to the husband at night; it sunk its teeth into his flesh so he couldn't get away. The husband was tired of the head following him and thought, "What am I going to do with this head?"

"I'll go visit the Macurap!" thought the man one day.

He went out secretly, but the head saw him and followed behind. They came to a river and the husband and the head stopped and looked down at the water. There was no bridge over the river, just a hanging vine – like a swing – to help people cross.

"Let me cross over first, then you grab the vine!" said the husband and the head agreed.

The husband went first and secretly cut the vine right in the middle. Then he threw it back to the head. I don't know how, the head didn't have feet or hands, but it got around. The head took the vine in its mouth and pushed off across the water, but the vine broke right over the middle of the river and the head fell into the water.

The head turned into a piranha. Piranha didn't exist before. *Iñen* is piranha; *andap* is head. That's why the Arua never ate piranha, because piranha was the head of the woman-who-turned-into-piranha. I don't know, maybe they eat it now . . .

The husband went to the Macurap. When he returned home he told everyone what he had done. They had to be careful with piranha, *Wandsep-andap*, Head-of-woman – they are dangerous.

The monkey

Narrator in Portuguese: Awünaru Odete Aruá

A man went with his wife to set traps for tinamous and monkeys. He imitated a monkey and the capuchin monkeys came. He shot an arrow and a monkey fell to the ground. He shot another arrow and another monkey fell. And another.

A little while later, his arrow fell far away and was lost. The hunter gathered together the monkeys he had killed and told his wife to wait while he went to look for his lost arrow.

His wife stayed behind. But she didn't have anything to do, so she took some straw and made a necklace, a bracelet, and a hat. She took a monkey and dressed him up with the necklace, the bracelet, and the hat.

"What a handsome monkey! If he were a person, he would be even more handsome!" she said.

She heard a rustling in the straw. She looked and saw a handsome young man standing before her.

"Who are you?" asked the young woman.

"I'm the one who should be asking you!" said the boy.

"I was talking to a monkey. I told him if he turned into a person he would be very handsome!"

"I am that same monkey! Come away with me!"

The two went away. Tree branches and vines were like paths on the ground to the monkey; for him, climbing up and down vines was like going up and down a mountainside.

A little while later, the husband came back and couldn't find his wife. He returned sadly home and paid no more attention to the game he had killed.

"Has anyone seen my wife?" he asked.

But no one had seen her. The man spent all his time looking for her, and a long time passed: one year, then two years. His wife was already growing hair on her hands and becoming a monkey. She even wanted to grow a tail.

One day the husband met the sloth.

"I don't know what this sloth is doing in my path – and me so miserable, without my wife – I'm going to kill this sloth!" he thought.

But the sloth said, "Don't kill me, I know where your wife is! She's with the monkeys and they're having a wild party! If you want me to get her for you, I will. All you have to do is give me an ax and some wax to spread on my bowstring." (The wax is resin – *borikáa* in Aruá language.)

The man went happily back to his hut to get an ax and some wax. Then he hurried back to see the sloth.

"Grandpa, I'm here!" he cried.

The husband and the sloth went on their way. Finally they saw the monkeys partying with the man's wife, and Ariá, the sloth, said:

"You stay here and I'll go where the monkeys are and ask to dance with your wife. I'll dance along different paths, so they won't be suspicious. I'll come back here later on and we can escape."

He went.

"Here comes Grandpa, here comes Grandpa!" shouted the monkeys when they saw the sloth coming. They were dancing and hugging the hunter's wife, several men in the same line (as is our custom).

"You have already danced enough with my granddaughter! Now it's my turn!" said the sloth.

"Come dance! Come join us!" shouted the monkeys.

"I want to dance alone with her and I don't want any of you dancing with us," he said.

The monkeys let him dance alone with her. They danced and danced.

They danced a long time in the courtyard, and then they went a little way along a path . . . and returned. That's what the sloth did so the monkeys wouldn't be suspicious. Soon he went along another trail, a little farther this time. He took her on various paths, taking a little longer each time. The monkeys trusted him; they stopped paying attention to him. Finally the sloth brought the girl to where her husband was waiting.

"See? It's your wife!" he cried.

The three of them ran away. The girl was already howling like a monkey, and she fainted when they arrived at the village.

The shamans took *rapé* and they took the wife's spirit, and did what they needed to do to revive her. When she woke up, she told them about how she had lived with the monkeys.

"I thought he was a real person, but I ended up living with the monkeys . . ."

The husband lost his wife.

The queen of the bees

Narrator in Portuguese: Awünaru Odete Aruá

Everything always happens to the chief's children!

One of the chief's sons went to chop down a tree with bees in it, the yellow bees that we call *canudo*. He chopped it down and took the honey.

He wasn't married yet. All the married men were very jealous of their wives and wouldn't let the chief's son even get near them. That's why he was sad, because the others were so jealous. He chopped down the tree and gazed at the honey and the bees with admiration. He exclaimed:

"What a beautiful bee! If this bee would turn into a woman, she would be beautiful! I wish it would turn into a woman to become my wife!"

The boy put the honey into a piece of bamboo, wrapped it up, and took it home. He arrived at dusk and gave the honey to his mother. Night fell and everyone went to sleep; the house grew quiet.

Meanwhile, in the jungle, the bee had turned into a woman. She entered the hut that night and tapped on the boy's hammock.

"Who are you?" he asked, admiring the beautiful young woman.

"It is I who am asking you!" she said.

"No!"

"And what was it you said in the jungle, while you were gathering honey?" she asked.

"I spoke to a bee! I said I wanted her to turn into a beautiful woman and make sweet *chicha* for me!"

The Bee-Woman said, "Well that's who I am!" and lay down with the boy in his hammock. They slept together.

The boy's mother woke up in the middle of the night and blew on the fire. She saw the two lovers lying together in the hammock.

"Who could this woman be? She's going to make trouble for my son! Could it be the wife of one of those jealous husbands? I don't want this woman sleeping with my son!"

But in the morning she didn't say anything. On the second night, everything happened exactly the same way. The Woman-Bee slept with the boy until morning and slipped away with the first ray of dawn. After the third night the boy's mother asked:

"My son, who is this woman who comes and sleeps with you every night?"

"She's not from around here, Mother. She is a bee who turned into a woman, because I wished her to!"

The boy's mother told his father. He said:

"Tomorrow I want her to spend the morning in our hut and make *chicha* for me."

The boy gave his lover the message:

"My father wants you to stay here in the morning with me and make *chicha* for him!"

She agreed and stayed. She was such a pretty young woman!

The husband took some corn down from the loft and the Woman-Bee husked and threshed it. She cooked it and mashed it. It is our women's custom to chew the raw corn a little to ferment the *chicha*, but the Woman-Bee only chewed it once (which is very little, usually they chew it more). She mashed the *chicha*, strained it into the mortar and poured some for her father-in-law.

"Tell everyone to drink my *chicha* nice and slowly. If they don't, they'll choke!" warned the Woman-Bee.

Everyone heeded her advice and drank the *chicha* very slowly, because it was very, very sweet.

The Woman-Bee made her *chicha* every day. But the third time she made the *chicha*, her own father-in-law, her husband's father, choked on it. He was very thirsty and drank too quickly. He choked on the Woman-Bee's *chicha* and died.

The Woman-Bee, mistress of the *chicha*, was ashamed and couldn't bear to look at anyone. She was ashamed because her father-in-law had choked on her *chicha*.

"Tonight is the last night I am going to sleep with you," she told her husband. "Tomorrow I'm going back home, because your father died from my *chicha*. He choked on my *chicha* and died. I'm going away."

The young man begged her to stay, but it didn't do any good. She left at dawn and her husband went with her. They arrived at the honey tree, where there was a house for her, and her husband went inside with her.

For us, even today, she is the queen of the bees, and the husband is the king of the bees.

Zakorobkap, the fly

Narrator in Portuguese: Awünaru Odete Aruá

In olden times flies didn't exist.

A little boy of seven had a mother, a father, and uncles. He was the chief's son. The boy started to think about something.

"Go make some *chicha*!" the boy's uncle ordered his wife, and went out hunting.

The wife put a pan full of corn on the fire and started to prepare the *chicha*. The husband went out hunting, and the boy, the man's nephew, stayed home. The boy started to cry and wouldn't stop. His aunt brought him some water, but he kept crying. The boy's mother did everything she could to try to make him feel better. Finally she figured out what the problem was.

"Sister-in-law, I think this boy wants to make love to you! Imagine, such a little boy!"

"Could it be?" wondered the aunt.

"Yes, that is what he wants!"

The aunt took a straw mat and carried it to a corner of the hut and lay down. The boy went over and lay down with her. Can you believe that they made love all day long, without stopping? And that from just that one day, the woman became pregnant with the boy's baby? Meanwhile, the husband was out hunting.

Toward evening the boy finally let the woman go. Then her husband arrived and threw the game he had killed in a corner, on the ground.

The aunt told her husband:

"I didn't do any work today. Your sister made the *chicha*, because your nephew wanted to play with me!"

The man stayed calm because his nephew was just a little boy. But time passed, and the aunt's belly grew larger and larger, and the boy was always around. But he never made love to his aunt again — it had been just that one day.

His uncle called him:

"Nephew, shall we go set a trap?"

(He wasn't a boy any more, now he was a grown young man.)

The two men walked until they came to a *tucumã* palm. The uncle caressed the boy and told him to stand still. Then he pushed the boy into the trap (a deep hole in the ground). The uncle gathered *tucumã* leaves and covered the trap and sealed it with *tucumã* thorns. The uncle went away and left the boy imprisoned by the thorns. He arrived home at dusk and the boy's mother asked:

"Where is your nephew?"

"He went with me but said he would come home early, by himself! He said he didn't feel like staying with me!" lied the uncle. "Didn't he arrive yet?"

After a few days the uncle went to see his nephew. The boy had died and his flesh had rotted and turned into flies. The flies were flying out of the hole of the trap.

"It is still little for what you did to me! I took my revenge on you and now you have turned into flies!" cried the uncle.

Two days later, the man's wife — the boy's aunt — had *Zakorobkap*, the Fly's baby. The uncle killed it and threw it away.

That is how there came to be flies. And that is why, whenever a fly sees meat, it lays its eggs right away — it is very fast. That is how it is until today. Flies, for us, are a person who turned into flies.

Djapé, the arrowhead, the man who ate his wives

Narrator in Portuguese: Awünaru Odete Aruá

A man ate his wives. He was kind of old, more than thirty. He married two young women, daughters of the tuxaua.

"Shall we go hunting?" he suggested.

The man took the two girls with him, he slept, and then he made a campground. He told his wives to wait for him while he was hunting, and he went into the jungle.

The man picked a leaf from a cabbage palm and started thrashing about with it in the jungle. He came back beating the palm leaf against the trees and making a lot of noise.

"A *caboclo*, an enemy, is coming to kill us!" he shouted from far away, to deceive his two wives.

The young women looked to see what was going on, and their husband came and hit them both over the head and killed them. He built a grill and cut the girls up like game and prepared them for cooking. Then he roasted them and spent the rest of the day eating them.

The next day, he finished eating his two wives and took their bones, and heaped them behind some *sapopemba* roots. He returned to the village and said his wives had run away because they were afraid of him.

He married two other girls (he only ate very young ones). After two days he brought the two new wives to the same place where he had killed and eaten the first ones. He said he was going hunting and asked them to wait for him.

He did the same thing he had done with his first wives: he picked a cabbage palm leaf and came back thrashing it about and making lots of noise.

"The Indians are going to attack us!" he cried.

And while the girls looked to see what was happening, the man killed them. He prepared them, and cooked them, and ate them. The husband grilled them slowly over the fire, scorching a few pieces of flesh at a time and eating them. He spent the whole day eating the girls, bite by bite.

He went home, then went to another village, and married two new wives. He took them to the same place and repeated everything.

That was the man's vice: eating young girls — always chiefs' daughters — each time from a different village. He always said the girls were afraid of him and ran away.

After the fourth wedding, the man told his new wives to stay in the campground and not to look behind the *sapopemba* roots. He said there was a beehive behind the tree and it would be very dangerous to disturb it. He also forbade them to run away as his other wives had.

The younger of the two girls was curious, and as soon as the man disappeared into the jungle, she decided to look behind the tree. She looked, and she saw the big pile of bones of the other wives.

"Sister! Come look!" she cried.

"So that is what's going on! He eats his wives!"

"Let's run away!"

"No, let's hide and wait."

The girls hid behind some trees and waited, and before long their husband came back beating a palm leaf.

"Girls! Be careful, the Indians are going to kill us!" he shouted.

The husband arrived at the campground but found no one there. He called out:

"Girls! Where are you?"

The older girl was about to answer when luckily the husband shouted out first:

"So you guessed! If you hadn't run away, I would have eaten you, like I ate the others!"

The younger girl said:

"You see what we escaped from?"

The man sat down and grabbed his own body.

"There's nothing for me to eat! And my own flesh is so tasty!"

The man took the blade of his arrow, cut off a piece of his arm, and ate it. He had been fat – but now his arm was thin. He roasted a piece and ate it, and thought it was delicious. He cut a piece from his other arm, grilled it, and ate it. Then he cut off a piece from his leg.

"This is really tasty! I'm hungry!"

He started cutting flesh from all over his body (in olden times we had chubby legs, but ever since that day, they became skinny).

The husband was still hungry and looked down at his belly.

"This belly must be delicious!" he said.

He cut from his neck down to his belly. He cut off so much that he was about to die. Before he died, he said (because he knew the girls must be hidden nearby):

"Return to your village and tell your father that the man who eats his wives ended up eating himself, that he killed himself, and turned into an arrowhead. Tell your father that when he comes to get me, to distribute me among his people, he must kill a lot of game, a whole lot of game. Come back here with your father and tell him to strip off some bark from the *jatobá* tree. Put the grilled meat where I am – where I will stay. Tell him to take a stick and swing me in the tree – so I'll come down to eat the game. I, the man who ate women, will turn into arrowheads, and your father can take as many as he wants."

The arrowheads hung from the tree, ready-made as in a factory, some decorated, others not. People didn't even have to make them; all they had to do was attach them to bamboo shafts. But if one of these arrowheads just scratched someone, it would wound him and he would die. It was very painful.

The man died and turned himself into arrowheads. The girls went away.

They told their father what had happened, and what the Husband-who-ate-his-wives had said to them. A few days passed, and they all went back to the campground.

The father spent several days in the jungle hunting and killed a lot of game. He grilled a lot of meat and put it in a big pile. He stripped some bark from a *jatobá* tree. Next he broke off a long stick to swing the man in the tree, so he would come eat. Before swinging him in the tree, the father said:

"Arrowhead, come eat! *Djapé, ewiraingá!*"

He swung the man in the tree and the arrowheads came down and ate the roasted meat, under the *jatobá* bark (it was like a little house). The father gathered the arrowheads with a pole because he couldn't go too close. He took as many of the arrowheads as he wanted and carried them home. He wanted to try out the arrowheads so he attached them to arrows and went hunting.

These arrowheads were good!

The father gave out the arrowheads, but warned his people to handle them carefully, not to scratch themselves. Everyone hunted carefully.

The father went back to the campground a second time with his daughters. He killed a lot of game and did everything just as he had before. He poked the arrowheads, and they came and ate the grilled meat. Then he took the arrowheads and put them in his house. He went a third time and did the same thing.

The chief was getting ready to go a fourth time, when the Stubborn One said:

"My friend, how did you find the arrowheads? I want to get some myself!"

"You can't! Take some from me. Later, when you are all more used to them, you can go like me!"

"I'm going!" cried the Stubborn One.

The Stubborn One insisted so much that finally the master of the arrowheads taught him exactly what to do. He told him not to forget the *jatobá* bark, because it was much safer that way.

The Stubborn One went, but only killed a small amount of game. He killed a little more in another place – but he didn't kill a lot of game, as the master did. He pulled off a leaf from the cabbage palm; instead of taking some *jatobá* bark, the Stubborn One took a leaf from the cabbage palm and called the arrowheads. He poked, and nothing happened. Once again he poked – nothing happened. The third time the Stubborn One poked, the creature appeared, panic-stricken – from rage, I think. It quickly ate the game, burst through the cabbage palm leaf, and ate the Stubborn One and his wife (who had been watching).

The master waited for the Stubborn One to return, but he never did. The master went with his daughters to take a look.

"I warned him! I told him not to go!" he said.

The master went to all the hunting camps and killed a lot of game. The next day he went to the campground of the arrowheads to see what would happen. He took bark from the *jatobá* tree and called to the arrowhead. But hardly anything came, only some ugly arrowheads. The beautiful arrowheads had changed. The master said:

"My son-in-law and I, the man who ate his wives, had already taught people who will be born in the future – they wouldn't have had to work to make arrowheads. All they had to do was come and get them. But because the Stubborn One didn't listen to me, these will be the arrowheads of those who have yet to born."

He took one of the ugly arrowheads and threw it on the ground. A *taquara* (bamboo) grew and that is how the arrowheads we use came into being.

"The children of the ones who have not yet been born will have to work hard to make arrows!"

And that's how it is today: it is a lot of work for us to make arrows.

Serek-Á, the mermaid

Narrator in Portuguese: Awünaru Odete Aruá

A girl's father gave her away to a man she didn't like. She really couldn't stand her new husband and always ran away from him. One day the husband's friend suggested:

"So your wife doesn't want you, my friend? I'll teach you how to make a special medicine and you can take your revenge on her!"

He gathered sap from the rubber tree, the wild rubber tree, the tonka-bean tree, and the *paxiúba-barriguda* palm tree. He mixed it all together, cooked it, and it got all sticky (the leaves of the *paxiúba-barriguda* palm make you itch like crazy).

The husband and his wife went to bed, but the wife got up – she didn't want her husband. So the husband got up and threw the sticky liquid all over his wife's body and she started to itch. It was unbearable. The poor girl scratched here, she scratched there . . . Finally she couldn't stand it any more and she went to the river bank. The unhappy wife kept scratching and washing herself, but it didn't help. The night passed, and the next day, and the girl's brother came to visit her.

"My sister! What a terrible thing your husband did to you!" he cried.

She was transformed: now she was half person, half snake – the top half was a person and the bottom half was a snake.

The brother wandered all over thinking about his sister – such a bad thing had been done to her! One day, as he was out walking sadly around, he came across a genip tree (in those times people only painted themselves with charcoal). The brother chewed the genipap and saw that it could be used as a dye. He gave some to his sister.

There was going to be a big party, a *chicha* feast, and the sister-snake asked her brother to chew the genipap so she could paint him. The boy chewed the genipap and gave the juice to his sister.

"Don't be afraid, my brother! Put the genipap sap in my throat and slip your body halfway into my mouth. Piss inside me, and I'll let you out," said the sister-snake.

The boy put the sap in his sister's mouth (by now she had turned completely into a snake). When she had finished painting him, the sister-snake told her brother to piss inside her. He pissed, and she spat him out. His body was painted all over.

"Go lie in the sun, my brother, to let the paint dry!" said the sister-snake.

The boy was still sad about what had happened to his sister. He kept walking around, and by chance he came across many animals: the jaguar, the parrot, and the macaw. He was walking because he was so sad about his sister and he ended up bringing home jaguar skin for hats and feathers to make a headdress.

The brother went to the big party, painted all over with the genipap. He was very handsome (the others were only painted with charcoal and weren't nearly as beautiful). He danced until the next morning.

Time passed and the boy gathered feathers and jaguar skins for another party. A *chicha* feast was coming up.

"Sister, I'm going to get more genipap so you can paint me again!" said the boy.

The sister was happy to do it. The boy did everything the same as the first time: entered his sister, pissed, came out, and went to dry himself in the sun. Later he made himself a beautiful headdress.

He was already teaching the people who are yet to be born; he was teaching us. That's how we were going to do things.

The boy went to get ready a third time and found the animals again: the jaguars, the macaws, and the parrots. He was the only one who knew how to find the animals, and the only one who knew about the genipap.

The sister painted her brother again. Now she lived by the river bank, in a bay in the river, under the water. Her brother called to her and she floated to the surface (only part of her body showed above the water).

It happened that way three times. There was a third party and the brother went, all dressed up with macaw feathers, and danced all night. It was the last party.

When the people were preparing for the fourth party, the brother-in-law, the one who had harmed the boy's sister, kept asking him how he painted himself. The brother-in-law bothered the brother so much that in the end he told him what to do. He explained how to enter inside the girl and piss inside her to get out. But the brother complained:

"You can't ask to be painted! My sister will want to go away! You can't, you have already harmed her enough!"

But the brother-in-law went and called to the Sister-Snake. He called and called, but she knew it wasn't her brother – it was her ex-husband's voice. She didn't want to come, and took a long time. But finally she appeared.

"Are you still going to ask me for something, after all the harm you have done to me?" she asked.

But it hadn't been the ex-husband's idea to make the magic itching potion, his friend had told him to do it. The husband wept, full of remorse, and the Sister-Snake agreed to paint him and told him to enter her without fear. She told him to piss when it was time to come out.

"Should I really piss inside your belly? Shouldn't I feel bad for you?" he asked.

And he didn't piss, so the Sister-Snake swallowed him whole and dove down deep into the water.

The brother waited and waited, but his brother-in-law didn't return, so he went to the river bank to call his sister.

"Sister, sister!" he called.

She came to the surface, but only stuck her little head out of the water.

"Where is the one who harmed you?" asked her brother.

"He is with me and won't ever return! Tell Daddy and Mommy! You know I wouldn't live with him before, but now, under the water, he is my husband. I won't give him back to you, no, I won't! You will all die, Daddy will die, and Mommy will die. Only he and I won't die. I'm going to take my husband away with me!"

It was the brother's turn to cry. Now his sister liked her husband. She had vomited him up and transformed him into a snake, just like her.

At midnight there was a loud rumbling as the happy snake couple, the boa constrictors, told their children what was to be. The little pool by the river bank turned into a bay – their happiness made it grow so big.

The people went to kill the snakes early the next morning. The father's people went to kill the two snakes – they didn't want them to have a chance to multiply. When they arrived at the water everything was quiet – the snakes had already escaped. But they left their snake-children behind along the way. The people would walk a little way, come across a snake, and kill it. Further ahead, another one. The snake couple kept going, leaving their young behind as they went. They went to the Guaporé River, and to the Mamoré River – they went far away, no one could reach them.

Before this, anacondas didn't exist. Boa constrictors didn't exist. Not a single kind of snake existed until this woman turned herself into a snake. Now we are afraid when we walk by the river.

Snakes know where there is game and how to hunt. They're afraid of people (but the ones who have never seen a person aren't afraid).

The boa constrictors' mother is Serek-á, the Mermaid. Her husband's name is Palib-bô, The-One-Who-Was- Swallowed-and-Came-Back-to-Life.

Love in the indigenous mythology of Rondônia: an anthology

A COMMENTARY ON *BARBECUED HUSBANDS*

Indigenous myths are told with great liberty in terms of erotic expression, unrestricted by any kind of censorship. They are characterized by the expression of themes dealing with sexuality, portrayed in a world and in the language of playfulness and a rich sensual imagination.

Thus the organization of indigenous myths around the theme of love seems a powerful way to entice the reader from a different cultural environment to dive into the unknown, into the tangle that is indigenous mythology. Sexuality is one of the fundamental topics of our time, a good pathway to awaken our curiosity about another way of thinking and living.

Are sexuality and love freer in indigenous society than in our own? Is there more equality between men and women, more possibility for harmony? This is the image we tend to have of indigenous life, and there are reasons for this: nudity and the body are accepted in the village without repression; affection, kinship, and community ties are dominant; there is no private property, and no pursuit or accumulation of material wealth; individual wants and needs are tempered by the social fabric, by the interests and power of the group; the sense of time, art, and ways of seeing are very different from those of industrial society.

If we use the myths to attempt to respond to these questions, we see that alongside the paradise-like aspects, violence, repression, conflict, war, taboos, and rigid rules for behavior also exist in indigenous life – all of which offer legitimate grounds for discussion.

Thinking about various aspects of indigenous romantic love can help us to appreciate the myths, as true stories or as fiction, and enhance the pleasure we experience when reading them; at the same time we can compare relations between men and women in different times and societies as we make our way through the various themes of romantic love.

Eroticism and repression

One of the first things that focuses our attention in this anthology of myths, contradicting our image of a sexually liberated and unrestrained indigenous society, is the repressive and moralistic character of many of the myths. The stories often have violent endings, usually following an uninhibited, playful depiction of sex and love – unusual portrayals from an unfettered imagination. Could it be that the liberty to think about and describe these forbidden pleasures functions as an escape valve for the imagination, afterwards establishing social norms that prohibit these same behaviors that bear such fascination?

The moralistic consequences occur, for example, in the stories about masturbation or sexual satisfaction that do not involve the opposite sex (or even the hero's own sex, for that matter).

A myth that is common to many peoples, such as the Nivaclé and the Kaxinauá, common as well in Rondônia, is about women taking their pleasure with worms.

The Tupari myth, "The *Cobra-cega*'s Lover," for example, ends badly for the young woman: she becomes pregnant, and is threatened by a myriad of worm fetuses that end up killing her.

The Macurap myth, "The Prick Made of *Muiratinga* Wood and the Frog *Páapap*," and the Tupari myth, "The Clay Pecker," are also dreadful. In both stories, a young woman makes herself an artificial penis that she talks to adoringly and makes love to every night. Jealous men spread hot pepper on the girl's inanimate lover, she grows desperate and promises never to do it again, or, in one of the stories, she dies.

Similar myths, documented by other anthropologists, exist among the Xingu peoples, for example among the Mehinaku (see Gregor 1985) and among the Kamaiurá (Junqueira 1979).

The Kaxinauá (D'Ans 1979) tell the story of the jaguar and the girl who is impregnated by a worm; the jaguar helps her get rid of the worm fetuses that have invaded her womb. The Nivaclé (Chase-Sardi 1981) also tell a story about a woman who makes love to a penis made of wax, much to the indignation of the men; the Waiampi tell of a woman who makes love to a worm (Grenand 1982).

The repression of adultery is also violent: in a Suruí myth, narrated in my book *The Unwritten Stories of the Suruí* (Mindlin 1985), a married woman makes love to a tapir; she is killed, and the tapir's penis is cut off and shoved into the vagina of her corpse.

Any type of lovemaking other than that between established couples within the indigenous systems of relationship, any lovemaking that evades reproduction, any lovemaking solely for pleasure, is not allowed. In the Tupari myth "The King-Vulture Rival," there is a crazy woman who is condemned because all she thinks about is making love to every man she sees; she even wants to make love to her own father. Finally she calls the monster Tianoá to lie down with her and he literally devours her.

Women are severely punished if they refuse to marry, or reject the men chosen for them, or don't want any man because the right one hasn't appeared.

One can't help but be strongly affected by the violence in the Tupari story of Piripidpit. A group of men beat a young woman to death in a kind of lynching, then eat her flesh in a banquet: her punishment for not accepting the man chosen for her. This story is told to Tupari girls from the time they are infants to teach them to obey their elders, and it is told as an event that really occurred. The older women told me how they were terrified by this story when they were children.

Myths of other peoples also describe severe penalties for women who reject their betrothed: a Suruí myth tells of a young woman who is tied up by the fiancé she despises, and although she changes her mind because of the suffering she undergoes, he does not pardon her and she turns into a bird (a trogon); or, in one of the most important Macurap stories, a young woman is transformed into a boa constrictor by her rejected fiancé; both the Jabuti and the Tupari tell a story of a rejected fiancé who cuts off the girl's clitoris and vulva and gives them to her mother to eat, as if they were game.

Men who find alternatives to women appear not to be punished so severely. The unlucky Macurap hunter (the theme of the unlucky hunter is very frequent) makes love to a *pau-âmago* tree, going so far as to be jealous of his tree lover; he beats and curses her, he sulks and pouts. But his only punishment is to be caught in the act by a friend and to be embarrassed. (It seems that making love to trees is commonplace: a man has sex with a calabash tree and that's how the first Suruí, Kabeud, and Samsam women are born.)

Lovers who are not human

An idea common to many of these stories is that the best lovers, male and female, do not come from this world. In the real world, sublime love is fleeting, and harmony is rare among humans.

In a Suruí myth, narrated in *The Unwritten Stories of the Suruí*, a pregnant woman unknowingly makes love to a spirit and gives birth to rat children. Thereafter it is taboo to make love to a pregnant woman. A Tupari myth tells the story of a young woman whose husband doesn't want her because she can't get pregnant. She feels miserable, runs away while she has her period, and finds a spirit lover who lives in an abandoned hut. In many other myths there are men who make love to Tarupás (Tupari spirits or ghosts), such as the beautiful, but very hairy, woman who makes men's genitals itch like crazy.

There is a Tupari myth, narrated in *Tuparis e Tarupás* (Mindlin 1993) and a very similar Macurap myth – truly erotic stories – in which a woman has a wonderful love affair, unaware that her lover is a spirit. The moral of these myths seems to be that a woman should not be allowed too much pleasure. In the Macurap version, a spirit visits the young woman every night. He slips his hand through the straw of her hut and plays with her clitoris, which grows to unmanageable proportions; her clitoris grows so big that it drags along the ground and makes it difficult for her to walk. Of course there is no way for the girl to hide what is happening and her parents resolve to catch the spirit red-handed; they grab him as he is about to caress their daughter and they cut off his arm. Because the villagers won't give the ghost back his arm, the world goes dark; there is perpetual night and the people run out of wood to keep their fires going. Now without light, the villagers are at the mercy of evil beings and end up giving the arm back to its owner. As for the girl's swollen clitoris, it is also cut off and turns into an electric eel (which could be a curious analogy for an orgasm).

This myth – and perhaps others – is difficult to understand if we consider it as a single story, standing alone. We need to go back to Lévi-Strauss, for example, and see this myth in the context of the opposing ideas and dialogues that the myths establish among themselves – to perceive them as part of a structured whole.

Love with beings from other worlds finds many echoes in our own literary tradition. We only have to think of Japanese stories such as *Kwaidan* (Hearn 1921) or those told in Lafcadio Hearn's *In Ghostly Japan* (1922); the Polish, *The Dybbuk* (Hirsch 1975); the accounts of Saint Teresa and her closeness to Jesus; the literature of terror, such as *Vathek* (Beckford 1929); *The Monk* (Lewis 1984); or Jan Potocki's *Saragossa Manuscript* (1960); and many other genres. But the world turning dark because a ghost is mutilated and upset requires us to look along a different path.

Lévi-Strauss sheds some light on the myths of darkness in his four volume *Mythologies*. One of the main themes explored in his *The Origin of Table*

Manners (1968) is the myth of the flying head. Lévi-Strauss gathers and dis-
cusses myths from both North and South America and demonstrates how the
mutilations are linked to the creation of heavenly bodies: myths that explain
the regularity of the seasons, of day and night, the map of the heavens, the
stars – in different ways, with distinctly opposing subjects and characters,
appearing very differently from one place to another, but all oriented toward
explanations of the universe.

In "The Ghost Lover and the girl with the Giant Clitoris," the regularity
of day and night is interrupted when a human girl unites, if only partially,
with a ghost lover. The equilibrium of the earth and the after-world is threatened. People touch some unknown power of supernatural beings and stability
is only regained when the Txopokod (ghost) becomes whole again. The final
mutilation of the girl, whose cut off clitoris becomes an electric eel, bears an
element of repression of sensuality: a repressed standard for feminine behavior becomes the norm.

Mother and daughter

The ties of family and kinship, with all the inherent conflicts, alliances, and
antagonisms, form the ground out of which all the myths spring.

Many of the plots involve mothers who meddle in the love lives of their
children. In the Suruí myth, "Ai-ai, the Horned Frog" (documented in *The
Unwritten Stories of the Suruí*), a myth also existing among the Gavião as well
as among various other peoples of the region, the mother opens up the piece
of bamboo where her daughter hides her frog lover during the day (at night
he turns into a handsome warrior). The lover turns into a frog for ever and
the daughter loses her lover – a kind of *Beauty and the Beast*. In the Macurap
"Akarandek, the Flying Head, or The Ravenous Wife," the mother, perhaps
with good intentions, buries her daughter's body without its head, and makes
her mutilation permanent.

The competition between mother and daughter reaches its height in this indigenous form in the Macurap story about the old woman who lusts after her son-in-law. She throws her daughter into a trap, a deep hole in the ground, and takes her place without her son-in-law noticing. The older woman can't laugh or open her mouth because she has no teeth, but it seems that she does fine with everything else. Her problem is that her gums bleed when she chews the manioc or corn to make the traditional drink, *chicha* – it ends up stained with blood. Meanwhile the daughter in her prison – which she later escapes from – learns important songs such as the Botxatoniã, the Rainbow or Snake. She teaches the songs to the Macurap people and becomes a heroine.

On the other hand, there is the giving, nurturing mother, as in the beautiful Macurap story of the woman who turns into a clay pot. Her uterus serves as a vessel for cooking a few hours each day – to the outrage and disgust of her son-in-law when he finds out where his food is being prepared. This pampering mother, similar to Demeter (with her daughter Persephone), presents her daughter with beautiful pottery the likes of which no one had ever seen before.

The adventurous feminists and their fear of the man with three penises

It is unthinkable not to marry or have a mate in indigenous society. The myths, however, are not very encouraging and the search for lasting love seems always to end in disaster. The myths portray an image of marriage not much more optimistic than in our 20th century literature.

There are adventurous women in the myths of various peoples of Rondônia – usually two or three women – who go out together in search of husbands. They go into the forest, come what may, facing wild beasts and monsters. They are brave, and travel with no warrior to protect them, but end up falling into all kinds of traps. There is always a smarter one and one who is easily deceived.

In the Macurap myth, the adventurers are two naïve aunts and their clever niece. The young women's evil sister-in-law lays down leaves pointing in the wrong direction, toward the land of the Txopokods, on a path that closes behind them as they walk. The three girls only meet men who deceive them, like the snake who offers them piss instead of *chicha*.

The niece is daring, always doing things that put the three young women in danger – but she always saves them. Finally they find a husband, but what a scary one! He has too much of what they want: he has three penises. Unlike her aunts, the niece resists as long as she can, but this time she can't find a way out. She can't find a safe place to sleep in this strange man's home and ends up in his hammock – all three women at once.

In the Suruí myths published in *The Unwritten Stories of the Suruí*, it is the first two women in the world – Kabeud and Samsam, daughters of a man and a gourd – who venture forth in search of a husband. But they find only false bait: the owl who cries and gives them tears instead of honey, the deer who gives them flesh from his own leg instead of game, the heron who gives them rats instead of fish, and so on. Samsam, the cleverer one, never lets herself be fooled and always sees the trap; she doesn't really make love – she only offers her fingers in a V shape. But Kabeud really makes love each time.

In the end, Samsam finally gives in, as does her sister, to Mekopitxay, the mythical jaguar. Their marriages don't end well – it couldn't be otherwise when human beings mix with a family of wild animals. The mother-in-law kills the two young women, and their sons, both of them the jaguar's children, avenge their mothers' deaths. They kill their grandmother, who is afraid of fire, and they turn into thunder. Only Mekopitxay, the poor jaguar, survives: alone in the world, without children, wives, or mother. He can't stay in the world of human beings or in the world of wild beasts – the two worlds are irreconcilable. He becomes a spirit.

Among the Tupari, the adventuress – only one this time – gets involved with a pygmy owl. She wants to marry the Amazonian wren, but she ends up with the owl after he marks her trail with leaves pointing the wrong way. She tries to trick him when she can: she gives him tears instead of honey, rats instead of fish, etc. Finally one day she decides to run away.

In the Xingu, the Kamaiurá tell a well-known variation of women made of pieces of wood who wander through the forest and end up marrying a jaguar (see Samain 1991; Junquiera 1979; Agostinho 1974).

Biology and feminine and masculine roles

It's curious how biology and social roles are perceived as one and the same, and are explained as a battle for power between the sexes. There are innumerable peoples (Tupari, Macurap, Suruí, Gavião, Arara, and many others) among whom, in archaic times, according to their myths, men were the ones who menstruated, until they threw the blood at the women.

Pregnancy did not exist, or was located in the foot (Macurap), or in the calf (Arara), or had to be learned. In myths from many different indigenous groups, women originally didn't have vaginas – they had to be created. In a myth documented by Caspar in 1948, that I published in *Tuparis and Tarupás*, Waledjat, one of the two Tupari demiurges, carves a woman out of wood and paints her inside with annatto dye: she becomes the first woman with a vagina. He makes a woman with no hole for his brother, who is furious.

Menstruation – but perhaps not pregnancy – is almost viewed as a disadvantage and a loss of prestige; the sex that menstruates is the one that has less power. In Suruí and Tupari myths, the women make fun of the menstruating men (the men have to stay in seclusion, while the women go wherever they want). The men pass a bloody hand over the women's vaginas (Suruí), or throw grass with blood on it as the women approach (Tupari), and the women start to menstruate instead of the men: they lose power, prestige, and freedom of movement.

SEDUCTION

"Botxatoniã, the Women of the Rainbow" offers an excursion into the world of romantic indigenous love, which we always imagine to be free, unrepressed, and fulfilling. It is one of the most beautiful Macurap stories, and its central themes are seduction and passion.

The story begins with presumably happy men and women in the village; they are married and have children. One day, the women are seduced by a magical being (aren't all lovers indeed magical beings?) who lives underwater and who they think is very handsome. In one of the translations of this myth, the women allow themselves to be seduced perhaps because their men are always out hunting, always far away and inattentive; in the other translation, the women venture the first step outside of their marriages.

The men find themselves abandoned and try to forget "the grief that pierces their hearts," according to the translator, and give in to the fire of new passions for women who also live underwater. The seducers and seductresses live in the water, like sirens belonging to other, non-indigenous, peoples. It should be noted that the women all fall in love with a single lover, while the men encounter many.

As time passes, both the men and women want to go back to how things were before. The "story" subtly gives us to understand that the men, as well as the women, have fallen for beings who are really illusions, spirits, ghosts: their intense passion has been misplaced. The women see how ugly their lover really is and kill him.

The men send an emissary to the women with a clear warning not to allow himself to be seduced, not even to allow a woman to touch him. But a young woman falls for him and he succumbs to temptation. Because of his weakness, as a kind of punishment of sensuality, the rupture between the sexes becomes final and the women remain without men for ever.

Punishment and seduction

What does the story of the Rainbow people (which can be seen as an image of love gone wrong) tell us? That love will never be reciprocated, or can only last for short periods of time? That it is always illusory because it invokes only apparitions, magical beings who don't really exist? Or is the object of the myth to penalize seduction because the couples end up apart for ever?

There are myths, however, in which the path of sensuality is the correct one. In a Carajá myth, for example, the hero shows only disdain for the single women he meets in his adventures who offer him their love. Everything goes wrong in his life until he follows the counsel of a magical being, who advises him to give in to the women's desires – only then will he have good luck. He shouldn't be afraid of the sensuality and urgency of feminine love – it will only help him (Peret 1979).

In the Macurap story, the heart of the plot is the sensual love that is refused, or improperly accepted – love always out of balance. First the men are rejected, but then the women want them back. The men stay away from the women and entertain themselves by hunting and walking through the forest. Later they are enticed by the beauty of the women underwater and the wonderful food they offer them. But time passes and the men start to long for their own wives, the very wives who caused them such suffering; but their wives are gone for ever – because of the misdeeds of a single person, the messenger.

The People of the Rainbow

The People of the Rainbow are the seductive women in this Macurap story. For the Macurap, a rainbow is a snake, which is the bridge between the land of the living and the land of the dead. Dead people, according to Macurap and Jabuti tradition, must cross a deep river where the Rainbow snake lives.

When the souls call to him, the snake makes a bridge for the travelers to cross over to the hereafter.

In the myth of "Botxatô," love is fleeting like a rainbow, an illusion that earth, water, and heaven are one (because the lovers are spirits who live underwater). At the same time, if it is true that the rainbow can be a link between now and the hereafter, between heaven and earth, then it follows that these same realms must remain for ever separate and distant – in the same way that it is a transgression for men or women to share their lives with magical beings. The cosmic order is linked to the rules of love.

THE ETERNAL BATTLE OF THE SEXES

"The *Koman* Song (The Frog Song)" (in the Macurap language, *koman* means a frog that lives in a lake) is a story that symbolizes the most violent hatred between the sexes. But why such a severe confrontation?

A group of little Macurap girls go to a lake and try to capture some little frogs, not knowing that they belong to an old woman Txopokod, an evil spirit. The old woman of the lake, named Katxuréu, incites the girls' mothers to kill and eat their husbands, one by one. She wants to avenge the theft of her frogs, but what motivates the women? What great offense have they suffered at the hands of their men that they would murder and eat them?

The forbidden territory of the old woman was invaded by the girls, who didn't know she was the mistress of the frogs. In many stories with which we are familiar, fairytales and others – for example *Hansel and Gretel* – this is how the hero's problems start: he enters the domain of a witch or an ogre.

And so the old woman bewitches the women, separating the wives from their husbands, as does the snake in the Judeo-Christian paradise of the Old Testament. She provokes hostility toward the men through the seduction of art: of music and painting.

In one version of this story, the old woman prepares body paint from genipap, which is linked, in many other myths, to incest. In other more common versions, the old woman's song and her bamboo flute are what attract the women, who learn her magic melodies.

In the beginning of the story, the girls persuade their mothers to follow them to the lake where the old woman lives. They participate in a kind of Dionysian ritual, reminding us of Euripedes' *Bacchae* or, on a lighter note, the women's revolt in Aristophanes' *Lysistrata*. What pleasure to kill and eat – in community with other women – their own husbands' flesh! It is worth noting that, according to some of the narrators, a number of the mothers eat their own sons.

Is it the old woman who instigates the banquet of human flesh to replace her little fish and frogs (even though the girls never really take her fish and frogs away)? If she wants to eat the men, we perceive them equally as food and sex objects.

Frogs are often linked with sex in these myths. There is a Jabuti story in which the hero is castrated while swimming in a river and receives a frog in place of his missing organ. One day he meets a *japó* bird who gives him a new penis, but it is so small that the results are dismal. Other frogs turn into husbands (in Suruí, Gavião, Macurap, Tupari, and other peoples' myths), similar to the frogs that turn into princes in fairytales.

What reason would the women have to carry out such a terrible command without the least resistance? The women separate themselves from their husbands, they murder them without regret, and without complaint about the men's power. There is no justification given in the myth for such profound resentment against the husbands.

The women's power and a world without women

Several of the stories tell of villages of only women or only men (although when the men are left alone there always turns out to be a young girl hidden somewhere among them). Harmony between the sexes seems so unattainable that the myths speak of life with only men or only women. How, then, will the species survive?

The men in these myths seem less concerned with reproduction and sex than with gluttony: they want good sweet *chicha*, as only the women can make it. This refers to the division of chores between the sexes, the only clear division of labor that exists in the villages. (Perhaps societal rules are guided by the myths.)

In "The *Koman* Song (The Frog Song)", the only reason the women are not all killed and womankind does not disappear completely, is because two young innocent sisters survive, rescued by their courageous brother (perhaps thinking of the next generation of women, of marrying his sisters' children). The moral component is strong: only "pure" women survive, the two girls who, by pure chance, do not eat their male relatives' flesh.

And so the myth alludes to a time, now considered flawed, when the women had power; then the women were threatening, but today they can be repressed.

The loss of women's power in ancient times appears in many myths.

Among the Munduruku (Murphy and Murphy 1974), there is a myth that reminds us a lot of "The *Koman* Song." This time three women hear music coming from a lake and capture three fish that turn into sacred flutes. The flutes give the women power over the men, who now have to cook and fetch water and firewood for them. They take over the men's houses, which until now they had been forbidden to enter. The women make the men come to their houses and have sex with them – the way the women tell them to (otherwise, then as now, the women were obliged to obey the men). Meanwhile the men continue to be the only ones to hunt, and because the flutes need to eat meat, the men force the women to give them the flutes (which in present times women are forbidden to own or use).

Among the Kamaiurá, in general, women are not allowed to play the *jacuí*, the sacred flute. If they see the *jacuí*, they will be raped by all the men.

In many indigenous societies in Rondônia, the separation between men and women is not as marked as in many other areas. There are no rituals that are hidden from or forbidden to women (such as the *jacuí*), and no feminine rituals, as among the Kaiapó, for painting the body. While the Munduruku and many other peoples have houses just for men, in Rondônia only the Nambiquara have small houses that are forbidden to women, where the men learn how to play the flutes that the women must never see.

The battle and enmity between men and women, who nevertheless need and depend on each other, reaches frightening dimensions in "The *Koman* Song." There is a scene in the story – which could be a scene in a film – in which the old woman bares her teeth in the middle of the lake and shows the few remaining avenging warriors the mouth with which she ate the rest of the men.

It's clearly possible to associate the oral and sexual types of eating with the vagina with teeth (which doesn't appear in these myths, but is common among other indigenous peoples). There is a Karajá myth about the sun's daughters, brides who have teeth in their vagina (Peret 1979); the Tukano tell a myth about piranha women, documented by Berta G. Ribeiro (1995); the Nivaclé tell of women who live in the water and eat with their vaginas until the men cause them to lose their teeth (Chase-Sardi 1981); and so on.

It is a symbolic story of the war between the sexes. It makes us wonder if it could ever be possible to escape the radical opposition between men and women.

The song from the story still exists and both men and women sing it. I recorded both a woman and a man singing it.

THE AMAZONS: WOMEN WITHOUT MEN

The story of the Kaledejaa-ipeb, the black women who live without men (a kind of Macurap Amazon tribe, living alone with their ferocious father), is a prime example of a portrayal of the marked separation between the sexes, while being at the same time a poetic love story. For the Macurap, the Kaledjaa, like the Txopokods, are a kind of spirit, or ghost.

One of the main characters is a maiden woman warrior – certainly a rare figure in the indigenous myths – who, however, only maintains her virginity a short time.

She is an extraordinary, loving, but extremely strong young woman – easily carrying loads that no man could manage – who meets a young warrior in the middle of the forest and brings him home to her village. She is the model of a perfect woman who combines both masculine and feminine qualities: the warmth and caring of her sisters with all the strength and abilities of a man. Her only defects are her terrifying father and the fact that she isn't human – she and her sisters are Txopokods (in this case, benevolent spirits, ready to teach men their secrets).

The novelty is that she does everything better than the warrior. She is without equal at hunting, fishing, and shooting arrows: everything that men do. She teaches her skills to her husband, the man she found in the forest, but shares him as a lover with her sisters (since he is the only man they have ever met). The women arm themselves and defend their lover against their father.

The young warrior realizes a fantasy common to many men: a whole village of women to himself, a loving, attentive, harem in the jungle, and a special, main lover who provides everything good, especially game – a Diana-Artemis mate. This lucky man finds himself in the kingdom of paradise; all he has to do is neutralize his father-in-law.

The secret

But these are ghost women, they are not real: they are friendly Txopokods who move around and disappear – they are magical beings. The young warrior divides his time between his women in the forest, with whom he now has children, and his family in the village where he was born. He should have kept his double life secret, but ends up revealing everything to the people in his village.

The hero doesn't keep his secret and so exposes his family of lovers to the dangerous presence of mortals. He is almost an antihero: he is passive and finally indiscreet. He seems like a toy in the hands of the women of the Txopokod village, while in the Indian village he is at the mercy of a Stubborn One, a killjoy, who spies on him and wants to imitate him. The Stubborn One pesters the young warrior so much that he finally tells where the enchanted women live.

What is the lesson to be learned? That a great love must be secret, in order to escape the evil eye? That the other world, the transcendental, the other life, can only survive outside the reach of society? That the eye of society hurts romantic life, and that is why the lovers are classified as Txopokods/ghosts? That which comes from dreams and fantasies must always remain marginal; if not, it would be almost impossible to resist the pressure of the reality principle.

And here again, as in many other stories, the fatal transgression: the hero talks too much and his life with his lovers and the wholeness of his life turn into a lost dream.

Other Amazons

The Tupari still believe that a group of women without men exists today, they don't know where. They believe that the women ran away from the village when – according to the myth, narrated in *Tuparis e Tarupás* – their husbands killed their lover, a tapir who seduced them. In retaliation, the women went off to live by themselves (the Tupari do not die out, but only because a man hides his little daughter, stopping the men from being single for ever and mankind from disappearing).

The Suruí tell another version of this story, narrated in *The Unwritten Stories of the Suruí*, that takes another twist, that doesn't end up with the women leaving their men. Only one woman is seduced by the tapir-Don Juan. Her husband kills the tapir and cuts off its penis; he hangs the penis from the doorway of the hut so it drips on his wife's head. Later he kills his wife and sticks the tapir's penis into the corpse's vagina, making her punishment an example for the others. The seduction, which in the Tupari myth is the origin of the tribe of women, is punished, but doesn't carry the danger of the complete separation of men and women.

There are stories told among other peoples, already published, which are variations on the theme of the tapir-lover and women without men. Among the Kayapó (Lukesch), a man seduces all the women and the betrayed husbands turn the man into a tapir and kill him. Out of grief, or in retaliation, the women turn themselves into fish.

Koch-Grünberg 1979: II, 110) describes the Taulipang Amazons (important in Mário de Andrade's *Macunaíma*, 1984) as beautiful women with long hair, using the word Amazon as an analogy. There are already references to these women in Carvajal and Orellana.

Among the Kamaiurá in the Xingu, the Amurikuma myth tells the mysterious story of a group of women who ran away in olden times, resentful when the men took too long returning from a fishing trip. Today the Kamaiurá call them the Mistresses-of-the-bow (Samain 1991). The Mehinaku, also in the Xingu, tell of women who left their men to fish and play sacred flutes, living in a village of only women – until they are conquered and raped by the men (Gregor 1985).

There is a very interesting Jabuti myth, included in the present anthology, about women who discover their husbands eating their own feces ("PakuredjeSui aoné"). The women are disgusted and go away to live without men; they become shamans and learn how to fly. Now without men, the women find their way to the spiritual kingdom, generally forbidden to women – and only experience this right because they discover that the men are dirty and contemptible.

WOMEN AND EXCESS

We are shocked by the myth of the flying head the first time we hear it.

A married woman separates into two parts every night: her head goes out looking for food in other huts and villages, while her body stays in her hammock, affectionately hugging her husband. Every morning she wakes up whole again with just a little blood sprinkled around – a mystery! In the middle of the night, apparently satiated, the head has returned and attached itself back to its body.

In the Tupari version (included in a previous book of mine), one night, after several adventures, the head comes home and can't stick itself back to its body, which has been burned by relatives. It turns itself into a nighthawk, or nightjar, a bird that is thought of as a bad omen. After a few days, the night-jar explains to her husband in somber whistles that she is his decapitated wife, and she takes him away to the kingdom of the nightjars, in the heavens. The husband, or the nightjar-wife, turns into a shining star, near the constellation we call Orion's Belt.

In the Macurap version, the girl's mother discovers the bloody body and buries it, thinking the husband has cut off her daughter's head. When the head comes back to the hammock, it has nowhere to go, so it attaches itself to the husband's shoulder. The head starts to rot, but is still insatiable, always asking for meat; it becomes a horrible torment for the husband. He becomes a man with two heads: his own and his wife's, stuck to his shoulder, rotting away.

To really understand this story, we need to examine it closely, to study it in detail, to study versions from many indigenous peoples.

If it weren't for the girl's mother, in the Macurap version, or other relatives in the Tupari version, perhaps the husband would never have a problem with this strange way of life. In the Macurap version, he knows that the head flies around – but he gets used to it. It is the internal family conflicts, for example mother versus son-in-law, that unleash the drama.

The nighthawk, in learning to rise to the heavens, links the worldly, human realm, with the celestial, the world of the hereafter, the terrifying world of spirits, of those who announce death and come after our corpses. A star appears which, in many of the myths, is the result of a mutilation. Disorder in the social word, with a bloody, devouring woman; new order in the celestial map – a new star emerges.

In the Macurap version, the nighthawk does not appear. We have instead the flying head becoming part of the husband's body. The voracious woman grabs on to the man and sticks to him and annoys him: another type of excess, of immoderate conduct, another lesson on what must not be done and on what frightens us – an unbearable odor, the superfluous lover, until now so desirable, now plagues and torments the man and he must free himself.

Lévi-Strauss and the flying head

The curious thing is that this dreadful myth, with its unexpected image, is ubiquitous in indigenous mythology, as much in North America as South America. Lévi-Strauss dedicated a lot of time and energy to studying this myth – especially in two books, *The Origin of Table Manners* and *The Jealous Potter* (1988).

The theme of the flying head became a classic in Brazil in *Macunaíma*, by Mário de Andrade. It relates a Kaxinauá myth, documented by Capistrano de Abreu (1941), about a decapitated head that decides to become the moon.

If Mário de Andrade made the horrific flying head familiar, it is Lévi-Strauss who shows that a myth, at first glance peculiar and perhaps ridiculous, is but one fragment of a veritable torrent of similar stories, transformations of the originals, with innovations, inversions, and various oppositions of different parts of the myths. What appears to be the creation of a fantastic, isolated imagination is really part of a whole.

A good part of both *The Origin of Table Manners* and *The Jealous Potter* is dedicated to the theme of the decapitated head. As we know, Lévi-Strauss is not interested in the interpretation of any one single myth. What interests him is the whole, the transformations of themes from one myth to another, the language developed among the myths themselves, the structure of the myths composed of the same contrasting motifs but holding different meanings and deriving from different points of view. Still, it is the severed head, and the moon it turns into, that illuminate these books.

Lévi-Strauss cites an interesting example of the gluttonous head that turns into a clutching woman, in which frogs turn into clingy wives. A curious Munduruku myth (Lévi-Strauss: 1, 65–6), told by Murphy and Murphy (1974), tells of a female frog that grabs a man with her vagina, turns herself into a woman, and seduces him. She asks him to warn her before he ejaculates; he obeys and comes out, but his penis is trapped and stretches. The woman-frog finally lets him go, but now he has to wrap his extremely long penis around his body in order to walk. In the end, some otters cure him.

It would seem that this myth has nothing to do with the severed head, but Lévi-Strauss registers many other myths about penises stretched to gigantic dimensions, elongated Eskimo testicles, mutilated penises, a Tacana penis so long it reaches the moon (Lévi-Strauss: 1, 67). He suggests that the severed head/clutching wife and the long penis are of symmetrical significance, one cut off, the other reaching for impossible destinations, both signs of unimagined excess or of too much greed or need. It's important to keep this idea in mind, for the myths of Rondônia hold nice surprises of penises that are most unusual, or disappointingly small.

The story of a long penis that reaches from the man's hut to a woman in the river makes the Tupari laugh. Many other peoples have similar myths. The Kaxinauá (D'Ans 1979: myth 41) have a myth of a sparrow with a penis and testicles so big that he has to keep them in a basket. His penis is so long that he stays in one room while he makes love to a woman in another; as he is always far away, his wife takes a lover without difficulty. The Suruí also tell a myth, included in *The Unwritten Stories of the Suruí*, about a penis that stretches.

The meaning of the greedy head

The flying head might be interpreted psychologically as a lesson on female voraciousness, excessive ravenous greed. It also represents a clingy, unloved woman who abuses her rights as a wife, making her husband live a horrible life with two heads.

A modern woman might extend these analogies, asking if the head thinks – its voracity might also be intellectual, wanting to know about everything everywhere, embracing the world, separating the woman from her domestic role and her erotic role at night in the hammock. It is not the case, however; the symbol of the voracious head probably does not hold this meaning for the indigenous peoples. The nightjar has an enormous mouth, as if it were ripped open, and can only be associated with greed or with sex. The head is used in the story in place of sexuality. Or is the story only about the nightly erotic adventures of a wife who is well behaved during the day?

THE DEAD HUSBAND

A counterpart to the myth of the flying head might be the myth of the dead husband who reappears. This time, instead of a clingy wife, it is the husband who doesn't want to let go of his still living wife.

In the Tupari myth, the husband's already decomposed corpse returns to lie down in his wife's hammock, to take what was once his. What once was love has become a burden ("Mon amour si léger prend le poids d'un supplice," as in the poem by Paul Éluard), and the once loving wife has to try many things to get rid of her dead husband (a fitting symbolic example for widows or women who have separated from their husbands).

DEAD BEFORE DEATH

There are various instances of the dead returning to the living in this anthology. But they have various meanings, and the returning dead are not always unwelcome creatures who must go away for ever. They are pre-death.

There is a Macurap myth (not included in this anthology) in which a dead man comes back to life, but before death existed. He becomes a newborn baby again, and as his mother feeds him he slowly becomes a live adult again. He comes, as the great narrator Odete Aruá says, to teach us "who are the ones yet to be born," to avoid death. But he is despised by a cranky old woman who never stops asking him for potatoes. Every time the dead-man-child's mother goes to the field to fetch food for him, the old woman asks him for potatoes. The old woman curses him; she tells him to die for real, and ever since then death exists. The child-dead-man's mother is very sad and accompanies him to the land of the dead, but she can only stay there with him for ever when she is stung by a spider and actually dies.

PASSION AND TRANSGRESSION

It would not be an exaggeration to say that the majority of the myths have something to do with incest; and that incest is, in these stories, the realization of desire and passion; it is what brings into being agricultural products, stars, rivers, art, and creation.

The cycle of the snake, the rainbow, and genipap

The snake is an extremely important theme in regions with lots of water, great rivers, and floods. In a Macurap myth, a young woman rejects her betrothed and in punishment he turns her into a boa constrictor that lives at the bottom of a lake. Her brother visits her and she teaches him the art of painting the body with genipap dye, but she has to swallow him almost up to his neck in order to paint him – a clearly phallic image (but inverted, because she is the snake, the phallic symbol); when the brother wants to get out of his sister-snake he has to urinate inside her. The rejected fiancé, after catching his would-be brother-in-law and trying to imitate him, can't urinate and dies inside the snake. The great – but unarticulated and prohibited – love between the brother and sister produces the art of painting the body with genipap, and ends tragically. (In the Aruá version, however, the sister-snake takes the fiancé she has swallowed underwater; she forgives him and falls in love with him. They run away!)

In the Tupari version, told in *Tuparis e Tarupás*, a mother and aunt raise a boy-snake. He swallows them almost whole – first his mother and then his aunt – in order to paint them with genipap dye.

The aunt insists that the snake-nephew swallow a little more of her each time and she finally dies in his belly. The boy is heartbroken and goes away, creating rivers wherever he goes; he is the rainbow's reflection and goes to the sky, because if he stayed on the ground everything would turn to water.

This snake-boy doesn't have a father – his mother becomes pregnant with the boy and many other little snakes when she eats a hog-plum floating on the water; she lets the other baby snakes go and only keeps him. As in many other stories in *Tuparis e Tarupás*, the mother and son end up happily alone together.

The incestuous love in this myth is between generations, and it is the aunt, not the mother (but almost a mother, because she is the mother's sister, and among the Tupari has the same status), who is completely swallowed, in an image of sexual fulfillment.

The moon

In another group of myths, genipap and incest are related. Genipap painted on a brother's face as a sign of incest is widespread in the Amazon. In the Suruí myth, transcribed in *The Unwritten Stories of the Suruí*, a girl in seclusion menstruating for the first time receives a lover every night, without knowing who he is. The girl's mother suggests she paint her visitor's face with genipap, and so she finds out that her lover is her own brother. The brother is ashamed and goes away to the sky and turns into the moon; the dark side of the moon is the genipap stain.

With small or sometimes major variations, this myth is told throughout the region: among the Gavião, Arara, Macurap, Tupari, Jabuti, Ajuru, and Aruá, as well as among many other groups such as the Kaxinauá, Taulipang, etc. (Campbell [1969] mentions a similar myth in Austria, where the transgressing brother is painted with charcoal.)

It is curious that genipap should be both art and the clear demarcation of what is prohibited – like the scars registering passage through the various stages of life, rules of behavior, or torture inscribed on the body, as Clastres writes about in *Society Against the State* (1987).

Frequently, as Lévi-Strauss insists, the planets, the moon, the sun, and stars are created because of human behavior, especially as a consequence of incest. The rainbow, and color, paint, art, and snakes, as well as genipap, unite incest with visible phenomena in the heavens.

The cycle of mothers who are crazy about honey, and again, the rainbow

The rainbow with its multicolored magic, and the sweetness of honey, are attributed, in a huge number of myths from the region, to the incestuous closeness between mother and son. They form the impulse for the founding of a new social order (the Macurap and Jabuti who speak Portuguese mention "o mundo novo," the new world), and the appearance of agricultural products and animals hitherto unknown, such as corn, peanuts, beans, tapirs, and other game animals.

The rainbow is taken for a snake, in this and other mythologies; we think for example, of Oxumaré, the African *orixá* (an African divinity). Some narrators say that the colors of a boa constrictor lying in the sun are just like the colors of the rainbow. And so, it is as if we were continuing the voyage through the genipap/snake cycle, the stories changing from one people to another.

One of the most beautiful Suruí myths, the first in *The Unwritten Stories of the Suruí*, is about a girl who, before reaching puberty, becomes pregnant when she touches an ant-bird's egg. Her son, still in her womb, asks her to gather some red *lolongá* fruit. The girl lies down, spreads her legs, and her son comes out in the form of a rainbow. He goes high up in the tree and knocks lots of fruit down to the ground. One day, the girl's and her son's relatives come upon them unawares and cut the rainbow. The son goes away to the sky, but a piece of him stays behind in the pregnant girl. This piece of rainbow teaches the men to plant corn. The unmarried women go looking for the corn, wind up lost in the fields, and turn into doves.

In another version, a mother – who has no husband – and her son take advantage of the solitude of the jungle. Although they are breaking the law, they are productive – they pick the *lolongá*, a very juicy, lusty fruit, and create corn and the rainbow.

This myth exists, in slightly different form each time, among other Tupi peoples in Rondônia: Gavião, Zoró, Arara, and Campé. Sometimes the rainbow is simply a snake, as in many Xingu versions, like the Kamaiurá and Mehinaku versions.

The Gavião (a Tupi-mondé people like the Suruí) version is very similar to the Suruí version. The Arara (who speak a Tupi language of the Ramarama family) version is more frightening and less erotic. The young woman is married to an old man, already has children, and becomes pregnant without knowing how. She is terrified when she discovers that she is carrying a snake inside her that comes and goes out of her womb as he pleases. On one of the snake's trips outside, he is killed by the young woman's brother and other relatives. The next day, the villagers discover that each piece of the dead snake gives birth to a person: this is the origin of white people – of non-Indians. The new race of people call to the young woman – their mother – but she refuses to go to them; she breaks the presents they have given her; she rejects her new children and later on they kill her. (Among the Mehinaku, in a myth told by Gregor (1985), the pieces of the dead snake, killed by the mother's sister, create the Suyá people; in the Kamaiurá version, told by Junqueira and Samain, the dead snake pieces become the Suyá and other peoples.) In *Diários índios* (1996, "Indian Diaries"), Darcy Ribeiro presents us with a beautiful Urubu-Kaapor version of a girl who is pregnant with a snake baby.

In the Jabuti myth (similar to the Aruá and Macurap versions), a wife is inexplicably eight months pregnant, even though she has just given birth. She asks her husband to gather some honey, but he thinks she has betrayed him because she is pregnant again so soon. The husband makes a magical gesture and his wife's hand gets stuck in the honey tree. Even though she is trapped, the woman still manages to give birth to a magical son who grows up overnight. The boy fetches water and tries to protect his mother and himself from the vultures that hover around them – but his mother dies. Later on, the lover/protector son becomes a demiurge who brings men peanuts and game animals from the sky. He takes revenge for his mother and kills his father.

In the Tupari version, told in *Tuparis e Tarupás*, the demiurge Arekuaion has two wives. He favors his younger wife, with whom he has no children, and despises Naoretá, the mother of his children. When Arekuaion gets honey for the family, however much Naoretá pleads with him to give honey to their children, he only gives it to his young wife. To punish Naoretá's greed, Arekuaion traps her arm in a beehive full of honey and turns her into a waterfall. Naoretá's children find out what really happened and set her free. The children start to hate their father, but Naoretá forgives him.

These mothers who are crazy about honey, who are too close to their small children, substituting them for their husbands (the children are babies who grow very quickly and in two days become ideal protectors), evoke another type of excess, of love or greed, that also appears in the myths of the young girl who is crazy about honey, told by Lévi-Strauss in *From Honey to Ashes* (1973).

Lévi-Strauss reminds us that the sweetness of honey has the special characteristic that one doesn't know whether it is tasty or whether it burns – like love. The Indians always associate expeditions to get honey with romantic adventure.

The immoderate mothers, just like the young women in the cycle of honey, or the greedy and clingy women in the flying head stories, want what society prohibits them from having. As the women confront this challenge, they unleash processes of creation and originate other stories. Just like the Virgin Mary, these women have miraculous sons who bring news to the world.

But the theme cycles and commentaries, although they may aspire to guide us through the myths, also have no end and turn into other stories. It is better to stick with the narratives themselves.

Bibliography

ABREU, J. (1941) Capistrano de. *Rã-txa hu-ni-ku-i*. Rio de Janeiro, Livraria Briguiet.

AGOSTINHO, Pedro. (1974) *Kwaríp. Mito e ritual no Alto Xingu*. São Paulo, EDUSP.

ANDRADE, Mário de. (1988) *Macunaíma, o herói sem nenhum caráter*. Edição Crítica, Telê Ancona Lopez, coordenadora. Trindade, Florianópolis, Editora da UFSC, Coleção Arquivos. (*Macunaíma, the Hero with No Character*. New York, Random House, 1984, translated by E.A. Goodland).

BARTHES, R. (1973) *Le Plaisir du texte*. Paris, Seuil. (*The Pleasure of the Text*. New York, Hill and Wang, 1975, translated by Richard Miller).

—— et al. (1977) *Poétique du récit*. Paris, Seuil.

BASSO, Ellen. (1985) *A Musical View of the Universe*. Philadelphia, University of Pennsylvania Press.

BASTIDE, Roger. (1961) *O Candomblé da Bahia*. São Paulo, Companhia Editora Nacional, Brasiliana 313.

—— (1971) *As religiões africanas no Brasil*. São Paolo, Pioneira/EDUSP. (The African Religions of Brazil. Baltimore, Johns Hopkins University Press, 1978, translated by Helen Sebba.)

BECKFORD, William. (1929) *Vathek*. London, Nonesuch Press.

BETTELHEIM, Charles. (1978) *A psicanálise dos contos de fadas*. Rio de Janeiro, Paz e Terra

BRINGHURST, Robert and REID, Bill. (1988) *The raven steals the light*. Vancouver, University of Washington Press.

CABRERA, Lydia. (1992) *El Monte*. Miami, Ediciones Universal.

CADOGAN, León and AUSTIN, A. López. (1965) *La literatura de los Guaraníes*. Mexico, Joaquin Mortiz.

CALVINO, Italo. (1993) *Fiabe italiane*. Milan, Mondadori. (*Italian Folktales*. New York, Harcourt Brace Jovanovich, 1980, translated by George Martin.)

CAMPBELL, Joseph. (1969) *The Masks of God. Primitive Mythology*. New York, Viking.

CASPAR, Franz. (1953) "Some Sex Beliefs and Practices of the Tupari Indians." In *Revista do Museu Paulista*, vol. 7, pp, 204–44, São Paulo.

——(1957) "A aculturação da tribo Tupari." In *Revista de Antropologia*, vol. 5 (2), pp 145-71, São Paulo.

—— (1958) "Puberty Rites among the Tupari Indians." In *Revista do Museu Paulista*, vol. 10, pp. 143–54. São Paulo.

——(1975) *Die Tupari*. Berlin and NewYork, Walter de Gruyter.

CHASE-SARDI, Miguel. (1981) *Pequeño Decameron Nivacle*. Asunción, Napa.

CLASTRES, Pierre. (1972) *Chronique des indiens Guayaki*. Paris, Plon. (*Chronicle of the Guayaki Indians*. New York, Zone Books, 1998, translated by Paul Auster.)

—— (1978) *A sociedade contra o Estado*. São Paulo, Francisco Alves. (*Society Against the State*. New York, Zone Books, Cambridge Mass., distributed by MIT Press, 1987, translated by Robert Hurley and Abe Stein.)

—— (1974) *Le Grand Parler. Mythes et chants sacrés des Indiens Guarani*. Paris, Editions du Seuil.

D'ANS, André Marcel. (1979) *Le Dit des vrais hommes*. Paris, Union Générale d'Éditions, 1018.

ELIADE, Mircea. (1960) *El chamanismo*. Mexico, Fondo de Cultura Económica. (*Shamanism*. New York, Bollingen Foundation, distributed by Pantheon Books, 1964, translated from French by Willard R. Trask.)

——(1972) *Mito e realidade*. São Paulo, Perspectiva. (*Myth and Reality*, Waveland Press, 1998).

FRANZ, Marie-Louise von. (1970) *Interpretation of Fairytales*. New York, Spring Publications, 1970.

FROBENIUS (1971) *African Nights. Black Erotic Folktales*. New York, Herder and Herder.

GALLOIS, Dominique T. (1986) *Migração, guerra e comércio: os Waiapi na Guiana*. São Paulo, FFLCH-USP.

GARIBAY K. and ANGEL M. (1964) *La literatura de los Aztecas*. Mexico, Joaquin Mortiz. (The Literature of the Aztecs, Mexico, 1996.)

GREGOR, Thomas. (1985) *Anxious Pleasures, the Sexual Lives of an Amazonian People*. Chicago, University of Chicago Press, 1985.

GRENAND, Françoise. (1982) *Et l'homme devint jaguar*. Paris, L'Harmattan.

HEARN, Lafcadio. (1921) *Kwaidan*. Tokyo, The "Ars" Bookshop.

——(1922) *In Ghostly Japan*. Boston, Little, Brown. [*c.* 1899].

HIRSCH, John. (1975) *The Dybbuk*. Winnipeg, Pequis Publishers.

JUNQUEIRA, Carmen. (1979) *Os Índios de Ipavu*. São Paulo, Ática.

KOCH-GRÜNBERG. (1979) *Del Roraima al Orinoco*. Caracas, Banco Central de Venezuela, 3 vols.

KUMU, Umúsin Panlõn and KENHÍRI, Tolamãn. (1980) *Antes o mundo não existia*. São Paulo, Cultura. Introduction by Berta G. Ribeiro.

LEÓN-PORTILLA, Miguel. (1964) *El reverso de la conquista*. Mexico, Joaquin Mortiz.

LÉVI-STRAUSS, Claude. (1964) *Le Cru et le cuit*. Paris, Plon. (*The Raw and the Cooked*. New York, Harper & Row, 1969, translated by John and Doreen Weightman.)

—— (1966) *Du miel aux cendres*. Paris, Plon. (*From Honey to Ashes*. New York, Harper & Row, 1973, translated by John and Doreen Weightman.)

—— (1968) *L'Origine des manières de table*. Paris, Plon. (The Origin of Table Manners. New York, Harper & Row, 1978, translated by John and Doreen Weightman.)

—— (1971) *L'Homme nu*. Paris, Plon. (The Naked Man. Chicago, University of Chicago Press, 1990, translated by John and Doreen Weightman.)

—— (1986) *A oleira ciumenta*. Sâo Paolo, Brasiliense. (*The Jealous Potter*. Chicago, University of Chicago Press, 1988, translated by Benedicte Chorier.)

—— (1993) *História de Lince*. São Paulo, Companhia das Letras. (The Story of the Lynx. Chicago, University of Chicago Press, 1995, translated by Catherine Tihanyi.)

—— (1986) *O olhar distanciado*. Lisbon, Edicções 70. (*The View from Afar*. New York, Basic Books, 1984, translated by Joachim Neugroschel and Phoebe Hoss.)

LEWIS, M.G. (1984) *The Monk*. London, Folio Society.

MARDRUS, J.C. (trans.). (1986) *Les mille et une nuits*. Paris, Laffont, 2 vols. (Book of the Thousand and One Nights. New York, Heritage Press, 1962, translated by Richard F. Burton.)

MÉTRAUX, Alfred. (1928) *La Réligion des Tupinambá*. Paris, Librairie Ernest Leroux.

MINDLIN, Betty. (1985) *Nós Paiter*. Petrópolis, Vozes.

—— (1993) *Tuparis e Tarupás*. São Paulo, Brasiliense/EDUSP/IAMÁ.

—— (1993) "Amor e Ruptura na Aldeia Indígena." In *Carta: falas, memórias / informe de distribuição restrita do Senador Darcy Ribeiro*. pp. 85–97.

—— (1994) "O aprendiz de origens e novidades": o professor indígena, uma experiência de escola diferenciada. In *Estudos Avançados*, 8 (20), pp. 233–53.

—— (1996) *Vozes da origem, Estórias sem escrita dos índios Suruí de Rondônia*. São Paulo, Ática/IAMÁ.

—— (1995) *Unwritten Stories of the Suruí Indians of Rondônia*. Austin, Institute of Latin American Studies (ILAS Special Publication).

—— (1996) "A cabeça voraz." In *Revista Estudos Avançados*, 10 (27); pp. 271–84, ilustrações de Adão Pinheiro.

—— (1999) *Terra Grávida*. Rio de Janeiro, Rosa dos Tempos.

—— (2001) *O primeiro homem*. São Paulo, Cosac & Naify.

—— (2001) *Couro dos espíritos*. São Paulo, SENAC/Terceiro Nome.

MURPHY, Yolanda and MURPHY, Robert F. (1974) *Women of the Forest*. New York, Columbia.

NIMUENDAJU UNKEL, Curt. (1987) *As lendas da criação e destruição do mundo*. São Paulo, Hucitec.

OLSON, D.R. and TORRANCE, N. (1991) *Literacy and Orality*. New York, Cambridge University Press.

PÉRET, Benjamin. (1960) *Anthologie des mythes, légendes et contes populaires d'Amérique*. Paris, Albin Michel.

ONG, Walter J. (1993) *Orality and Literacy. The Technologizing of the Word*. London and New York, Routledge.

PERET, João. (1979) *Mitos e lendas Karajá*. Rio de Janeiro.

POTOCKI, Jan. (1960) *The Saragossa Manuscript, a Collection of Weird Tales*. New York, Orion Press.

PROPP, Vladimir Ja. (1983) *Les Racines historiques du conte merveilleux*. Paris, Gallimard. (*Theory and History of Folklore*. Minneapolis, University of Minnesota Press, 1984, translated by Ariadna Y. Martin, Richard P. Martin and several others.)

RADIN, Paul. (1972) *The Trickster*. New York, Schocken.

——(ed.). (1983) *African Folktales*. New York, Schocken.

REICHEL-DOLMATOFF, Gerardo. (1971) *Amazonian Cosmos. The Sexual and Religious Symbolism of the Tukano Indians*. Chicago, University of Chicago Press.

RIBEIRO, Berta G. (1995) *Os índios das águas pretas*. São Paulo, Companhia das Letras/EDUSP.

RIBEIRO, Darcy. (1980) *Kadiwéu*. Petrópolis, Vozes.

——(1996) *Diários índios. Os Urubus-Kaapor*. São Paulo, Companhia das Letras.

RODRIGUES, Aryon Dall'Igna. (1986) *Línguas brasileiras*. São Paulo, Edições Loyola.

SAGUIER, Rubén Bareiro. (1980) *Literatura Guarani del Paraguay*. Biblioteca Caracas, Ayacucho.

SAMAIN, (1991) *Moronetá Kamaiurá*. Rio de Janeiro, Lidador.

SODI M., Demetrio. (1964) *La literatura de los Mayas*. Mexico, Joaquin Mortiz.

STRAND, Mark. (1971) *18 Poems from the Quechua*. Cambridge, Halty Ferguson.

VÁSQUEZ, A.B. and RENDÓN, S. (trans.) (1965) *El libro de los libros de Chilam Balam*. Mexico, Fondo de Cultura Económica.

VERGER, Pierre Fatumbi. (1954) *Dieux d'Afrique*. Paris, Hartmann.

——(1985) *Lendas africanas dos orixás*. São Paulo, Corrupio.

VERNANT, Jean-Pierre and NAQUET, Pierre Vidal. (1988) *Mito e tragédia na Grécia antiga*. São Paulo, Brasiliense. (*Myth and Tragedy in Ancient Greece*. New York, Zone Books, Cambridge, Mass., distributed by MIT Press, 1988, translated by Janet Lloyd.)

WALLACE, Anthony F.C. (1972) *Death and Rebirth of the Seneca*. New York, Vintage.

WILBERT, Johannes and SIMONEAU, Karin (ed.). (1983) *Folk Literature of the Bororo Indians*. Los Angeles, University of California.

—— (1984). *Folk Literature of the Gê Indians*. Los Angeles, University of California, 2 vols.

Profiles of the narrators and translators

JABUTI / ARIKAPU

Abobai Paturi Jabuti

Paturi is the older of two great Jabuti shaman brothers who are always together. He is perhaps eighty years old and so represents life in the jungle before colonization; he was a baby when the first employees of the rubber companies made contact with the Jabuti in their huts. He says that the visitors held him in their laps and told his mother, "This little boy will work for me when he grows up and will cut down rubber trees." He left the village when he was a young man to work in the Paulo Saldanha rubber plantation, and says that if he were paid today for all the work he did, he would be rich. He lived on the São Luís rubber plantation until he was taken by FUNAI (the former Federal Bureau for Indian Affairs) to the Guaporé Indigenous Area, around 1968.

Paturi speaks almost no Portuguese. He tells very long stories, full of life, all in his native language. Today he is a widower, is restless and walks a lot; he is looked after by his children and grandchildren.

Armando Moero Jabuti

Armando, the son of Wadjidjika and Kubahi, is a talented native teacher. He speaks both Jabuti and eloquent Portuguese, and reads and writes as well. He was born in 1970, and grew up and studied in the Guaporé Indigenous Area.

But because he married Wudkuneká Regina, daughter of Buraini and Menkaiká Macurap, he now lives in the village of Gregório, in the Rio Branco Indigenous Area, where only one other Jabuti man lives. He was born to be a chief, to lead his community along new paths in their relations to the city, but he is part of an ethnic minority. He has been my tireless collaborator in the research of native traditions, and is full of an insatiable curiosity. He helped tremendously with the recording and translations, and is at the same time an expressive storyteller in his own right. His dream is to become a shaman.

Erowé Alonso Jabuti

Alonso is Paturi's younger brother, also born in the village, before "the contact." He lost his mother at birth and was brought up here and there by other women who also died while he was still a child. He was taken as a boy by the rubber plantation managers to work at the Paulo Saldanha center. From there he also went from time to time to the São Luís rubber plantation. He says he would be rich if he had been paid for all the work he did, but at the time did not understand how he was being exploited. He only earned small amounts of food, and did not have the right to till and plant a plot for himself, or to have *chicha* feasts or parties.

While in the village on a short leave from work on the rubber plantation, he caught measles during the epidemic; he says he was saved by his uncles and by the spirits of shamans of olden times who came to him as he was about to enter on the path of souls.

His father, also Paturi's father (they had different mothers), was a shaman who lived long enough to move to São Luís, where he died, it is said, from a magic spell. Alonso followed his father's path and became a shaman while he still lived in the village.

Alonso died in 2001 – he must have been around seventy years old. He spoke an expressive Portuguese, with the grammar of those born in the jungle, making himself understood – better yet with the help of interpreters. He told stories that went on and on for ever, and was capable of speaking for days on end – in his own language as well as in Portuguese – with an urgency of immediate communication, without translation.

His name, Erowé, is the water spirit's name.

Kubahi Raimundo Jabuti

Raimundo is Armando Moero Jabuti's father. He has to take special care of his village; he cannot abandon it or its animals will fall prey to jaguars. It is called Baía das Onças (literally, Jaguar Bay), in the Guaporé Indigenous Area – a beautiful area in the middle of the jungle on the bank of a river. He was the chief of the Jabuti for many years, the title now held by his brother, Saturnino. He was born in a hut, but speaks Portuguese quite well. His elderly parents lived a long time, and from them Raimundo learned the Jabuti traditions. His mother died in 1993 and Raimundo tells how he accompanied her right to the threshold of the path of souls. He tells his stories in Jabuti.

Pacoré Nazaré Jabuti

Pacoré translates for her husband, the shaman Ajuru Pororoca. Their children, Alberto and Sérgio, speak Ajuru poorly and Jabuti well. Pacoré translates her husband's stories into Jabuti, and in turn their sons translate them into Portuguese. Pacoré was born in a hut and went to São Luís as a little girl, while her family remained in the village. Her mother died young, before the measles came, and her father died in the great epidemic. She says she caught the measles but miraculously survived. Pacoré is a beautiful woman, probably seventy years old or more, and displays a seductive grace around her husband.

Wadjidjika Nazaré Arikapu

Nazaré was born in the jungle, in the round hut of the Arikapu. When she was very young she started a new life in the rubber plantations of Paulo

Saldanha, where her mother died. Her father was a Jabuti shaman. She is a cheerful girl-like matriarch, and displays a constant vivacity and happiness. She told (and sang) stories in Jabuti, in Arikapu, and in Portuguese, describing old-time customs and rituals from her varied repertoire, spinning her tales while working constantly.

AJURU

Alberto Ajuru

Son of Galib Pororoca Ajuru and Marina Jabuti, he translated from Ajuru to Portuguese.

Aperadjakob Antonio Ajuru

One of three Ajuru shamans in the Guaporé Indigenous Area who arrived in 1985, after being expelled from their non-demarcated land, close to Rolim de Moura, in Serrito. They reunited in Guaporé with other relatives already living there, such as Galib Pororoca. They know a great deal about Ajuru history, but speak very little Portuguese; there was no one who could adequately translate their stories, because most of their children speak almost no Ajuru.

Galib Pororoca Gurib Ajuru

One of the three highly respected Ajuru shamans. Today he is paralyzed, but continues to perform ritual blessings. He doesn't speak Portuguese, is quite deaf, but loves to tell stories, squatting on his shaman's stool. He was born in an Ajuru hut, in the region of the Mequens River, near Rolim de Moura, Serrito – from where the two other shamans, Antonio and Durafogo, were expelled in 1985. Like everyone else, he left the village to work in the rubber plantations. He worked on the Terebinto plantation, then moved to São Luís, where his sons, Sérgio and Alberto, were born. His other three children were born when he already lived in Guaporé, in the 1970s.

Sérgio Ajuru

Son of Galib Pororoca Gurib Ajuru and Marina Jabuti, he translated to the Portuguese from the Jabuti.

ARUÁ

Awünaru Odete Aruá

A great orator and storyteller who possesses all the qualities of a chief: Awünaru is extremely intelligent, charming, and welcoming. Although still young, he is the last keeper of the memory of his language and tradition. His father, João Chapchap Aruá, was a great shaman, but died in 1990. Today there are very few older Aruá who still speak the language: five in the Guaporé Indigenous Area, and only one, Anísio Aruá, living in the Rio Branco Indigenous Area. The younger generation, who because they have Aruá fathers are considered part of the Aruá group, are all children of mixed marriages – Aruá with Jabuti or Macurap – and not one speaks the Aruá native language.

Even among the older Aruá, only Awünaru Odete remembers the stories well and tells them to the children, in a creative and lively Portuguese.

Awünaru was born in the Rio Branco Indigenous Area in 1957 and left for the Guaporé Indigenous Area in 1973. During a certain period he participated in many indigenous meetings in the city, and was always thoughtful and convincing – a respected leader. But by 1995, it had been some time since he had left the village, and he returned home to work in the fields, concentrating on feeding his and Teresa's (daughter of Abobai Jabuti) eight children.

The walls of Awünaru's hut were covered with newspaper clippings and political notices. He is well informed and reads and writes Portuguese well. He told stories for days on end in a warm, welcoming manner, always with one of his children by his side – a listener who might participate and express his doubts at the just the right time. He was always asking, "Do you think people will like my stories? Is there anyone who could tell so many, and so well as I?"

His way of telling stories is virtually unchanged in my written rendition.

MACURAP

Aienuiká Rosalina Aruá

Aienuiká is the daughter of Wariteroká Rosa Macurap and Anísio Aruá, and is beautiful like her mother. She speaks Macurap well (but not Aruá) and knows lots of stories; she both told stories and helped with the translations. She is married to Naru Fernando Kanoé, a teacher in the village of São Luís, who had already written down some of the Macurap stories she had told him.

Aiawid Waldemir Macurap

Son of Amampeküb and Iniká Isabel, Waldemir helped with the translations.

Alcides Macurap

Translated various stories told by Iaxuí Miton Pedro Mutum Macurap, and following his wife Ewiri's example, as often as he could, was part of a small group of enthusiastic listeners in the Guaporé Indigenous Area Center.

Amampeküb Aningui Basílio Macurap

Nicknamed Niika or Aningui, he must be between sixty and seventy years old. Today he lives in the Rio Branco Indigenous Area, after having spent some time in the Mequens Indigenous Area. He was the first to tell me some of the long Macurap stories, in his native language, along with his wife Iniká Isabel (who is older than him); their son Waldemir translated the stories into Portuguese.

Aroteri Teresa Macurap

Doroidom's inconsolable widow, Sawerô Basílio Macurap's mother, and Meinkaiká Juraci Macurap's stepmother. Aroteri lives in Baía das Onças, in the Guaporé Indigenous Area. She told stories in Macurap – translated by Sawerô – while weeping with longing for her dead husband.

Biweiniká Atiré Macurap

Translated her mother's (Überiká Sapé, whom she closely resembles) stories with pleasure and charm.

Buraini Andere Macurap

A wonderful storyteller, he is the son of the famous Andere Macurap who in the 1930s led the enslaved Indians in a revolt against the cruelty of the rubber bosses, killing foremen and settlers who lived on their land. Buraini was born in his parents' hut in the jungle, probably around 1940. His mother died shortly after he was born, it is said from a magic spell; his father died later from measles. He knows all of Macurap history, and it is to him that the Macurap owe the fact that their current homeland in Gregório, their traditional land, was preserved. The SPI (Serviço de Proteção aos Índios, Federal Agency for the Protection of Indians (1910–67)) as well as FUNAI (Fundação Nacional do Índio, Federal Bureau for Indian Affairs (until the seventies)) constantly tried to move them from there to the Guaporé River, to free their land for occupation by rubber plantations. Some families gave in, but Buraini Andere refused.

Ewiri Margarida Macurap

Translated a large number of the stories told by Iaxuí Miton Pedro Mutum Macurap into a very beautiful Portuguese, always with a child at her breast and with tremendous patience.

Graciliano Macurap

Son of Buraini and Meinkaiká, Graciliano lives in the Guaporé Indigenous Area, and helped with the translations.

Iaxuí Miton Pedro Mutum Macurap

Mutum was born before "the contact" in a Macurap hut, perhaps between 1925 and 1930. He was about ten years old when he was taken to work on the rubber plantations. When the anthropologist Franz Caspar visited Rio Branco, the Macurap had already left their village and were living in São Luís. Mutum guided Caspar to the Tupari village. He was still young and wasn't yet a shaman; perhaps he never completed his apprenticeship as a shaman, because he doesn't take *rapé* (snuff) and I have never seen him participate in a healing ceremony. He is, however, one of the most respected Macurap in terms of his knowledge, and freely describes creation and the world of souls. His skin is tanned and leathery from hard work in the fields in the hot sun; it is pitted all over as if he had had smallpox, and the skin on his arms sheds like a snake's – an attribute, according to Odete, of one of the mythical Aruá demiurges. Mutum speaks very little Portuguese; all of his very beautiful stories were told in Macurap, for days and nights on end, translated on the spot by various people.

Menkaiká Juraci Macurap

Menkaiká and her husband, Buraini Andere, are tireless standard-bearers for Macurap culture, insisting on preserving their language and customs. At every party, and whenever people get together to sing, Menkaiká and Buraini mourn the passing of an era, of an ancient vision that only they and a handful of others (mostly between fifty and seventy years old) still retain today. Menkaiká is the daughter of Doroidom Wenceslau, who died in 1994. She was born in São Luís perhaps around 1940, already in the era of slavery on the rubber plantations. After her mother died of measles Menkaiká was brought up far away from her father by her oldest sister, both in the distant settlements of Rio Branco and in Colorado. When she moved to Laranjal to work as a cook for the Indians' bosses, she met some old Macurap women who were her cousins. They taught her how to speak her mother's language well and she regained her identity as a Macurap woman who takes great pride in her origins. The wife of the owner of the rubber plantation, Rivoredo (who was also, at the same time, a functionary of the SPI), wanted to send Menkaiká to Minas Gerais to work as a maid in the city. But Doroidom, her father, wouldn't let her go and sent for her to go to São Luís; she rediscovered her father, who she thought had died of measles. She soon married Buraini Andere and they had seven children; now they have many grandchildren, some of whom they raised themselves. She got to know her father-in-law Andere Macurap's hut before it disappeared.

Niendeded João Macurap

One of the Macurap chiefs, who helped with various translations.

Rosilda Aruá

Rosilda is another of Rosa and Anísio's daughters, is married to Rui Kanoé, and lives in the headquarters of the Guaporé Indigenous Area. She speaks both Macurap and Portuguese and translates with ease and grace.

Sawerô Basílio Macurap

Son of Doroidom and Aroteri Macurap, Sawerô lives in a small settlement near Baía das Onças, in the Guaporé Indigenous Area. He helped his mother tell her stories and translated them into Portuguese, adding his own versions as well.

Überiká Sapé Macurap

The oldest of the Macurap, widow of Marripe, a famous Macurap singer (whom I met, but unfortunately never had the chance to record). Überiká was the first to open the Macurap world to me, recounting the beautiful mythology of her people for me in her native language, translated by her daughter, who must have been twelve years younger than she was. She lived in Manduca, a settlement in the Rio Branco Indigenous Area, next to Palhal, Etxowe Tupari's village, in the Biological Reserve of Guaporé. She died in 2001.

Wariteroká Rosa Macurap

Daughter of the late Alfredo Dias Macurap, who told me several stories in São Luís, and the late Madalena Aruá, whom I also knew. She grew up on the São Luís rubber plantation and heard many stories from not only the older Macurap, but also the Aruá, and the old man Chapchap, in the era of slave labor. She knows a great deal, teaches her children, and loves to talk. She is gentle, tall, thin, and pretty, and has an elegant bearing, although she considers herself old. She is married to Anísio Aruá, and lives in the São Luís settlement, now the FUNAI outpost.

TUPARI

Etxowe Etelvina Tupari

She lives in the last existing village on the Branco River, in the middle of the Biological Preserve of Guaporé, some distance down the Branco River, almost where it meets the Guaporé River. We can calculate that she was born in 1936, according to the censuses done by Caspar, and therefore reached adulthood and married before living on the rubber plantation. These days she seems like an adolescent, always happy and skipping around, shaking her head and hair in the wind. Her repertoire is impressive – she let loose with a flood of stories about women, and every time Moam started to tell a story in his halting Portuguese, Etxowe took over in her more expressive Portuguese.

Isaías Tarimã Tupari

A talented native teacher. He had never had any formal education when he came to the bilingual courses first given by IAMÁ (Institute for Anthropology and the Environment, a non-profit, non-government-affiliated organization) in 1992. He has been working steadily and productively as a teacher since 1993, and is one of the main creators of written Tupari; he has been doing research on the narratives, experimenting with recording and writing the myths in his native language as well as Portuguese. He was born in 1967 in the Laranjal settlement, today the Biological Preserve of Guaporé. He is the son of the late Maindjuari Biguá Tupari, who, together with Konkuat Antonio Tupari was one of the chief narrators of *Tuparis and Tarupás*.

Kabátoa Tupari

Daughter of shaman Waitó, grand master of the anthropologist Franz Caspar in 1948, Kabátoa was born in 1938, and is two years younger than her brother Konkuat. Kabátoa represents the older generation of women and is talkative and cheerful in spite of the tragedies she has lived through. She likes to joke and knows many stories that she learned from her father. Unlike Konkuat, who speaks beautiful Portuguese, she really only speaks her native language; Tarimã and others translated for her. She is married to José Tiraí Tupari, who is almost the same age as she is, and since 1995 considers himself an apprentice shaman, participating in numerous *rapé* sessions.

Moam Luís Tupari

Etxowe's husband, quite a bit older than she, was born in 1926, according to data provided by Caspar. He began his apprenticeship to become a shaman as a young man, before "contact", and used to take *rapé* and heal people. He used to say, however, that when his uncle, the great shaman Waitó, died in 1955, he had not completed certain important steps to become a full-fledged shaman; he did not consider himself to be a real doctor like the shaman Iubé Tupari, who was born in 1918 and had already become a shaman when "the contact" was made, or like Mamoa Arikapu, to whom, incidentally, he bore a great physical resemblance. He knew the tradition very well and told his stories in a not always understandable Portuguese, with very little in his native language. He died in 2000.

Naoretá Marlene Tupari

Etxowe's and Moam's daughter, Naoretá has her mother's good humor, in spite of the difficulty of her life. She has quite a number of children and grandchildren, is a non-Indian's widow, and provides for her children herself. She speaks Portuguese very well. She was both a narrator and translator.

The six indigenous peoples
of the narrators

AJURU, ARIKAPU, ARUÁ, JABUTI, MACURAP, TUPARI

The narrators of the stories in this anthology belong to six different peoples who live in Rondônia, near Brazil's border of Bolivia, in the Rio Branco and Guaporé Indigenous Areas. In 1995, there were approximately 350 people living in the Rio Branco Indigenous Area, and somewhat fewer than four hundred in the Guaporé Indigenous Area. Our best source of information about the history and first contact of these peoples with non-Indians comes from Swiss anthropologist Franz Caspar, who visited them in 1948, and again in 1955, finding the Tupari still living in their huts.

The Macurap were the first to be contacted by the colonizers, and were already working in conditions of semi-slavery on the rubber plantations (such as the Paulo Saldanha plantation, mentioned by many narrators) in the 1920s, under the regime of the rubber barons. At the time of Caspar's visits, the Arikapu, Jabuti, Aruá, Tupari, and some Macurap still lived in their huts, working sporadically on the rubber plantations to acquire knives, clothes, and various objects made of metal. At the end of the 1940s, the SPI enticed these peoples to leave their native lands and villages to work as near-slaves on the São Luís rubber plantation, which is today one of the larger villages in the Rio Branco Indigenous Area. Shortly after moving from their huts, they were stricken by an epidemic of measles that killed three hundred to four hundred people in just a few days. The Arikapu and Aruá were nearly wiped out, and the Jabuti, Tupari, and Macurap were reduced to very small populations.

The SPI moved many of the survivors to the Ricardo Franco outpost, on the banks of the Guaporé River on the Bolivian border – in the area now demarcated as the Guaporé Indigenous Area. However, the large majority of Macurap and Tupari continued on in the São Luís rubber plantation and in other settlements along the Branco River (a tributary of the Guaporé River). Like the Cajuí, Colorado, and Laranjal, they worked for the rubber barons exploiting lands that, in truth, belonged to them.

In the 1970s, the FUNAI tried to move everyone from the Rio Branco settlements to the Guaporé area, to avoid the difficult task of demarcating the Rio Branco area. Fortunately, many Macurap – like Andere – and many Tupari – like Konkuat – refused to go; otherwise they would have lost their lands around the Branco River, which were demarcated in the 1980s. In 1985, once their land had been demarcated, the Tupari and Macurap forced the rubber plantation (that had invaded the Rio Branco Indigenous Area since the time of the SPI) and its workers to leave. It was an impressive event: the Indians united and forcibly but non-violently moved the rubber workers and their families one by one. The workers were humble people, indifferent to which plantation they worked on, and had little motive to resist. Since then, the Indians have become the true owners of their land.

The territory of the Tupari, Jabuti, and Arikapu – from which they were removed and brought to São Luís – is farther towards the east, but the traditional lands of the Macurap and Aruá were exactly where the São Luís rubber plantation was erected: a tragic site for all of these peoples. The Ajuru, as well as the Kampé, come from the regions around the Mequens and Colorado rivers, near today's city of Rolim de Moura. The Kanoé come from near the Tanaru River, also near the Mequens River. No Kampé narratives appear in this volume, and there is no longer anyone who tells them; fragments of some Kampé stories were published in my *Tuparis e Tarupás*.

This is a very brief outline of the story that explains the current mixture of peoples and languages in the Guaporé and Rio Branco Indigenous Areas. The

Guaporé Area was opened, around 1935, to receive the remnants of the populations of the villages that had been destroyed in the region. Among the narrators of this book, Francisco Kanoé was one of the first to be transported there. Later on, many Arikapu and Jabuti arrived; later still, the Aruá and Ajuru.

Today, all of these peoples have an important, if still limited, relationship with the urban world. Until 1985 – when the illegal exploitation of wood, mahogany in particular, began in the Indigenous Area – the inhabitants of the Rio Branco Indigenous Area rarely left their villages. Despite the many years since their first contact with the outside world, the Indians' isolation – in the rubber settlements in the forest – was great. Many, especially women, spoke little Portuguese. Today, they are entering the market economy and travel frequently to nearby cities, such as Ji-Paraná, Alta Floresta, and others. They sell rubber, handicrafts, and flour; they buy food, clothes, and ammunition. Fortunately food in the region is still abundant. The major effort toward the preservation of the Indians' traditions, since 1991, is the multicultural, multilingual development work done by indigenous teachers, teaching literacy and other subjects in the various native languages as well as Portuguese, organized by IAMÁ, the Institute for Anthropology and the Environment, a non-profit, non-government-affiliated organization, until 1996, and by the government educational agencies since 1998.

The situation is similar in the Guaporé Indigenous Area. The main difference is the absence of the exploitation of timber. There is no mahogany in the region, and transport to the nearest cities – Guajará-Mirim and Costa Marques, both on the Bolivian border – is only by river and quite difficult.

The narrators' languages

Tupari, Macurap, and Ajuru are all languages of the same Tupari family of the Tupi trunk, as are Sakirabiar and Kampé. There is a strong concentration of Tupi languages in the region. (Arara belongs to a family of the Tupi trunk called Rama-rama. Gavião, together with Suruí, Aruá, Zoró, and Cinta-larga, belongs to the Tupi-mondé family.) Jabuti and Arikapu are isolated languages.

There may be around 180 people who speak Tupari, seventy who speak Macurap, and fifty who speak Jabuti (but these are rough estimates). The three languages are very much alive, and there are many Macurap who live outside of the Indigenous Areas. There are no more than five people who speak Aruá, no more than seven who speak Ajuru, four older people who speak Arikapu, two or three who speak Kampé, and only one who speaks Kanoé (other than isolated Indians who have recently been discovered). The situation is very different in the Arara/Tupi-mondé cultural area. Arara is spoken by almost two hundred people, Suruí by almost seven hundred, Gavião by 450, Zoró by 350, and Cinta-larga by approximately eight hundred people. Written versions of the indigenous languages are being developed only for groups that number at least fifty people.

The language and style of the narratives

I took greater liberty in the writing of the myths in this anthology than in my previous works from the same region, *The Unwritten Stories of the Suruí* and *Tuparis and Tarupás*.

The Suruí book required a great deal of translation work: I recorded the stories in the native language, then came the long laborious task of transcribing the recordings (creating a phonetic Suruí); later the stories were translated into Portuguese with the help of interpreters and making use of my own knowledge of the Suruí language. Other translations are possible using the original recordings and transcriptions, and I hope that the work will be done by many people, with other narrators telling the same stories. Clearly, the written style reflects my own way of writing, and there is often a kind of cultural translation, necessary to familiarize the reader with various aspects of indigenous life. I also tried, as much as possible with my limited ability, to give the stories a literary rather than literal rendering – while remaining faithful to the original text.

The Tupari book was a very different experience, based on a shorter research period, with fewer field trips. I didn't speak the language, and the narrators spoke Portuguese very well. In addition, I was unable to record some of the stories and recreated them from notes. The book was written with the intention to preserve the style and the tasteful Portuguese of the narrators.

In the present volume, I was carried along by still different circumstances.

I worked with peoples speaking twelve different languages (some of these peoples are not represented in this book, such as the Suruí, Kampé, Gavião, Kanoé, Zoró, and Arara), and was solicited to listen to a great number of narratives. My research flowed along like waters in a flood and I recorded perhaps three hundred hours of narratives, almost always in the indigenous languages.

The translations were done, not word for word, following transcriptions of the language – as in the case of the Suruí – but by interpreters, generally people with great creative and expressive gifts, who listened to the narratives along with me (also by others, listening to the tapes a second and third time). In the writing of the stories, I took into account the narrators' and translators' style and language (Portuguese), along with my own imagination, to try to portray the atmosphere and environment of the myths. Some of the stories are therefore, to a certain extent, re-creations in the way they are written; I remained faithful, however, to the original content without inventing material. I experimented with many different ways of writing the myths and I tried to recreate the enchantment I felt when listening to the narrators tell their stories. I also tried to use everything I know, rather than restrict myself to a written language that does not yet exist. This does not mean that I did not remain faithful to both the form and content – I didn't make anything up, but I followed a mood.

A narrator may tell several different versions of a story, and of course other narrators tell still other versions. I chose one version of each story, being careful not to mix or alter the plots, aware that apparently inconsequential details can be crucial. On a couple of occasions, however, I did blend the variations when the content was very similar.

When several narrators contributed important pieces to a particular story, their names appear in the credits. But even when the name of only one narrator appears, I owe my comprehension of the story to various narrators – they are all authors, each with his/her own style. It is a communal effort by many storytellers.

A small number of the stories were told in Portuguese. This is the case for the Aruá stories, because the only narrator, Awünaru Odete Aruá, can of course tell the stories in his own language, but also speaks perfect Portuguese. He preferred to tell the stories directly in Portuguese, and I tried to communicate his style without interfering. Erowé Alonso Jabuti, although less fluent than Odete, was very creative, and also wanted to relate a large part of his repertoire in Portuguese. Most of the Tupari told their stories in Portuguese (which they have mastered quite well).

It is my hope, as in the case of my previous works, that these stories will be translated again and again, using the recordings I made in the various languages as a base, or making and using new recordings. I have preserved the recordings and translations of each narrative and of each narrator, and my documentation is a type of museum or archive for Indians or other researchers. The whole book can be rewritten by Indians or by others.

Translator's note:
sex and translation

COMPARING ENGLISH, PORTUGUESE, AND THE INDIGENOUS LANGUAGES

In Portuguese, the verb *comer*, "to eat," can also mean to have sex. Although the expression is not particularly pleasant or romantic, it is very common for men to say that they "eat" their women (it is almost never used by women referring to men). This mixture of orality, gluttony, eating, and sex is fundamental to the book, starting with the title, *Barbecued Husbands* (*Moqueca de Maridos*); the women literally eat their husbands, but in the figurative sense they are making love. Myths like "The Flying Head," "The Greedy Wife," and myths about flesh eating, such as "Djapé, the Arrow Head, the Man Who Ate His Wives," confirm the fine lines that separate the erotic appetite, lust for food, and sensuality.

Eroticism and gluttony are mingled in the indigenous languages as well. One of the words for wife, in many of the languages, could be translated as my-daily-meal.

This double meaning does not exist in English (although "to eat" is common slang for cunnilingus, it is not in general usage for coitus). This gives us food for thought about the relationship, the proximity or distance, between the worlds of the body and of the soul as they exist in each society.

Glossary

MACURAP

akaké: penis sheath or case

Akaké: mythical character, the husband with three penises

Akarandek: the Flying Head, a mythical character

Amatxutxé: an underwater being, the seducer of the women in the story of the Rainbow

arembô: a kind of monkey

Ateab: name of the unlucky hunter

awandá: boa constrictor

awatô: grandpa

baratxüxá: rattlesnake

Boariped, Mboapiped: chief, name of a chief

botxatô: rainbow, also snake

Botxatoniã: People of the Rainbow

Djokaid: name of the *Caburé*'s wife's lover

dowari: spirits of the dead, souls

Iarekô: name of the boy who made love to his mother-in-law without realizing

kaledjaa: phantom, ghost

Kaledjaa-Ipeb: mythical black women, spirit women living without men

Katxuréu: mythical character, name of the old woman who devoured men

kawaimã: transgression, crime

koman: a species of frog; a mythical song of the old woman, Katxuréu, women's song

kupiporô: rabbit

nhã: mommy

omeré: vocative for husband

páapap: species of frog

Paiawi: Iarekô's wife, the girl whose mother stole her husband

Peniom: name of the boy who married the *tocororô* bird

Pibei: name of the lucky hunter

Piribubid: name of the winds' sister, mythical character in the story of Akaké

piron: a type of tinamou

Pitigboré: Cold Man, a mythical character
popoa: pygmy owl (*caburé* in Portuguese)
socó: heron
tocororô: a kind of bird
txadpunpurim: vine snake
txaniá: pussy, vagina
Txopokod: spirit, phantom, ghost, threatening being
Uri: the Moon, the boy who turned into the moon
wakotutxé piõ: a type of bird
Watxuri: name of the old man who became the Morning Star or the Pleiades

TUPARI

Akiã: the narrator Etxowe's great-grandmother, mutilated by the Pawatü
Arekuainonsin: name of a warrior guest of the Tupari
cao-cao: a type of bird
epaitsit: spirits of the dead, walking, wandering souls – dangerous to the living – that don't go
    to Patopkiã, the land of the dead
Haüwud: name of the head hunter
Huari: name of a Tupari shaman
Kempãi: mythical old woman with only one breast
Kenkat: a large snake
Kiribô: a Pawatü chief
Koiaküb: name of a warrior guest of the Tupari
Moroiá: Piripidpit's cruel fiancé
pabit: souls, spirits of the dead
Paküa: name of a dead Tupari warrior
Patopkiã: land of the dead
Pawatü: mythical people, or real enemy of the Tupari, spirits
Piripidpit: name of a girl who didn't want to marry her betrothed
punhakam: a kind of grass
tamará: a straw loincloth
Tampot: the man with the long cock
Tarupá: spirit, phantom, ghost, threatening being; the white man
Tereü: the warrior Paküa's already dead wife
Tianoá: mythical monster/nighthawk
Waledjat and Wap: the two friends or demiurge brothers, mythical characters, whose story is
    narrated in *Tuparis e Tarupás*, mentioned in the final essay

AJURU

Amekô: jaguar

Amekotxewé: the jaguar father-in-law of the girl in the story of the brother and sister kidnapped by a *Wainkô*

dáb: a kind of snake

Eriá, Iguá, Iguariá: name of a people who were the Ajuru's neighbors – it means "those who live in the field"

gáptara: rattlesnake

Karuê: name of a bay in the story of the enchanted girl

mekahon: *pico-de-jaca*, a kind of snake

Kubiotxi: name of the gluttonous woman

Nangüeretá: the flying head, a mythical character

Pibiro: the master of the wax, a mythical being of the heavens

Pacuri: the Moon, the brother who committed incest and turned into the moon

tororô: a kind of frog

Sírio: the master of genipap, a mythical character

Wainkô: phantom, spirit, ghost, apparition

waiküb: companion

JABUTI

Bedjapziá: the master of the wasps, a mythical character

Berewekoronti: name of a cruel husband, a character

Bidjidji: a small mythical spider

curau: nighthawk

dekëkëtã: thunder

Djikontxerô: the flying head, a mythical character

henon: vocative for girl friend, female companion

heté: menstruating

hipopsihi: spirit, phantom, apparition, ghost

Hibonoti: the Old *Japó* bird, a mythical character

Kero-opeho: a mythical character who gets castrated

kunonhonká: name of a tree known in Portuguese as *pente-de-macaco* (literally monkey's comb)

Kurawatin-ine: the morning star, a mythical character, brother of Tiwawá

nekohon: *pico-de-jaca*, a kind of snake

nerutë: a little boa constrictor

Nerutë Upahë: the boy-snake, a mythical character

oné: a kind of bird

otore: lungfish (*mussu* in Portuguese)
pakuredjerui aoné: women without men that turn into birds, mythical characters
Tiwawá: the evening star
Wanoti: the jaguar of olden times, a mythical character
wirá: companion, friend, compadre

ARIKAPU

namwü hoa: women without men
pakukawá: a kind of small tinamou (*macucau* in Portuguese)
Pakukawá Djepariá: a mythical character, an old woman who turns into an undulated tinamou

ARUÁ

andap: head
Ako-son: an indigenous people mentioned by the Aruá
ariá: a sloth
awa-sá: a fish known in the region as *tamboatá*
bagapbagawa man: lightning bugs
borikáa: a resin used on arrows
djapé: arrowhead, bamboo
ewairingá!: come eat!
iñen: piranha
Membé Ai-ai: the master of the pigs, a mythical character
Palib-bô: mythical character, The One Who Was Swallowed and Then Reborn
Poá: an indigenous people mentioned by the Aruá
Serek-á: a mermaid, mother of boa constrictors, a mythical character
txapô: grass
wandsep-andap: piranhas, women's heads
wãnʒei warandé: women without men
wasa: anteater
wasa, ema piwa ongoro!: Anteater, come eat the *sapopemba* root's liver!
ʒakorobkap: a kind of fly

ENGLISH

annatto: a tropical tree which yields annatto dye; also known as anatto or arnotto
coati: a small, flesh-eating animal resembling a raccoon, but with a longer body and a long
    flexible snout

Contact, the: the first contact with white people

genip tree: a tree that yields the genipap fruit, which produces a black dye used for body painting

genipap: the fruit of the genip tree which yields a black dye used for body painting; if the dye is not washed off within a few hours it cannot be removed for several days

paca: name for various small rodents

tamarin: a marmoset that resembles a squirrel and has long silky hair

PORTUGUESE

angico: a tree with very useful wood

apuí: a type of tree whose bark discharges latex

caboclo: Indian, in regional or old Portuguese; or a person with mixed Indian and white origins

Caburé: gnome or pygmy owl

capemba: leaf of a palm tree, used as a vessel

cavalo-de-cão: also known as *marimbondo-caçador*, a common name for a kind of wasp that is widely distributed geographically and has many other names

capoeirão: a kind of deer

chicha: a fermented drink made from corn, yams, manioc, potatoes, or sweet potatoes; it owes its fermentation to raw pieces of vegetable that the women chew and throw into the soup; the Indians drink it in great quantities and vomit it up, which produces intoxication

cobra-cega: popular name (literally, blind-snake) for a limbless amphibian that lives in the ground and feeds on larvae, worms, and insects; it is also commonly known as *cobra de duas cabeças* (literally, snake with two heads); both of these common names are derived from the fact that the creature's eyes are hidden, causing it to appear blind and making it difficult to distinguish one end from the other; (there is no English name for this creature that only exists in the tropics – its Latin name is *Siphonops annulatus*)

compadre: godfather (in relation to godchild's parents)

cuatipuru: common name for any one of a number of tropical squirrels or chipmunks

embira: common name for several types of plants known for producing a strong, rope-like fiber

emboá: regional name for a dangerous little insect with many legs, similar to a centipede

FUNAI: Fundação Nacional do Índio, the Federal Bureau for Indian Affairs

gongos: the local name for a kind of edible larvae

inajá: a kind of palm tree

jabuti: land turtle (and Jabuti, the people)

jacuí: a sacred ritual flute played by Xingu peoples

jararaca: venomous snake

jatobá: a kind of tree

laranjinha: a small tree also known as *espinho-de-vintém lolongá*: a small red fruit that grows in a very high tree

macucao: undulated tinamou

mamuí: a kind of tree

mandim: a nasal pronunciation of *mandi*, common name for several varieties of Brazilian catfish which make a crying sound when they come out of the water

mangaba: edible fruit of the *mangabeira* tree, which yields latex

mangabeira: a tree that yields latex

marajá: common name given to various palm trees, or another name for *tucumã*

marico: a straw pocketbook or basket woven by the women

moqueca: either a kind of stew or roasted (barbecued) meat; the title of this book in Portuguese is *Moqueca de Maridos* (literally: *Barbecued Husbands*)

muiratinga: a kind of tree

mussu: lungfish

orixá: African divinity

ouricuri: a kind of palm tree where *gongos* live; its stalks are also used to make salt (not the same as the tree of the same name in the northeast of Brazil)

orelha-de-pau: mushrooms that grow in tree trunks, literally tree-ears

pamonha: a kind of pancake made from corn

pariri: a fruit with soft, aromatic flesh

pau-âmago: a type of tree

paxiúba-barriguda: a kind of palm tree (literally fat-bellied palm tree)

pente-de-macaco: a kind of plant (literally monkey's comb)

pico-de-jaca: a venomous snake

pinguelo: clitoris, in the north/northeast of Brazil; penis, in the south of Brazil; literally trigger

rapé: snuff – used in rituals by shamans

sapopemba: a thick root that circles the trunks of many trees in the rain forest

SPI: Serviço de Proteção aos Índios, Federal Agency for the Protection of Indians (1910–67)

tacacá: a kind of soup made of tapioca and *tucupi* (manioc juice and pepper)

tanajura: female or queen sauba ants, both the male and female sauba ants are edible, but the females bite

tapuru: a kind edible larvae cultivated by the Tupari

taquara: bamboo

taxi: local name for the ant tree

timbó: timbo, a woody vine whose bark contains a poison the Indians use to kill fish

traíra: a species of voracious freshwater fish

tucum: a type of palm tree

tucumã: a kind of palm tree

tuxaua: chief

veado-roxo: a kind of deer, literally purple deer, from *veado*, deer, and *roxo*, purple